FOR THE
LOVE
OF THE
GODS

© Alex Williams

ABOUT THE AUTHOR

Brandy Williams (Washington) is a Pagan Theurgist and a Woman Magician. She is passionate about sharing the knowledge of the gods and particularly passionate about making magical traditions accessible to women. She has been an active organizer, teacher, and writer for more than thirty years, presenting frequently at conferences in the magical communities. Her books include *Practical Magic for Beginners* and *The Woman Magician.*

Williams works in Western Traditional Magic as a Thelemite, Golden Dawn Magician, and Witch. She cofounded the sororal order Sisters of Seshat, is the founder and director of Seattle Pagan Scholars, and is a past president of Covenant of the Goddess. Since 2001, she has been active in Ordo Templi Orientis, having served as a master of Vortex Oasis and on Anahata Rose Croix Chapter. Williams is an ordained priestess in Eccclesia Gnostica Catholica and celebrates the Gnostic Mass with Vortex Oasis.

In her spare time, she sings with the Medieval Womens Choir and keeps bees.

FOR THE LOVE OF THE GODS

OF THE GODS

The History and Modern Practice of Theurgy
OUR PAGAN INTERITANCE

BRANDY WILLIAMS

Llewellyn Publications
Woodbury, Minnesota

FIRST EDITION
First Printing, 2016

Book design by Bob Gaul
Cover art by superstock/866-11423/©Christie's Images Ltd./Christie's Images Ltd.
Cover design by Lisa Novak
Editing by Laura Graves

Llewellyn Publications is a registered trademark of Llewellyn Worldwide Ltd.

Library of Congress Cataloging-in-Publication Data
Names: Williams, Brandy, 1956– author.
Title: For the love of the gods : the history and modern practice of theurgy
/ Brandy Williams.
Description: First Edition. | Woodbury : Llewellyn Worldwide, Ltd, 2016. |
Includes bibliographical references and index.
Identifiers: LCCN 2016017113 (print) | LCCN 2016025633 (ebook) | ISBN
9780738744698 | ISBN 9780738749778 ()
Subjects: LCSH: Theurgy.
Classification: LCC BF1623.T56 W55 2016 (print) | LCC BF1623.T56 (ebook) |
DDC 203/.2—dc23
LC record available at https://lccn.loc.gov/2016017113

Llewellyn Publications
A Division of Llewellyn Worldwide Ltd.
2143 Wooddale Drive
Woodbury, MN 55125-2989
www.llewellyn.com

Printed in the United States of America

CONTENTS

PART TWO: The Living Tradition

ACKNOWLEDGMENTS

I am indebted to all the teachers in this book and to the many people I have learned from in the past and in the present. Three teachers in particular have been very kind to me in my own research and practice. Bruce McLennan, my first teacher (through the Internet) who brought Hypatia to life; whenever I have a particularly thorny question he unfailingly directs me on the right path. Tony Mierzwicki, an extraordinary teacher, meticulously recreates practice for the love of the gods. Richard Reidy's Kemetic rituals brought the practice of creating living statues within the reach of contemporary practitioners; his recent passing has robbed us of a great mind and a good friend.

Glenn Turner took me seriously as a theurgist. Her ongoing belief in me has given me the courage to present and write on the subject.

Editor Elysia Gallo tells me what I need to hear and always makes my work better. I am privileged to work with her.

Alex and Ted live without me for extended periods while I write and still lavish on me their unwavering physical, emotional, and spiritual support. Without their love, my work would be significantly less joyful.

INTRODUCTION

The gods call us, and we answer. We are drawn to learn about them, approach them, move into their presence. As our love for them grows, we seek teachers who can show us the path to know them even more intimately.

Pagan instruction in the way of the gods historically passed from teacher to student, person to person. But the deliberate suppression of Pagan religion seems to have broken our connection with their teachings. What happens to the story of our lives if what we are called to do was not passed to us by our ancestors? We feel a rupture, a loss of continuity, a lack of authenticity. This is what has happened to Pagan religion in the monotheistic world. How can we bridge the gap between what we want to do and the people who could teach us how to do it?

What if there was no gap?

Theurgy is a Pagan religious and magical practice that was passed from teacher to student. Although some have declared that the connection to our Pagan past was destroyed, this book links contemporary rituals with ancient teachers, reclaiming Pagan theurgic practice in the continuity of history.

Part One of this book, "Stories from the Ancestors," tells our history from a Pagan perspective. Why tell this history in stories? We can learn philosophy from texts and rituals from academic and popular descriptions, but critical analysis keeps the teachers themselves at a distance. When we immerse ourselves in the lives of the teachers, we can recreate the experience of being in their presence, learning from them directly.

Part Two of this book, "The Living Tradition," describes the specific theurgic rituals that bring us into the presence of the gods. The teachers instruct us how to engage in study, prayer, and ritual to raise our souls to the experience of the gods and of the One. As we learn from them, we realize that our practice keeps the Pagan theurgic tradition alive.

Theurgy participates in the project to restore Pagan religion. Together with indigenous peoples, reconstructionists, and those who create new paths, theurgists embody Pagan religion in living practice today.

While theurgy is open to all humans—this cannot be emphasized enough—it developed in cities among people who travelled between cultures. For that reason, it is especially welcoming to those of us who live in urban environments far from the lands where our ancestors were born. Theurgy embraces people of all genders, ethnicities, ages, and abilities. Theurgy welcomes those who envision the gods in humanlike form and those who perceive the gods as universal forces. This cosmopolitan, inclusive, and inspiring path provides us continuity with the past and a path to experience the divine.

Pagan religion never died. The historic attempt to suppress Pagan religion was unsuccessful. The techniques of theurgy are self-healing and continually renew the tradition. Telling stories of the teachers returns to us the continuity of our history and connects us to our ancestors. It heals the sense of isolation and lack of genuineness. Through the lives of the teachers we can understand ourselves as the inheritors of a sophisticated and ancient tradition that is living and thriving today.

The great teacher Plato said the true goal of a life is to become good, to center our lives not on material gain but on spiritual understanding. As our love for the gods draws us, we seek to become like the gods ourselves, suffused with their light, dwelling within the happy presence of the divine.

PART ONE

STORIES FROM
THE ANCESTORS

We call on those who have come before us,
Ancestors of our bodies and spirits.
We are the ones who walk in the world now,
The link between the future and the past.
As we walk on our living journey
Grant us the support that ancestors can give.

To contemporary Pagans, the word "ancestors" often means the people connected to our bodies—that is, our mothers and fathers and their mothers and fathers as far back as we can reach. We advise one another to research our family lines, to discover our people, to find the divinity that calls to us through our blood. This discovery may be easy for some, difficult for others, impossible for those whose ancestors were stolen from their homelands and brought to Europe and America as slaves.

There is another way to look at our ancestors, the ancestors of our souls, a chosen family of the spirit. Any ancestor who speaks to us can form part of that lineage. This does not depend on our physical bloodline and no one can exclude us from that relationship.

Pagan theology has a category of people who stand out above the rest, who contribute so much and live such exemplary lives that they occupy a space between humans and spirits. The term for these people is "heroes," and especially, "teachers."

To ancient Pagans, teachers were not simply people who imparted knowledge. They were also spiritual guides. They themselves glowed with the energy of the gods they invoked, serving as intermediaries between students and the gods. They were called by titles such as "Divine" and "Savior." They inspired respect but also reverence and even love. Individually they can guide us; collectively they form the golden chain connecting us to our human past and the knowledge of the ultimate source of our souls.

We can and must study the works the teachers left behind, but if we limit ourselves to reading the texts, we're simply walking back down the road of understanding with the mind only. We also need to understand the context of those works. Where did they live? What gods did they worship and how? What was happening in the world that affected their work?

We tend to treat the texts of the ancients as if they exist outside of space and time, floating in a mind-only world. But the people who wrote those works had a physical life. They were children once, they had great triumphs and terrible losses, and they had flaws. We need to understand who they were, how they lived, what their friends thought of them, where they succeeded and where they failed. We need to hear their stories.

Telling the stories of the teachers of theurgy from a Pagan perspective strengthens the golden chain that connects them to us. It is an act of reclaiming, bringing back to life the lives that have come before us, framing a Pagan context for our own relationships with the gods. We learn from the teachers and they show us the way.

The Neo-Platonic teachers all insisted that their knowledge was rooted in Egypt. We begin our study of the lives of the teachers in Kemet, with the practices in the temples where priestesses and priests approached the living presence of the gods.

ONE

PRIESTESS OF KEMET

Three women ruled Thebes for nearly two centuries. From 700 BCE to 525 BCE Shepenupet, Nitocris, and Ankhesneferibre held the reins of power.

Their names are rendered in many different ways by scholars. Douglas Blake, an independent scholar, translates the cartouche of Nitocris as *Nt-ikrty mrti Mwt*, "by virtue of Neit beloved of Mut." I have Anglicized the name here as *Neitokrity* to highlight her connection with the goddess of her childhood town. Neitokrity was among the most powerful women who ever lived and she dedicated her life to the service of a god.

I GIVE YOU MY DAUGHTER

When Krity was a young child, she sailed with her father to Waset. Her first glimpse of the temple was through a soldier's legs. Her father's army surrounded her as they marched toward the open gates of Ipet-Iset, the sublime house of the god. It was dazzling: stone pylons rose toward the sky, figures of the gods strode across the face of the temple in a rainbow of colors, gigantic statues of pharaoh flanked the gate. She fairly gawked.

Her father led his army through the gate without pausing and marched into a vast walled courtyard open to the sky. As they penetrated more deeply into the temple, they found themselves in a forest of massive pillars supporting a gigantic stone roof; slits in the roof let rays of sunlight filter in, but the light never reached the floor, and the room was forbiddingly dim. The army stopped for a moment to let the soldiers light torches.

Finally they faced the entrance to the holiest of holies, the shrine where the god himself lived. A man and a woman stood side by side in front of the door, blocking their path. The man's round face was rigid, his arms folded across his chest. He was impressive, but the woman was formidable, fully as tall as him and as proud, holding her head high under a massive double serpent crown.

The marching soldiers stopped. Shadows flickered in the torchlight. The temple of the great god was so quiet Krity could hear her own breathing.

The man facing them beat his chest once. "Mentuemhat," he said. "Fourth priest of Amun, governor and protector of Waset." He inclined his head toward the woman standing next to him. "Shepenupet, wife of Amun-Re, creator of the world."

So you say, Krity thought; she knew her own patron goddess Neit had actually created the world.

Her father beat his chest once too. "Psamtik," he said. "Pharaoh of Kemet."

"Pharaoh of Sau," Mentuemhat countered, refusing to acknowledge the man in front of him as the leader of his country.

Shepenupet took a step forward. Even in the dim hall Krity could see her eyes blazing. "You may not pass!" she thundered. "Amun is in his house and you may not enter!" Krity hid behind a soldier, shaking with fear.

Mentuemhat held his arms out straight as if to stop the entire army by himself. "The temple has been robbed. There is no more gold to be taken, no more silver on the walls, nothing is left. What do you want with us? Do you mean to take the wife of the god from the house of her husband? We stand against you! We will not permit it!"

"I am pharaoh!" Psamtik shouted. Krity hid her head behind a soldier's leg. More quietly Psamtik went on, "I come to restore Ma'at. I do not come to take. I come to give."

There was silence in the hall.

Psamtik said, "Neitokrity, step forward."

Hoping no one could see how badly she was shaking, Krity slowly slipped between the soldiers to stand at her father's side. Psamtik took her hand and held it up. "This is my daughter," Psamtik said. "I have brought her to give to you."

After a long moment Shepenupet exhaled and her shoulders dropped. "A man who brings his daughter does not mean to sack a city," she said, her voice shaking a little. Only then did Krity realize that the formidable woman was scared too.

Psamtik said conversationally, "This is a mighty and terrible place and the child is afraid. Is there somewhere we can go to talk?"

Geographic and Historic Egypt

Krity's Kemet was very similar to our Egypt today. Travelers can still visit the great temple at Karnak. We can watch farmers tilling the fields along the river using methods three thousand years old.

To understand Egypt you have to understand the river. The Nile flows peacefully from Sudan through Egypt's deserts to the Mediterranean Sea in the north. Kemet, "the Black Land," is the gift of the Nile, a truism that is emphatically reinforced by a flight over the country: there is a strip of blue water, a narrow band of green on either side, then reddish rock out to the horizon.

The country of Egypt, modern Misr, ancient Kemet, is situated in North Africa. It is bordered by Libya to the west, Sudan to the south, Israel to the east, and the Mediterranean Sea to the north, with Greece across the sea.

Egypt encompasses three geographical regions: Lower Egypt, Upper Egypt, and Nubia. This is confusing until you get used to it, as "Lower Egypt" is actually in the north, and the river Nile is one of the few in the world that flow from south to north. Lower Egypt describes the Nile delta and the seaport of Alexandria, whose ancient buildings are now submerged. It also includes the cities of Memphis (ancient Men-Nefer), Sais (ancient Sau), and the modern capital Cairo. "Upper Egypt" lies south and includes the modern city of Luxor, which the Greeks called Thebes and the people of Kemet called Waset.

Nile agriculture provided a stable basis for the Kemetic economy. Historian James Burke called ancient Kemet "the world's longest running good times." From the earliest historical period until Roman times, the culture of Kemet remained essentially unchanged no matter who ruled the country.

The record keepers of Kemet began their historical sequence with the Pharaoh Menes. Everything that happened before him is referred to as "pre-dynastic." Menes united Lower Egypt and Upper Egypt about 3100 BCE. Egyptian dynastic history is generally presented in four time periods: the Old, Middle, New Kingdoms, and the Late Period, with times in between when Egypt was ruled by outsiders or there was no clear rulership.

Good times for all meant especially good times for women. Throughout the Dynastic period, women chose their husbands, divorced without fault, and received support if their husbands left the marriage. Women represented themselves legally, shared equally in property during marriage and bequeathed it on their deaths. Land and titles passed through the mother, so ambitious men married women with royal ties.

Women served as priestesses and pharaohs. In the dangerous times when Kemet was invaded and the male pharaohs killed, the women of the royal families stepped up to rule the country, lead armies, and expel the invaders. They also led during times of peace. For example, the

Pharaoh Hatshepsut enjoyed a long reign, building huge monuments that are among the most popular tourist attractions today.

Many royal women bore the title *hemet neter*, "God's Wife," but it wasn't until the Nubian pharaohs that the bearer of that title assumed both political and religious authority in Waset.

PEOPLE OF KEMET

Krity and her father relaxed in the shade of a courtyard beside a shimmering tiled pool. Palm trees rustled overhead while young servants dashed about offering them water, plates of cheese, and honey cakes.

Mentuemhat adjusted his black shoulder-length wig. Shepenupet said kindly, "It's on straight, Mentu."

He patted her hand in response. "Nu, you're in your own house. You can take off your crown." Krity thought they sounded like comfortable old friends.

The priestess laid aside her crown and sighed. "My, but that's a heavy thing," she said. She cast a shrewd glance at Psamtik. "As you have come to know, I think."

"I have faced down the king of Assyria," Psamtik said. "Neitokrity, who was that?"

Krity startled and dropped the date she was holding. In her mind the courtyard vanished and the walls of her childhood home enclosed her while her mother's voice beat the names into her head, repeating them over and over until her daughter got them right. "Assurbanipal," she blurted.

Nu looked up at the sky as if seeing another scene. "Assurbanipal came as an enemy. He burned Waset, the beautiful city. He took so many captives." She turned haunted eyes to Psamtik. "When I walk the streets I still smell the smoke. Even after ten years. And the streets are so empty."

"And yet he did not take you captive," Psamtik said, taking a bite of cheese. "How did you do it?"

Nu shook her head. "All night I stood in the doorway of the Holy of Holies, just as I did today, while the soldiers ran through the temple. They never came near me." Her eyes filled with tears. "It was Amun. The great god protected me. They never laid hands on me."

"Well, we didn't oppose him, either," Mentu said mildly. "He meant to punish Kemet and pay his troops, but he didn't see us as his sworn enemies."

"The middle way," Psamtik agreed. "Neither serve nor oppose. This is the way I have chosen as well. I didn't go to war with Assurbanipal. But I did invite the Assyrian troops to leave the Black Land. Politely."

For the first time Nu laughed. "Did they leave politely?" She sobered again. "Assurbanipal placed you on the throne of Sau."

"I am not Assyrian," Psamtik countered. "I am a man of Kemet and my duty is to the Black Land. My father taught me that."

"A king of my family killed your father," Nu said conversationally. "Neitokrity, who was that?"

Krity's stomach trembled. "Tanwetamani," she quavered. History was very different when the people you were talking about were in the room.

Psamtik leaned back and folded his arms. "And so you think, this man's father was killed by my family. This man was placed on the throne of Sau by the king of Assyria. How can I trust him?"

"You come from the north," Nu said. "The invaders always come from the north. The saviors always come from the south and they're my family. You're not my family."

Psamtik leaned forward eagerly. "Tie our two families together. Adopt my daughter as your heir."

Nu reared back. "I have an heir!" she said. "Amenirdis! She's already been presented to the god and to the people as god's wife after me. Do you mean to rob her of that?"

"I will not do what should not be done," Psamtik said. "I will not remove an heir from her place. Amenirdis will be god's wife after you. Neitokrity will be god's wife after her."

"No," Nu said firmly, crossing her arms on her chest.

"Kemet is stronger when the two lands are united. North and south. Sau and Waset." Still Nu shook her head. Psamtik added, "She comes with a dowry."

Nu started to make an angry reply, but Mentu held up his hand. "What kind of dowry?"

"Lands from eleven districts," Psamtik said. "Lands and all their products, beer, bread, geese, oxen, cakes, vegetables. And gold, silver, jewels."

Mentu turned to Nu with eyes glittering with tears. "We can attract people to rebuild Waset. We can feed our people, and we can feed the god. We can refill the scribal school with students."

Nu argued, "We have kept Ipet-Iset pure. We never missed even a single day of the service of the god. He has eaten every meal."

Mentu smiled wanly. "Even now the meals are so meager we are often left hungry."

Psamtik said nothing. He watched them and waited.

Nu turned to Krity. The eyes of the priestess burned with the light of the god. "Why do you come here?" she demanded. "Girl who would be my daughter. Do you come to rule? Do you come to serve?"

Krity considered her answer carefully. If she said she came to rule, Shepenupet would mistrust her. If she said she came to serve, the god's wife would control her for the rest of her life. Neit, she prayed, help me to know what to say. In answer to her prayer the words she should speak dropped into her mind like stones in a pool. She said, "I come to learn."

Nu leaned back, studying her for a long time. Finally she said, "I can work with that."

Nubia

The relationship between Egypt and Nubia has always been complicated. Lower, northern Nubia lies between the first and second cataracts of the Nile. Cataracts are rocky interruptions of the smooth flow of the river where boats have to be towed against the current or ported over the rocks. The area around the third cataract, the Dongola Reach, was in ancient times a fertile area teeming with wildlife, giraffe, lion, rhinoceros. The rulers of Kemet pushed into the area, drove out the Nubian natives, and made use of the resources they found there, including Nubian gold.

In the Old Kingdom, climate change caused desiccation and the withdrawal of large animals, which are now found only farther south in Africa. Kemet's forces withdrew from the area and the native peoples returned. For some centuries the pharaohs of Egypt traded with the rulers of Nubia. Egyptian and Nubian rulers shared leadership styles, religious ideas, and a penchant for building monuments; the kings and queens of Nubia built hundreds of pyramids, many of which still stand.

The Kemet-Nubia trade was disrupted during the hundred years of Egyptian civil war in the First Intermediate Period. Demand developed in Egypt for Nubian mercenaries, particularly their fine archers, pictured in rows on Egyptian monuments. After the reunification of the country that launched the Middle Kingdom, Egypt once again occupied lower Nubia, building fortifications to control the important trade routes, although this time Nubians remained resident.

The beginning of the Second Intermediate Period coincided with the emergence of the Nubian kingdom of Kush, centered around the city of Kerma at the fourth cataract of the Nile. The rulers of Kush allied with the Hyksos who had invaded Kemet and pushed the pharaohs out of Lower Nubia. In the New Kingdom a Kemetic family dynasty based in Waset, Thebes, succeeded in driving the Hyksos from Kemet and secured the border with Kush. Throughout the New Kingdom, Kush and

Kemet contested the area south of Waset, and the rulers of Kemet captured and enslaved Kushite warriors.

Later in the New Kingdom, relations between Kemet and Kush were friendlier and Kushite royal families were educated at Kemetic courts. It is difficult to trace Nubian families in the later New Kingdom since they adopted Egyptian names and appear in the records as indistinguishable from Egyptians. Upper-class families assimilated into the Egyptian bureaucracy and married into the Egyptian royal families. In many real senses Nubia and Egypt, Kush and Kemet, shared a single culture.

In the Third Intermediate Period, foreigners invaded Kemet; first Libya, then the Persian Empire. As Kemet weakened, another strong dynasty emerged in Kush based in the new city of Napata. Kushite armies marched into Kemet, secured Waset, and pushed as far north as Sau in the Nile delta. Although rulership changed, daily life and culture did not; Napata and Waset both honored Amun as the deity of the cities, and Kushite rulers continued the strong traditions of Kemet.

While women sometimes ruled in Kemet, the traditions of queenship were even stronger in Kush. Kushite pharaohs established a strong ruling dynasty of women in Waset, daughters of the pharaohs who were loyal to the family dynasty, serving both as secular leaders and as priestesses, "God's Wives of Amun." Each priestess adopted her successor, securing the succession and indicating as well a strong sense of spiritual guidance between the women.

When the Kemetic pharaoh Psamtik succeeded in pushing the Persians out of the country, he secured Sau for a native Kemetic dynasty for the first time in centuries, but a Kushite priestess still ruled Waset. Psamtik persuaded Shepenupet to adopt his daughter as her successor. Neitokrity was young enough that it is likely her mother came with her to Waset to care for her as she grew into her new role.

LEARNING MA'AT

When Krity was an older child she went to school. The morning call woke her before dawn. Her mother heard her stirring on her cot and said, "Go back to sleep. It's only the call to the bakers." Krity didn't care that Nu had adopted her. Mehetnusekhet would always be her real mother.

At the second call her mother shook her cot. Krity struggled awake and wriggled into a scruffy everyday robe. She scurried out to the table to share a breakfast of fruit, bread, and water.

Before she was even finished, scrawny Pabasa poked his head in the door. "Come on! We're going to be late!" Krity jumped up and gave her mother a quick, fierce hug before dashing out the door.

The two ran down the path toward the House of Life. They were just in time to snag seats along the wall, a prized location as they could lean up against it when the teachers weren't looking. The first teacher rapped on his lap board. "Seshat opens the House of Life. Come to us Thoth!"

"Come to us Thoth," the students repeated dutifully. "Grant us skill in your ways. Being a scribe is better than all other ways."

The teacher distributed pottery shards to the students, yesterday's copy lesson that had been corrected with red ink. "Copy these again," he said. "When you are done, write this." He propped up a slab of pottery with the text of the day. "The maxims of Ptahotep, maxim five."

Krity groaned. "How many of those are there?" she whispered to Pabasa.

Pabasa grinned and whispered back, "Stop whining. There are only thirty-seven of them."

Her voice rose. "Thirty-seven! And this is number five?"

Their teacher glared at them and hissed them to silence. Krity bent her head over her palette, carefully mixed her ink, and copied the inscription on her pottery shard. She loved the way the meaning unfolded as the pen scratched over the clay. She repeated the words to herself as they came clear.

The teacher said severely, "Neitokrity, if you're going to speak the text, recite it to all of us."

Krity cleared her throat. "Ma'at is great, Ma'at was established in the time of Osiris, in the end Ma'at remains."

The teacher continued the lesson. "What is Ma'at?"

"The goddess of justice," Krity said.

The teacher frowned. "I didn't say *who*. I said *what*."

"Ma'at is the way of justice," Krity corrected herself.

A priest appeared in the door. "We need a Seshat," he announced.

The teacher jerked his head at Krity. Sighing, she got up. "Why do I always have to be Seshat," she grumbled. The goddess of libraries and the female scribe, Seshat measured the temple's length. In practice, that often meant her human representative stood in the hot sun holding one end of a cord while a priest recited prayers at the other end. As the school's only girl student, Krity often ended up in the role.

The priest said, "You will hold the cord for your own house of eternity. Isn't that enough reason?"

The chapel under construction had been started for Shepenupet's first heir Amenirdis. But Amenirdis wasn't around anymore, she'd found a king to marry back in Kush, so the tomb was going to be Krity's instead. Krity supposed she ought to be grateful—not everyone had a house in which to live for eternity—but it was a sunny day in the young years of her life, and she'd rather have stayed in the cool room with her friends.

The Kemetic Academy

During Pharaonic times Kemet was considered by Greeks and Romans to be the most advanced civilization in the world. Greek philosophers and educators such as Thales, Hippocrates, Pythagoras, and Plato travelled to Kemet to learn.

The temples were the schools. While much Eurocentric scholarship has investigated the religious practices in the temples, Afrocentric scholars recover the depth of function of these centers of knowledge. Dr. Molefi Kete Asante is Professor of the Department of African American Studies at

Temple University. Among his seventy books, the slim volume *The Egyptian Philosophers* gives us a glimpse into the subjects the Greeks went to Kemet to learn, including science, philosophy, and medicine.

Temples in the ancient world often doubled as hospitals. On the Greek island of Kos people came to a temple of the god Asklepios to dream and be healed. One of the healers there, an "asclepiad," was Hippocrates. We remember him because of the vow that begins "I swear by Apollo the physician and Asklepios and Hygeia and Panacea and all the gods and goddesses." That part gets left out today, but physicians still take the Hippocratic oath to heal to the best of their ability.

Hippocrates learned from Egyptian medical texts. He may have travelled to Kemet himself, to the medical temple of Imhotep at Memphis to study at the temple library. He certainly knew that Asklepios was the Greek form of Imhotep. Imhotep was a man honored as a god after a long life filled with accomplishments. Known today primarily as the architect of the step pyramid at Saqqara, he was also a healer serving in the temple at Memphis, pioneering treatments, and writing medical treatises.

Even more than an architect and a healer, Imhotep was known as one of the great philosophers of Kemet. As might be expected for someone who lived in 2600 BCE, Imhotep's philosophical works have largely disappeared. Asante points to the famous "Harper's Song" found in the tomb of Pharaoh Intef which quotes Imhotep as saying that we should be happy while we live, keep ourselves clean, remain peaceful, and use the gifts of the gods, knowing we return to the gods upon our death.

Women also learned and taught in the medical temples. In *Hypatia's Heritage*, Margaret Alic cites a tablet found at the temple of Sais reading: "I have come from the school of medicine at Heliopolis, and have studied at the woman's school at Sais where the divine mothers have taught me how to cure diseases." This chance survival documents women's contributions to medicine in Egypt; how many other subjects did they teach?

The temple curricula taught more than medicine, science, and religion. In *Maat, The Moral Ideal in Ancient Egypt*, Maulana Karenga points to Kemet as a wellspring of philosophy. Ma'at developed throughout the pharaonic period but in all periods remained the foundational religious/spiritual conception of the Kemetic people.

Karenga establishes the idea of Ma'at as the way of rightness. Ma'at is a spiritual and moral principle similar to the ideas of other religions, justice in Islam, dharma in Hinduism, agape in Christianity. Ma'at is a description of the natural order like the Homeric *dike*, Chinese *tao*, and Hindu *rta*. Ma'at is connected as well to the idea of morality, like the conception of *iwa* or character in Ifá, and the Dinka *cieng* or way of life.

Karenga situates key Kemetic texts as philosophical texts. These include the Shabaka Text, the Pyramid and Coffin Texts, the Declarations of Virtue, and the Declarations of Innocence in the Books of Coming Forth by Day. He draws from these traditions to articulate a Way of Worthiness. He offers this conception as a contribution to the restoration of the Ma'at-ian ethical tradition.

SERVING THE DIVINE

When Krity grew into her womanhood, she joined the choir of the temple. In the morning two young servant women took Krity to the small bathing chamber where they washed her, shaved any hair that had managed to sprout on her body, and anointed her with oil. Her mother Mehetnusekhet plaited Krity's hair, then helped her put on her fine white linen robes.

Mehet stayed behind in the house while Krity joined the procession of priestesses and priests streaming into the temple. Krity took her place in the chorus of priestesses who shook the sistrum. The offerings were already heaped on the tables—meat and cheese, fruit and beer, bread and honey. Krity's mouth watered, but it was not yet time for her to eat; first the god must take his share.

The soloist began the Morning Song. "Wake, all you neteru, awake! Amun amouni, great god Amun, awake!"

"Amun amouni," Krity sang with the rest of the chorus. They drew out the vowels, ahhhhhhhhhhh mun, ahhhhhhhhhhh mouni, floating on a long string of melody, pulling them all into a mind-stilling trance.

The song seemed to go on forever. Finally the High Priest of Amun threw the bolt to the holy of holies. A priest handed him a lit oil lamp. The High Priest entered the sanctuary and set the oil lamp in it. He removed a single tray of food and handed it back to the waiting priests. They handed back to him a new tray of food. Then several priests bowed their way into the sanctuary to remove the god's linens, anoint him, and wrap him again.

Krity stood on her toes to try to catch a glimpse of the god, looking over the tall shoulders of the priests. She thought she saw a flash in the shadows and drew in a sharp breath. The god seemed to know she was there. Did he know she would one day be his wife?

The High Priest held up a censer offering incense to the god and then held up a tiny statue of Ma'at, offering Ma'at to the god. Finally he stepped back and gave way to Shepenupet, splendid in her new gold necklaces and jeweled bracelets. The God's Wife walked into the holy of holies and closed the door behind her. From without they could hear the rattle of her sistrum.

Some time passed. Krity fidgeted. Someone sneezed.

Shepenupet emerged again, nodded regally to the High Priest, and left the sanctuary. Krity had gotten up the courage to ask her what she did while she was alone with the god, but Nu had not answered. Did she dance? Sing? Sometimes Krity thought she heard a sistrum. Mostly there was just silence. Some of the young priests made lewd jokes, making Krity squirm.

The High Priest offered more incense, spilled water on the floor, swept the floor and sprinkled sand on it. Then he closed the sanctuary, leaving behind the tray of food and the burning lamp.

By the time Krity got back to her house, her share of the morning's offerings had been delivered. Her mother turned a shining face toward her, proud of her daughter's work. "Look, food from the gods," she said, offering Krity a plate of fruit.

Kemetic Temples and Priesthood

Temples in Kemet were served by a full-time professional priesthood. Each temple housed a main deity with chapels dedicated to other deities as well. At Ipet-Iset, the deity in the holiest center of the temple was Amun, but he had an additional chapel in a trio with the goddess Mut and the child moon-god Khonsu. The war-god Mentu was also honored at the temple.

Common people, those not in the royal family or priesthood, did not have access to the inner temple where the deity was housed and fed, much as they did not have access to the palace of the pharaoh. They could enter the outer courtyard and address the god. In later dynasties chapels were built for the use of the unpurified commoner that might contain a statue of the deity, a statue of pharaoh, or just a carving of an ear in the wall. These chapels are sometimes called "Chapel of the Hearing Ear."

The professional priesthood, full and part time, maintained purity by shaving all hair and bathing every morning; at Karnak the priesthood bathed in the sacred lake.

Each morning the temple priesthood would approach the statues, providing them with clothing, feeding them, and providing less tangible offerings including music, singing, and the idea of justice and order, Ma'at. Serge Sauneron provides a description of these rituals in *The Priests of Ancient Egypt*.

Robert Ritner's indispensable work *The Mechanics of Ancient Egyptian Magical Practice* discusses the work of temple priests and priestesses outside the temples. While some of the priesthood resided near the temple and worked there year-round, others served a shift at the temple for a few months, then returned to their homes, where they were called on to perform ritual and healing work in their communities.

The temple walls and papyri are inscribed with instructions on how to perform rites for the gods who lived there. The most important rite was the one that invited deity into the statue, literally bringing the god to life, the Opening of the Mouth. This could also be performed on the mummies of pharaohs and other members of the royal family to bring them into the presence of the gods in the afterlife. The ritual ensured that the eyes could see and the mouth could receive food offerings. E. A. Budge provided a translation of the ritual in *The Book of Opening the Mouth: The Egyptian Texts with English Translations*; Mark Smith updated the effort in *The Liturgy of Opening the Mouth for Breathing*.

At first it was only royalty who joined the gods upon death. The Pyramid Texts of the Old Kingdom assisted the deceased royalty in their afterlife journey to join the sun god on his daily journey. These texts have been translated by Samuel Mercer, R. O. Faulkner, and Miriam Lichtheim. By the Middle Kingdom the secret had leaked, and well-placed families could have these texts drawn on their coffins to help them gain access to the realm of the stars in the afterlife. These have been translated by R.O. Faulkner in *The Coffin Texts*. Maulana Karenga extensively analyses these texts in *Maat, The Moral Idea in Ancient Egypt*.

By the New Kingdom, the rituals guiding the deceased in their journeys had become available to everyone as funerary scrolls. The 1250 BCE Papyrus of Ani, titled *Book of Going Forth By Day*, is the most complete of these texts. Ernest Arthur Wallis Budge provided a translation as *The Book of the Dead*.

The Papyrus of Ani no longer survives thanks to Budge's careless treatment of the text during his tenure at the British Museum. In an act of colonialist acquisition he purchased the scroll, cut it up, had it mounted on wood, and displayed it in a hall where direct sunlight destroyed the original papyrus. Fortunately, he had commissioned a copy. This copy has been produced in several new editions. Karenga also analyses this text in his work *Maat*.

By the Late Period, the sacred writings were in widespread use among common people. Kemetic priestesses and priests used the texts in rituals to aid people in their daily lives. These made their way onto scraps of papyrus written in demotic script, a late cursive form of hieroglyphic.

As increasing numbers of Greeks visited and settled in Egypt, Greek magicians began to learn these spells, and copy them onto papyrus. A number of these papyrus spells written in both Greek and demotic Egyptian were collected in *The Greek Magical Papyri in Translation* edited by Hans Dieter Betz. These papyri include spells for healing, instructions for inducing trance, and rituals for calling Kemetic and Greek deities into the bodies of small statues for the magician's use.

Just as the sacred texts used by royal families in pyramids made their way out into general use over time, the texts that brought the deity to life in the grand temple became a spell to bring the deity to life in a small shrine in the home. Richard Reidy's excellent contemporary work *Eternal Egypt: Ancient Rituals for the Modern World* bridges these worlds. Reidy adapts the Opening of the Mouth ritual for bringing deity into a home statue. The priestess or priest then performs temple rituals for the deity, bringing the deity food, clothing, and incense daily in an intense and dedicated devotional.

FLOOD

Krity panted up the stairs of the pylon. For some reason Nu had decided to have their lesson up here today.

When Krity reached the top, she found Shepenupet leaning against the wall looking out over the river. Nu didn't talk, so Krity leaned against the wall too. Watching the river rise was always exhilarating and frightening. The slowly swelling waters swept away the carefully tended gardens and edged toward the houses of the town. Then the water stopped, crept back into the river's banks, and the people came down to the newly deposited black soil to plant their crops again.

On bad years, the water rose too high and washed into the houses while the families carried their belongings to safety. Or the waters barely rose at all and the new fertile mud did not come, leaving the farmers to scratch the depleted soil and try to make it produce again.

This year the flood had come, which was good. All through the hot summer months the people waited to see how high it would rise, splashing in the cool waters, grateful for the river's gifts but eager to get back to the work of growing food again.

"There," Nu said suddenly. Krity looked where she was pointing. She could just make out a thin mound of mud rising up from the river. "It's peaked. The flood has peaked."

Every year the world was made new again. First the flood came, a chaos of water. Then the land emerged and the waters gave way to green growing things, order, life. Ma'at.

"Amun spoke the word and the world was created," Nu murmured.

"Neit," Krity countered, still stubbornly clinging to the goddess of her childhood. "Neit created the world."

Nu laughed. "Neit created the world," she agreed. "And so did Ptah. But you live in Amun's house so it might be a good idea to thank him." She exhaled as if she had held a month's long breath. "We have done our work correctly. It's a good year," she said.

Kemetic Cosmology

Today Cairo's airport sits in a suburb of that sprawling metropolis, and every visitor who flies to Cairo lands there. In ancient times, this suburb was its own city, known to the Egyptians as Iunu, and to the Greeks as the "city of the sun," Heliopolis. In ancient times, this city was a religious center and home to an early and vigorous cosmology known as the Heliopolitan cosmology.

This Heliopolitan story is reproduced in several places, most completely in the Book of Knowing the Manifestations of Ra and of Overthrowing the Serpent Apophis, translated by R. O. Faulkner as the Bremner-Rhind Papyrus. The story begins when Atum-Re-Kephra mounts the primal hill. This god spit out Shu, air, and Tefnut, moisture. Shu and Tefnut created Geb, earth, and Nut, sky, who in turn created Osiris, Isis, Set, and Nephthys. These deities form the central core of the Kemetic deities.

In his work *Maat,* Karenga analyses the gender of the creator deities. He quotes Coffin Text 132 as saying Amen-Re *made* as male and *birthed* as female, acting as both father and mother. Neit, he says, also encompasses male as well as female qualities. Both women and men are made in the image of the divine.

In *The Egyptian Philosophers* Molefi Kete Asante explicitly connects the Kemetic cosmology stories with the annual inundation of the Nile. Rain falls every year in the African highlands, washing soil into the river. Before the Aswan dam was built, these waters flooded down along the river to the Nile delta and thus to the sea. During the flood, water covered vast tracts of land. As the waters receded, a mound of earth could be seen to form within the water, and then the river returned to its banks. The cosmology story of the Egyptian people exactly described this process: water covered everything, then earth emerged, the self-created deity of life. Asante makes the point that the Greeks adapted this cosmology story to feature the elements water, earth, air, and fire.

What has happened since the Aswan dam was built? The fertile soil builds up on the Nubian side of the dam, burying the villages that were flooded when the dam was created. Farmers spread expensive fertilizer created from petroleum on the land to return a measure of fertility. The flood has been tamed at a cost difficult to sustain.

Asante notes that every thinker, whether philosopher, theologian, or scientist, must grapple with the origin of the world. Greek philosophers returned to Kemetic cosmology as a nourishing source again and again over the millennia, just as the flood nourished the land. For example the ogdoad and the image of the lotus rising from the mud re-appear in Iamblichus's work *On the Egyptian Mysteries*.

There is one more story to tell here, possibly the most famous story to come out of Kemet. It is the story of Isis and Osiris, brother and sister, wife and husband, and the love that transcends death.

Osiris ruled the fertile land with compassion and wisdom. Mad with jealousy, his brother Set murdered Osiris and scattered his limbs throughout the land. Isis mourned, crying out for him, seeking him everywhere. Her sister Nephthys joined her in her search. Even though Set was her husband, Nephthys joined forces with her sister, choosing to act to restore Ma'at.

The two sisters managed to collect all the pieces of Osiris and re-assembled them. This body gave the ba of Osiris a place to return. Isis Great of Magic fanned her wings and brought the breath of life back to his lungs. Then Isis lay with her husband for one final night, a triumph of love, a triumph of magic, a triumph of life over death.

Beyond that one night he could not stay in the green land of day. Osiris went to the Duat, the desert land of the dead, to rule the red land of night as he had ruled on earth when he lived.

Meanwhile Isis realized she had conceived. Knowing that an heir would threaten Set's right to hold the throne, she hid in the rushes beside the Nile until she gave birth. She named the boy Horus and raised him in secret until he was fully grown.

When Horus achieved his full growth, Isis told him the story of his life. Filled with righteous anger, Horus stormed into the court of Set, challenged his uncle, and rushed upon him in battle. Set fought with the cunning of an accomplished murderer, but Horus fought with the strength of young justice. Horus triumphed, toppling Set from the throne, and took his place as ruler of the land of day.

Stories differ about what happened next. In some stories Set and Horus are still fighting. In others each rule half of Kemet, Upper and

Lower. We also find Horus as the sun, Re-Horakty, travelling over the heavens in his boat during the day, then travelling through the Duat every night. In his dangerous nightly journey he is accompanied by many deities, among them Set, who stands at the bow of the boat and defends Re-Horakty with his spear.

The story is retold in many versions through many sources. It is clear that it dates to at least 2500 BCE, and there is no reason to believe it is not older. It was loved in ancient times and is loved today. The image of Isis holding Horus on her lap is the image of mother and child, thousands of years older than the image of Mary holding Jesus. The grief of Isis speaks to everyone who has ever lost a loved one. The triumph of her magic, one more night with the one who has been lost, is the boon we all desperately dream.

DUTIES

Shepenupet waited impatiently in the door. Mehetnusekhet fussed with her robe while Neitokrity shied away from her like any adolescent chafing under her mother's touch. "The bakers aren't even up yet," Krity complained. "Why do I have to go?"

Nu and Mehet traded an exasperated glance. Mehet said, "Because it is your duty."

"A god's wife seems to have a lot of duties," she grumbled. Nu and Mehet laughed together.

As Nu and Krity followed the path toward the river, the cool breeze of the pre-dawn touched their faces. A shadow among the shadows blocked their path. Nu paused, then seemed to recognize something in the shape of his shoulders. "Ibi," she said heavily.

"You are avoiding me," he accused.

"I go to my mother's house of eternity to pay my respects. There is a time for this conversation, and it is not here and now."

The lightening sky revealed the scowl on his face. "Psamtik requires an answer. I require an answer."

"Are you Psamtik's steward?" she demanded. "Or are you mine?"

"I am both. The Black Land is one," he countered.

She sighed. "I will meet with you today." An edge crept into her voice. "Now will you let us pass?"

"My lady?" Priests gathered around them protectively.

Ibi stepped out of the path. "Today," he said warningly.

Nu waited until they were well out of earshot before she muttered, "I need a bodyguard to protect me from my own steward." She looked down at Krity. "When the time comes to appoint your steward, try to make sure he is yours and not the pharaoh's," she said. "Even if the pharaoh is of your family and *especially* if he is not."

The priests helped them into the little boat and rowed them across to the West Bank toward the houses of the ancestors. The priests carried baskets of tools and food as they all walked toward the funeral chapels. It was a long walk.

Finally they reached the temples at Djanet, Medinet Habu. Krity thought they would go straight to the house of Amenirdis the first, Nu's spiritual mother. Instead Nu turned toward the Mansion of Millions of Years, the funerary temple of Ramses III. "I want to show you something," Nu said. The frieze she pointed at captured suffering in stone—bound men bowed their heads before the triumphant pharaoh. "Do you know who they are?"

This was always a tricky question from Nu. "Enemies of the pharaoh?" Krity ventured.

"Some of them are my people," Nu said. "For many centuries the pharaohs of Kemet have turned to the south for gold and for soldiers. When we did not go willingly we were enslaved."

Krity winced. She knew she was supposed to rejoice that the pharaoh had conquered his enemies, but the men carved into the stone seemed so wretched.

"Your ways have become our ways and you have learned from us. We who were slaves became pharaohs. We drove away the enemies of Kemet. We rebuilt the temples. We restored Ma'at." Nu took Krity's brown hand between her black ones. "Now you and I stand here together, both of us serving the same gods. Mother, daughter, together," she said. "In my family women rule as queens. The daughters of Kush have ruled Waset. Rule after me, not as a servant, not as your father's daughter, but as a queen."

"My father is a good man," Krity said immediately.

"He keeps Ma'at," Nu agreed, and waited.

Krity felt something in her shift. She had not seen her father since he returned to Sau, but she saw Nu every day. Nu, who had survived Assurbanipal and had stood up to Psamtik. Nu who served Amun every day, as Krity would in her own time. Slowly she said, "Pabasa."

"Pabasa?" Nu said.

"I want him for my steward," she said.

Nu gave her measured look. "I know he is your brother," she said, using the word which meant "lover." When Krity started, Nu went on, "It's none of my business or anyone else's either, don't let anyone tell you differently. But he will marry, and you're married to the god, so it can't be to you. Will you be able to work with him when he's not your brother anymore?"

Krity didn't answer immediately. It was a new idea.

Nu gave her a crooked half-smile. "Now let's go make our offerings to Amenirdis." She sighed. "I hope she will grant me some insight into how I should answer Ibi."

Colonialization

The people of Nubia have always been black. They are depicted on monuments as black, and Nubian skin is among the deepest black humans can produce.

Shepenupet was Nubian. Neitokrity's family came from the delta near Libya, where generations of conquest and intermarriage had introduced different genes. She was likely to have been lighter in color, but she was still African.

Everyone agrees Shepenupet was black, but not every scholar agrees that Neitokrity could be described as black. Eurocentric history claims Kemet for Europe. Egypt forms part of the Mediterranean culture, the wellspring of civilization. In this narrative Egypt is a special case, cut off from the rest of Africa by the cataracts of the Nile, belonging more to Greece and Rome than to Nubia or southern Africa. Racism detected a distinct difference between Nubia and Egypt: Nubia belongs to sub-Saharan Africa and is inhabited by "true Negroid" peoples. The peoples of Egypt, on the other hand, were of mixed "Caucasoid" and Arabic genes, not "Negroid." They weren't black; they were *light skinned* enough to be counted as white.

Cheikh Ante Diop thought the peoples of Egypt were black and are black today. In *The African Origin of Civilization: Myth or Reality*, he noted that the ancient Egyptian people did not think of themselves as separate from Africa but as relatives of the inhabitants of Kush and Napata and Meroë. Their art depicts a range of skin tones, and their writings pay no attention to skin color.

In his introduction to Karenga's monumental work *Maat*, Jan Assman notes that the dialogue of Europe with Kemet has had three distinct phases. First, during Pharaonic times, both the Greeks and Romans considered Egypt to be the most advanced civilization in the world. Second, in the Renaissance, a romantic interest in antiquity led to the European appropriation of Egypt as part of the Mediterranean classical heritage.

Third, the modern archaeological recovery of Egyptian artifacts and scripts established Egyptology as an academic discipline.

Afrocentric scholars are opening a fourth phase of dialogue, recovering the philosophers of Kemet both in historic context and as contributors to contemporary discourse. In *Maat*, Karenga writes as a Seba or moral teacher. He explicitly rejects the Eurocentric viewpoint that privileges Greece, treating Kemetic culture as a site for academic study. He points out that Eurocentric scholarship focuses on the mythopoeic aspects of Egyptian thought while denying its cultural depth and intellectual insight. He seeks to restore the place of Kemet as a wellspring of philosophy, contributing to contemporary religious discussion.

Many scholars in the magical communities have come to realize that we owe a debt to Kemet, that failing to acknowledge it continues the colonialization of Kemet by Europe, and that it is our duty to uphold Ma'at. We understand Kemet as the black land, the people of Kemet as black, the accomplishments of Kemet as the greatest in the ancient world, and ourselves as only students.

ALONE WITH AMUN

Aging Shepenupet eventually turned over most of her duties to her adult successor.

Krity trembled a little as she waited for the High Priest to offer Ma'at to Amun. Finally her turn came to step into the shrine. She fumbled with the massive door; the man winced and helped her close it.

The flickering lamp lit the room and played over the face of Amun. He stood erect, regal, his eyes staring into her soul. Her heart beat very quickly. She'd never been alone with the god before and Nu hadn't answered any of her questions about what to do. "When the time comes, you will know," she always said.

The sistrum! Krity lifted the rattle in her trembling hands and shook it twice. The sound echoed loudly in the small chamber and she stopped, confused. "I don't know what you want," she said to Amun.

She thought she heard something in her mind but she wasn't sure. "Say that again?"

Later, in the heat of midday, she found herself crouching on a mat while an aged priest methodically chopped herbs on a reed board. She waited patiently, not interrupting him, until he finally deigned to notice her. "Incense for Mut," he said.

Krity cleared her throat. "Wise one, I need your help," she said.

He didn't look up at her. "I wondered when you would come."

"Nu won't tell me." He said nothing to this. Krity rushed on, "I saw the god today. He said—" She hesitated, then plunged on. "He told me to quiet my mind."

Was that a smile she saw on his face? It was gone in an instant. "That task may require years to master."

"Then let's start," Krity said.

He held her eyes for a long moment. "Very well. Settle the body, still the mind, contemplate the divine. What does it mean to settle the body?"

Stilling the Mind

Every great religion instructs us to still our minds. The task of those who seek to hear the divine is to clear out enough of ourselves that the divine can actually be heard.

The magical papyri from Greece and Egypt make long invocations to the deities. They are composed of words of course, but they also include sounds that seem nonsensical to us. First, there are long strings of vowels. Chanting to vowel sounds, a musical technique called "melisma," comes to us in the European world from medieval times, liturgical chants connected to the chants of ancient Greece. It is arguable that the vowel sounds in the spells partly serve the same function, to create a trance state within the singer.

The spells also specify popping and hissing sounds. Long strings of P's are followed by strings of S's. They aren't nearly as pretty as the vowel sounds and don't have as clear a modern counterpart. Peter Kingsley has an idea that sheds light on these. In his work *In the Dark Places of Wisdom*, Kingsley notes that the hissing sound was described by a word that means "flute." Actually, the word is translated more as "pipe"; it's the sound a harsh flute makes.

The earliest Greek philosophers discussed the music of the spheres, describing not a beautiful melody but a hissing sound. In 1964, two Bell labs scientists (Arno Penzias and Robert Wilson) noticed a low hiss in the horn antenna they had built. Scientists eventually decided this hiss was the residual effect of the Big Bang. They named it Cosmic Microwave Background—the music of the spheres!

Kingsley notes that humans hiss at one another when we want each other to be silent. Those pops and hisses in the magical papyri may be techniques for calling the perpetually busy mind to be silent long enough to hear the divine. Hissing features in the ritual practice of theurgy, as we seek to quiet our minds to listen to the gods.

A YOUNG SESHAT

Krity stomped up the stairs. The insufferable, snobby, unhelpful—*stomp*! The High Priest of Amun insisted on lingering over his office while the priests waited and the food became cold. She had only a few minutes each day in the presence of the god striving to hear his voice while she tamed the beehive of her thoughts.

Somewhere up above she heard a sniffle.

Gathering her linen skirt in her hands, Krity moved silently now, easing herself out onto the roof of the pylon. A small girl tucked her head in her knees, crying. Gently Krity said, "Good morning." The girl startled like a bird and leapt up to run, but Krity filled the door. "Sit down," Krity said, and the girl dropped instantly as if commanded.

Krity leaned on the pylon wall, breathing the morning air. "I love to come up here," she said. "It helps me think. Actually, it helps me practice not thinking." Krity glanced at the trembling girl and realized she was understanding none of this. She tried again. "What's your name?"

"Ru. Irtyru."

"Ru, why are you crying?"

"I want to be a scribe!" she burst out. "My father says it's better than all other ways."

Krity smiled, thinking of Pabasa. Scribes thought so much of themselves. "Why can't you be a scribe?"

"I went to school with my father, but the teacher wouldn't take me. He said girls can't go to school."

Rule after me, Nu said. Krity drew herself up to her full height. She had had it with self-important priests. "There's always a Seshat," she said. "In fact, I think there ought to be more than one, don't you?" She held out her hand. "Let's go see about that."

Chance Survivals

Kemetic history covers many thousands of years. What do we really know of the lives that were lived there? Scholars generalize based on the few bits of evidence that have chanced to survive. Many sources have said there were no female scribes in Egypt. Then a female scribe was found.

Until recently Tomb TT390 was part of someone's house. People still live on the dusty hills, still dig in tombs to find treasures to sell, still re-use the old buildings to house their families. This is what happened to Irtyru's tomb. When the government offered the family a chance to move to a better house in 2006, an archaeological team began to excavate the original tombs. The South Asasif Conservation Project led by Dr. Elena Pischikova and Katherine Blakeney continues to shore up the tombs and has already restored some of the friezes. The inscriptions identify one of the tombs' owner as a scribe and chief attendant to Neitokrity. There is an offering inscription to Irtyru's father, while Neitokrity is present in many scenes; clearly Irtyru honored them both.

In a 2014 blog post entitled "Irtieru and the Woman in Black Garments," one of the Dr. Pischikova's team members confessed to listening for Irtyru's whisper to point out where to place the restored blocks. Irtyru is still called on to fulfill the office of Seshat.

BURYING MOTHERS

Women who live long enough come to the time when we stand at the head of our family, when all our mothers are ancestors now.

Irtyru stood stock still in the harsh sun holding her end of the line. Neitokrity held the other end of the line in one hand and a papyrus in the other, chanting the prayer.

Finally it was done. Krity and Ru stepped back while the masons moved in to block out the room. "I thought that was your house of eternity," Ru said, pointing at the big chapel next door.

"It was going to be," Krity said. "I'm giving it to Mehetnusekhet so I need a room of my own." Her eyes stung. It was still hard to believe that her mother wasn't going to be waiting for her at home.

She looked down at the girl. "Shall we pay our respects to Shepenupet? You would have liked her. She was spunky like you."

The girl stood solemnly with her while they looked up at the friezes. Neitokrity started to read out the inscriptions, but stopped. "You read them," she said to Ru. Slowly the girl puzzled out the words. "Hemet neter," God's wife, "you with the true voice, your sister Isis is filled with joy when she sees you. She protects you. She gives you breath as she gave Osiris breath."

When the girl had finished, there was silence in the chapel. Ru said quietly, "Do you miss her?"

A quiet joy filled Krity's heart, washing away her grief and comforting her. "How can I miss her when she is still here?" When Mehet's temple was complete, she could visit her too.

The Kemetic Soul

For the people of Kemet, the dead didn't leave.

The Kemetic conceptions of the afterlife involve relatively complicated conceptions of the makeup of each individual person. In "The New Kingdom 'Divine' Temple," Lanny Bell explores the importance of ancestor culture. Death did not sever the relationship of the living to the deceased; instead, they continued to play a vital role in the life of the family. You could be comfortable living above a tomb or in one.

The person was composed of multiple parts. First of course was the body, which on death would become the corpse and could be preserved by mummification. There was also the shade, drawn as a silhouette of the body, indicating the incarnation of life in the body. There was the name, expressing the true essence of the individual, which could be spoken to provide life to the deceased. Many tombs, temples, and stelas inscribe names and a prayer to the passer-by to speak them. There was also the heart, which served some of the same functions the head does for us as the seat of the individual's intellect and feelings. The books of the dead that detail the journey of the afterlife describe the weighing of the heart of the individual to determine whether the individual had lived a virtuous life.

In addition to body, shade, name, and heart were three components that are less familiar to us: the *ka*, the *akh*, and the *ba*.

The *ka* (life force), did not belong to the individual and left the body at death. This was the connection of the individual to the ancestral line, to the first ancestor, and to the gods who created that ancestor. Each living individual formed a link in the family line between the past—ancestors who had come before—and the future, those who would come after in the family line. All the members of that ancestral line, dead, living, and not yet born, make up the ka.

The modern conception of the soul does not map neatly onto any of the Kemetic/Egyptian parts of the soul, but the closest analogue may be the *ba*. Depicted as a bird with the head of a human, it was closely tied to the body, inhabiting the body during life and separated from the body at death. Bell calls the ba the "spiritual body."

The *akh* was associated with the recently dead and was worshipped in ancestor shrines in the home by family members who continued to closely feel their presence. It was the akh who could intercede for the family, or in the case of angry spirits who were not properly buried, disturb the living.

In his work *The Ancient Pyramid Texts* James Allen explains that the pharaoh's akh was godlike in life and joined the gods among the stars on death. Lesser individuals could aspire to this condition if the ba could rejoin its ka, the force of life. It was the function of the spells contained in the Pyramid Texts to accomplish that reunification. Each morning the sun emerged from the death of darkness to be reborn; the ba-ka could also go forth by day.

As access to the spells to reunify the parts of the deceased trickled out into the general populace, families took on the duties of feeding the dead, just as the gods were fed in their temples each day. Food left for the deceased could strengthen the ka-force in the ba. Tombs of pharaohs included stores of physical food, private tombs were sometimes equipped with altars where food could be left by the living, while images of food on tombs and stelas also nourished the deceased.

Each time we speak the name of one of the priestesses and priests who came before us, we stand in as their spiritual children, fulfilling their desire to be remembered, to be literally brought together again so that they might live forever.

SUCCESSION

As Neitokrity aged, she thought more and more about how to secure the power of her office. She had managed to choose her own steward and control her own property. But how would her successor fare?

The priests and priestesses of Amun gathered in the open courtyard, all of them, the first and second and third and fourth prophets, the chanters, the sem priests who opened the mouths of the gods and the dead so that they could live. Their chatter filled the air. Krity lifted one arm, and they all fell silent. Well, they should! She'd known all of them since they were children. She'd served the temple for many decades now. Long enough to have completed the course of training in the temple. Long enough to have learned how to silence her mind. Silencing a crowd was easy compared to that.

"We have gathered to greet our new High Priest of Amun," she said. Her eye fell on the Harkheb, cramped with age, smirking next to his hand-picked successor. Cramped in spirit too; just yesterday as Krity stood with quiet mind in the presence of the god, soaring on the wings of his presence, Harkheb banged on the door for her to hurry up so he could have his breakfast, and broke her trance.

Krity reached back and grabbed Ankhesneferibre's hand. "You know her," she said, "this is my spiritual daughter." She was the pharaoh's choice for her successor, just as Krity had been the pharaoh's choice. "You all know how hard Ani has worked to learn the office I hold."

Harkheb fidgeted, clearly anxious for her to get on with it.

"Our priest has chosen his successor." The old man stood up straighter. "I affirm Paser as the next High Priest of Amun. However, this choice is also mine to make." Krity took a deep breath. "Due to her diligence, her great energy, and her clear devotion to Amun, I appoint Ankhesneferibre to the office of High Priest, to succeed Paser in the office."

"No!" the Harkheb said violently. Hori next to him shook his fist angrily. One of the older men—was it the teacher of the scribes?—called out, "A woman?! The high priest?"

Krity's steward Pabasa called out, "Why not?" Krity flashed him a smile.

"Yes, why not?" Ru called out, squeezing her own daughter's ink-stained hand.

For a tense moment Krity held Harkheb's eyes. Then he shrugged. He had what he wanted; it wasn't worth fighting over. Paser grumbled, but he had what he wanted as well, and it wasn't a good start to oppose the God's Wife in public. The priests and priestesses took their cue and straggled out of the courtyard to go back to their business. Why not?

"There," Krity said fondly to Ankhesneferibre. "Now no one will rush you to finish when you are with the god."

THE LESSONS OF NEITOKRITY

What can we learn from studying the life of Nt-ikrty mrti Mwt? While we know some things about her life through chance survivals of a few texts and images, there are huge gaps in our knowledge. How scholars approach Kemetic history often says as much about the scholar as the subject.

We know something about the social context of the servants of the god. The first lesson is how insignificant it was to the people and to the gods that they were Kushite or Saite, black or brown. Even today we still hear scholars say publicly "Egyptians weren't black Africans, they were Caucasian." Contemporary theurgists need to step up and call that kind of privilege out. The peoples of Kemet were African and peoples of color and our philosophical ancestors.

Another important lesson is how central women were to Kemetic religious life. Eurocentric history writes women out of the story. We constantly fight to regain and retain our own heritage. It is not uncommon to read that there were no women scribes, even after the discovery of Irtyru's tomb. The women who ruled Waset in Krity's time wielded significant political power. Ankhesneferibre simultaneously held the two highest religious offices. One of my favorite images comes from Nefertari's tomb, where she makes an offering to Hathor, a priestess offering to a goddess. In Kemet women acted with authority in the temple and without.

We know that the clergy could live at the temple year-round or could serve part time. The holders of the offices wielded political and spiritual power, and the priestly bureaucracy could make or break a pharaoh.

These offices were not just political but also deeply spiritual. The form that spirituality took is hazy to us, but we can recover some idea both from contemporary African practice and from similar traditions around the world. This spirituality was and is rooted in a strong moral sense that focuses on community, honoring the sacred, and sustaining life.

The priestesses and priests of Kemet served gods living in statues. The technique of calling a deity into a statue passed into the magical papyri. Greek theurgists learned the technique from Kemetic teachers, and it has been adapted by people like Richard Reidy for use today.

We know what the priestesses and priests did from the outside—we have clear images and descriptions of the offerings they made. But we don't know what they did from the inside. What did the God's Wife do when alone with the god? How did the priestesses and priests prepare for their offices? Their Greek visitors tell us the course of study in the temple at Waset took forty years to complete. What was taught there?

Since Plato and Iamblichus pointed to Kemet as the source of their philosophical, spiritual, religious knowledge and practice, we can infer that many or most theurgic techniques trace to ancient Kemetic teachings. Plato laid down the philosophical basis, describing successive meditations on the nature of the cosmos. Iamblichus described how to use that philosophy to approach the gods in the temples without and in the chambers of the mind. Studying their work may shed light on what the Kemetic priestesses and priests did in the dark silence of the temples.

Notes on the Story

While we have some record of Neitokrity's life, we don't have films or diaries or letters as we would from a more contemporary subject of biography. As with every dramatization, this story contains extrapolations. Some scholars would agree with these choices, some would argue for a different choice.

Mariam F. Ayad's *God's Wife, God's Servant* is an excellent place to begin study of these powerful women. In *The Black Pharaohs*, Robert Morkot explores the complicated relationship between Kemet and Kush, detailing the struggle between the family dynasties of north and south.

The adoption of Neitokrity by Shepenupet is recorded on the walls of the temple. The record describes Neitokrity's arrival by ship along with all the goods Psamtik sent with her. The record does not mention the negotiations that preceded her adoption and implies she came later; placing her in the temple at that time is a bit of dramatic license.

It is a mystery how Shepenupet survived the Persian sack of Waset, and how she remained in power even though the Kushite faction that enthroned her was overcome by their Saite rivals. She must have been a formidable politician as well as an effective priestess.

In "Celibacy and Adoption Among God's Wives of Amun and Singers in the Temples of Amun," Emily Teeter points to evidence for two mothers of the women, one physical and one spiritual. I have here portrayed Mehetnusekhet as Krity's biological mother and Shepenupet as her adoptive, spiritual mother. While we don't know that Mehetnusekhet accompanied her daughter to Waset, Neitokrity was quite young when she was adopted by Shepenupet and would have needed care. The inclusion of Mehetnusekhet's chapel among the tombs of the God's Wives argues for a continual and loving relationship.

While there is no record of Neitokrity learning the scribal trade, there is also no reason to think the most powerful priestess in Waset would not have received every education possible. We know she employed women scribes, most notably Irtyru.

Images depict Seshat and the pharaoh each holding an end of the cord to mark the location of the walls of new temples. As priests took the place of the pharaoh in ritual, there is no reason why a god's wife or a girl scribe could not take the role of Seshat, the patron goddess of scribes.

Vowel chanting is used around the world to still the mind; medieval European manuscripts describe vowel chants. There doesn't seem to be evidence that the Kemetic priesthood used the technique but it seems a reasonable supposition.

Since God's Wives did not marry and did not bear their successors as their own biological daughters, but instead adopted their successors, some scholars argue that they remained virgins throughout their lives. Emily Teeter questions the assumption that the priestesses of Amun were necessarily celibate. Some singers are known to have had children. I note that Kemetic culture celebrated sexuality, and powerful women, like powerful men, tend to take the lovers they want.

While scholars like Asante and Karenga work to restore the teachings of ancient Kemet, there isn't a lot of detail about what the teachers actually taught. The full course of study at the University of Waset took forty years. With a temple at the center of that teaching, surely some of the curriculum included meditation techniques.

TWO

PLATO

A hundred years after Ankhesneferibre's death, the Persians had conquered Kemet again. Once again they were pushed out by native pharaohs, this time with the aid of Greek mercenaries. Plato was born into a world at war. He lived 427–347 BCE, child of a wealthy Athenian family, but his family's position could not entirely shield him from the chaos of the times.

A DEATH IN THE FAMILY

The day everything changed the boy woke up, slipped into a brightly colored linen shift, threw on a cloak, stuck his feet into sandals, and scrambled down the ladder to the kitchen. His sister was waiting for him at the table. "Aristocles! You're late," she said, shoving a hunk of bread at him. He dipped it into water mixed with a little wine and ate as much as he could, wiped his hand on it, and threw it onto the floor. Potone pulled at his hand. "Come on," she said, running out of the room with him, while behind them a slave quietly cleaned up the mess on the floor.

"He's home," Aristocles said to his sister in a low voice. *He* was Ariston, their father. To the public he was a great man, a politician, the son of kings. Aristocles and Potone knew a different Ariston. The night he tried to force his wife to have sex with him, Perictione shouted loud enough to wake up the whole house. Potone climbed into bed with Aristocles and the two of them shivered as they listened to the argument. Later their mother told them their father had changed; Apollo had come to him in a dream and told him to behave chastely.

Chastely to his wife, at least. "There's going to be a symposium," Aristocles said. He hated the drinking parties that kept the whole house awake all night. His father's friends would cram into the men's room of the house and shout "More wine!" while the male slaves poured them drinks, the women slaves worked in the kitchen all night turning out food, musicians played flutes and drums, and hired women came to dance and sing and roll about on the couches with the men.

"You know what he said to me?" Aristocles went on. "He said 'aren't you in school yet, boy?'"

"Oh no!" Potone said. Their older brothers already went to school. When Aristocles finally joined them their father had said he would dismiss their tutor, and Potone's education would be over. She'd join the women in the weaving room making cloth for the family and learning how to run a household. But she loved to learn. She listened raptly to the tutor's stories about the Persian wars, especially the exploits of Artemesia, the warrior queen who fought with the Persians. She bent her head over the tablet, making marks on the wax with the stylus, determined to read and write.

"I told him I'm not old enough, but I don't think he believed me," Aristocles said. Their father was often gone, finding the house in the city claustrophobic, spending most of his time with the other politicians or touring the country estates that provided the family's wealth.

Their tutor was not waiting for them in the craft room. Instead their mother sat on a bench, her eyes red with crying, supported by a slave woman. Aristocles and Potone traded an alarmed look, then crept up to her and sat at her feet. "Your father is dead," Perictione said.

"Good!" Potone said. It was exactly what Aristocles was thinking.

Perictione shook her head. "Now we are alone in the world," she said. "Your brothers are too young to represent the house." Only men could serve on the political councils and speak in court. "I can't manage the estates. This is a rich and noble family and there will be many who descend on us to try to take some of it for themselves."

Aristocles felt helpless. He wished he was old enough to defend his mother and his sister. What would happen to them?

A few days later Perictione called all her children into the men's room. Usually women didn't use the room but it was the only place they could all gather. Glaukon and Adeimantis had already taken the couch, leaving Aristocles and Potone to sit on the floor. "You remember Pyrilampes," their mother said. "My uncle. He's ambassador to Persia, he's just back from court."

Stiff with age, Pyrilampes greeted Glaukon and Adeimantis gravely. When his eyes fell on Aristocles he grinned. "Bee lips!" he said. Aristocles grimaced. Of all the stories the man would remember! One morning when Glaukon had come in to wake him up he found bees on Aristocles's lips. His mother said it meant he would be a great poet. Glaukon said it was because he had stolen a honey cake before going to bed.

Perictione said, "Pyrilampes is your new father." Glaukon and Adeimantis traded a glance. Aristocles looked anxiously at his mother. What did that mean? "He has agreed to step in to protect our household. Now the estates will remain in the family. You'll all be able to continue your education." Seeing Potone bite her lips, Perictione said, "Yes, all. We can afford to keep your tutor, Potone. My daughter will be literate, like me." Her eyes fell on her youngest son. "But Aristocles will have to go to school."

Classical Greece

Athens, the birthplace of democracy! The shining city where geniuses built the foundations of civilization! For centuries Eurocentric scholars have glorified the accomplishments of the city's privileged elite. In our modern time, however, scholars with other viewpoints have called into question this picture of Athens.

The classical Greek world was composed of an alliance of cities, each of which had a distinct character. Athenian "democracy" extended only to male citizens; women were either confined to their homes and estates or served as prostitutes to the men who engaged in public discourse, while the city itself was powered by the labor of slaves. European history remembers Athens's rival and ally Sparta primarily for the bravery of its warriors, but in Sparta women received a literate and physical education and conducted the affairs of the town and their estates while the men were off at war. The cities around Athens periodically allied with each other and Athens's other enemies to resist the aggression of the Athenian Empire.

The Greek cities in the Mediterranean bordered the Persian Empire, a vast alliance extending across Central Asia, Africa, and parts of Europe. The Persians built on the success of the Mesopotamian empires preceding them. For hundreds of years goods moved throughout the Persian world on peaceful trade routes. While the official religion of the Persian Empire was Zoroastrianism, Persian emperors permitted their subject peoples to keep their own religions and ancestral customs.

The Greek and Persian empires went to war in the fifth century BCE. While children of Eurocentric education are taught to cheer for the Greeks and applaud the bravery of the Spartans (especially the 300 who held the pass at Thermopylae), the Persian Empire at that time was significantly more cosmopolitan and tolerant than the Greek. In the end neither empire conquered the other, and after several decades of war a peace treaty firmed up the borders, one of the first divisions of East and West.

In the later fifth century BCE, Sparta and Athens went to war, an event that diminished the prosperity of the Peloponnesian peninsula. Sparta won and imposed strict controls on Athens. It was in that world where Plato grew to adulthood.

TRIAL OF A TEACHER

When Aristocles entered the gymnasium bathing room he found both his brothers waiting for him. A slave stepped forward to douse his glowing skin with oil and then scrape it off. Adeimantis looked up and down his brother's naked girth and said, "Hello, *Plato*."

Unlike "bee lips", the nickname *broad* didn't sting him. "The better to throw you with, dear brother," he laughed.

Glaukon said, "How did the bout go?"

"I won," Plato said. "I always win."

Adeimantis grinned. "That's my brother!" he said. "You're the best wrestler in Athens. You should go to the Isthmian Games again."

"I don't have the heart after the war," Plato said. Only a few years before, he'd fought in the Athenian army that lost to the Spartans in the latest battle of the Peloponnesian Wars.

Glaukon quelled Adeimantis with a glance. "That's not what we're here to talk about," he said. "Are you heading out to Socrates's house again?"

"Of course," Plato said, turning so the slave could oil his back.

"Maybe you shouldn't," Glaukon said.

"Why not?" Plato said. "He's a fine philosopher."

"If that's what you call it," Adeimantis said. Glaukon glared at him again.

"Look, the rumors aren't true," Plato said. "He's not an atheist. He doesn't spend all day on the couch with his students either. Not that he'd be the first teacher to do that," he added. Older men often picked youths for lovers, trading clothes and political favors for emotional and physical intimacy. Thanks to his mother's uncle, Plato's family continued to be among the wealthiest in Athens, and Plato believed he didn't need favors from anyone.

"Socrates is a spiritual man," he went on. "He's an initiate of the priestess Diotima who serves the gods. He meditates—he can sit for hours. He hears messages in dreams and acts on them. His daimonion guides his actions."

"His daimonion?" Adeimantis said. "You mean his daimon, the guardian spirit?"

Plato nodded. "He met his daimon as a child, and the daimon speaks to him in his mind. He always does what the daimon tells him to do. Or rather, doesn't do what the daimon tells him not to do."

"That doesn't sound right," Adeimantis said doubtfully.

Glaukon took over. "The city has turned against him. They blame his students for helping Sparta install the tyrants." Sparta had handpicked thirty Athenians to rule the city. Their bloody rule had won them the title "the Thirty Tyrants." "Ever since the tyrants were overthrown the city has been punishing the people who were associated with them."

"I don't follow them," Plato said, putting on his chiton. "They were too violent. I can't support that anymore."

"You left, but Uncle Charmides didn't and a lot of people remember that," Glaukon said.

"We've always been a powerful family. We always will be," Plato said. "I'm going into politics myself."

"Just stay in the gymnasium today," Glaukon said. "One of the Pythagorean teachers is lecturing."

Plato laughed. "More tales of the mythical traveler? He'll tell us to stop eating meat," he said. "That's not a wrestler's diet. I'll see you at home." He shoved his feet into his sandals and turned to go.

Adeimantis grabbed at his arm. "You love Socrates," he said accusingly.

Plato met his gaze calmly. "Of course I love him," he said. "He's the best man I've ever known."

He didn't become alarmed until he saw the soldiers standing in front of Socrates' house. "Plato," one of them said. "You should go home. No lectures today."

He tried to push past them. "Where's Socrates?" His voice rose. "What's happened to him?"

The man looked sympathetic. "He's been arrested," he said.

"What?" Plato couldn't hide his shock. "On what charge?"

"Corrupting the youth."

"I'm his student. I'll vouch for him," Plato said.

The man said quietly, "You're one of the youth he's corrupting."

Plato managed to make it to the court just before the formal charges were read. "This indictment and affidavit is sworn by Meletus, the son of Meletus of Pitthos, against Socrates, the son of Sophroniscus of Alopece: Socrates is guilty of refusing to recognize the gods recognized by the state, and of introducing new divinities. He is also guilty of corrupting the youth. The penalty demanded is death."

Plato pushed his way onto the bench among his friends who crowded over to make room for him. "New divinities," one of them muttered. "They don't know what they're talking about."

Plato grew increasingly agitated as three accusers stood and passionately condemned Socrates. It seemed that his primary crime was teaching Critias, the leader of the Thirty Tyrants, although there was plenty of stuff in there about his impious behavior too.

Finally Socrates rose to give his own defense. He seemed frailer than Plato had ever seen him, showing every one of his seventy years, but his voice rose strongly. Plato leaned forward, trying to commit to memory every word his teacher said. Socrates spoke for three hours about his love for Athens. He admitted it was true that he did not attend the religious festivals of the city, but he loved and honored the gods. It was just that he knew the gods through the works of his daimon.

Once he pointed up into the benches. "There are my students," he said. "If I corrupt the youth, why don't they accuse me?"

Plato's friend elbowed him. "Look, they're staring at us."

Plato saw that many men in the assemblage were glaring at them. For the first time he felt the weight of disapproval. "I wish I was old enough to sit on the council," he muttered. He realized that he *did* need political favors; once again he was too young, helpless to help his teacher.

His friend raised his eyebrows. "You are far from the most famous Plato in Athens."

Finally the water in the water clock ran out and Socrates had to stop. The jurors threw their clay ballot disks into one of two pots, one for guilty and one for innocent. The count was close, but in the end, the verdict was guilty.

The jurors had to decide what his punishment would be. The accusers stood and demanded Socrates be put to death. Socrates stood to offer the usual counter-punishment. Everyone expected he would ask to be exiled, which would probably be accepted. Instead he said, "Punish me with free meals for life."

The crowd roared. "What is he doing?" Plato shouted. "He's provoking them!"

His friend said, "I think he's saying he's innocent."

Another friend said, "I think he *wants* them to kill him."

When the noise finally died down, one of his accusers said, "That's not a punishment, it's a reward. Propose a real punishment."

"One silver coin," Socrates said, throwing it down on the ground in front of him.

The crowd roared again. Plato leapt to his feet and ran to his teacher's side. "One silver coin, and these," he said, emptying his pouch. His friends pushed their way down to the floor and emptied their pouches too. In the end there were only thirty silver coins.

The jurors voted again, choosing between death and a punishment of thirty silver coins. This time the verdict was overwhelming: death by drinking poison hemlock.

The soldiers led Socrates away to a jail cell. His students followed, crowding around the couch while he lay his head down. The hand that reached for the cup of hemlock was steady. "Don't be afraid of my death," he told them. "I'm not."

Plato said, "Why did you do it?"

Socrates said calmly, "My daimonion didn't tell me not to."

When Plato arrived home Potone threw herself on him. "I was so worried about you!"

Gently he pulled her arms from his neck. "I live," he said. "My teacher does not."

"I tried to spare you," Glaukon said. "You should have listened to the Pythagorean."

Pythagoras. The name gave Plato an idea. The old philosopher was said to have travelled the world. The city that had turned on Plato's teacher seemed a prison to him now. "I'll follow him," Plato said. "I'm leaving the city."

Pythagoras

More than a hundred years before Plato, Pythagoras was born on an island off the coast of Turkey. The port city of Samos engaged in seaborne trade around a quarter of the world. In "The Paths of the Ancient Sages" Peter Kingsley points out that the temple of Hera on Samos stored objects from around the known world, including Babylonia, Syria, Asia, India, and Egypt. It is not surprising that Pythagoras acquired a taste for travel at the beginning of his life.

We know Pythagoras's life from the accounts of three biographers who lived many centuries after he died: Diogenes Laertius, Porphyry, and Iamblichus. All of them documented his extensive journeys across the ancient world from Egypt to India. Iamblichus says he learned divine rites and worship of the gods from the Chaldeans. While it became a Eurocentric scholastic fashion to question whether Pythagoras ever traveled at all, Kingsley points out that reports of his travels date back to his own lifetime.

In middle age, Pythagoras settled in Corona, a city in Italy, and began to teach. In *Pythagorean Women* Sarah Pomeroy details his teaching methodology. First he addressed the men, then the women separately, then the children, including girls and boys, at a time when it was unusual for girls and women to receive formal education. Pomeroy points out that the reforms he instituted in daily life would have to be adopted by the whole family, including the women. These reforms included giving up ostentatious clothing and jewelry, wearing linen rather than wool, and strict monogamy. This last was an innovation in a culture where men routinely visited prostitutes and maintained concubines. Pythagoras also countered the idea that women were made unclean by sex by saying that women were pure enough to engage in ritual even after sex with their husbands, although not after sex with anyone else.

The followers of Pythagoras were divided into outer and inner circles. The outer circles lived at home and attended his lectures by day. The inner circle lived in a community of families that followed his way of life, including strict vegetarianism and holding property in common.

In his paper "The Death of Pythagoras," Bruce Pennington notes there are as many as ten versions of Pythagoras's death. In some, a spurned student rouses the populace against him. Others say he lived to be a hundred and taught his philosophy to Empedocles, the Greek philosopher who said that the world is composed of the elements, earth, water, air, and fire.

The school of Pythagoras continued in southern Italy, where his followers became fervent devotees of the Orphic Mysteries. Plato spent some time among them in his own travels and would later draw heavily on their ideas and the imagery of the mysteries for his own work.

A NEW BEGINNING

Plato peered anxiously at the slaves carrying his luggage sacks off the ship. "Careful with that!" he called out. One of those sacks held the accounts he had laboriously recorded of Socrates's trial and as much of his teacher's wisdom as he could dig out of his memory.

He'd started the journey with friends, other students of Socrates, but none of them had come with him this far. In Italy he'd spent time with Pythagorean teachers. They had taught him that this one life was but a waypoint on the cycle of birth, death, and rebirth. They said Pythagoras had learned this teaching in India. Only virtuous living and spiritual initiation could win a soul free from the cycle. This was strange to Plato, who like every Greek knew that the soul entered the dark underworld after death where it could wander lost, or be saved by knowledge imparted by initiation and be brought to Persephone's realm.

The Pythagoreans taught Plato that the mysteries of the universe could be understood through the knowledge of numbers, that philosophy imparts divine wisdom, and that the soul could rise to union with the divine. These things Pythagoras had learned not from India, but from Egypt, and these were the teachings he most valued.

The Pythagorean teachers had reminded Plato that his true calling was to learn. He was no longer running away from Athens. He was running toward knowledge.

"Greetings!" The voice spoke Greek, but the man was as far from Greek as Plato could imagine. His skin was so black it shone in the merciless desert sun. "Welcome to Thebes!" The city too was as far from Greece as he could imagine, with buildings made of clay stretching for miles along the banks of the river.

"'Thebes' is what we call it. You call it 'Waset,' don't you?" Plato said, stepping off the boat. "City of a hundred gates." He'd learned the land called "Egypt" in his own tongue was called "Kemet" by its own people, after the fertile black soil deposited by the yearly flooding of the Nile.

"The city has fewer gates since the Persians came," his guide said, falling in with him along the path into the city. "Thebes is no longer the city it once was."

"We've had some trouble with them ourselves," Plato said dryly.

The man laughed. "And we thank you for your aid!" Egypt had only recently thrown off Persian rule with Greek assistance and had re-instated Kemetic pharaohs. "I presume you're in the army yourself?"

"Not since my youth," Plato said. "I'm a student, not a mercenary."

The man blinked at him. "A man from Greece, and you are here to study?"

"I am told this is the finest school in the world."

"Of course," the man said, "but … are you ready?"

Plato drew himself up. "I was schooled in Athens by Socrates and in Italy by the Pythagoreans. I am sure I can learn what you have to teach in a year or two."

His guide laughed and changed the subject. "You have sailed a long time."

"Eleven days from Heliopolis," Plato said. The travel guide written by Herodotus had said the trip would only take nine, and Plato rather held it against him. It had been a cramped boat.

"Then you are ready to rest," his guide said. "I can show you a good place to stay. Run by a relative of my sister, very cheap—" He ran his eyes over Plato's finely woven cloak and said, "Er, very comfortable."

Later in the day as he walked toward the temple, Plato thought he had travelled enough that he should have become accustomed to the sight of women on the streets by now. In Athens there were only a few and they were not respectable. In Thebes respectable women were everywhere, beautiful brown and black women in linen dresses, with jewels around their necks and jeweled colors on their eyes and cheeks. They not only ran households, they ran businesses! They married who they wanted, travelled where they wanted, owned property, represented themselves in court, and seemed to live as freely as men.

The temple itself was impressive. The columns rose twice as high as the Parthenon, stone walls carved with figures and signs, all painted in bright colors. Six gigantic statues of men guarded the gate, all identical, except the two flanking the gate, who were seated.

As he stepped through the gate into the vast courtyard, an Egyptian woman greeted him in Greek. "Hail, traveler. What have you come to seek?"

He'd thought he was a man of the world, but a woman greeting him so openly in public surprised him. "I've come to speak to your teachers," he said.

"I am a teacher," she said. He expected her to next ask him what he wanted to learn, but instead she said, "What makes you worthy to be taught?"

"I am Aristocles, son of Ariston," he said. "My family has been powerful in Athens for a hundred years."

The woman smiled gently. "Do you see the guardians at the gate?" she said. "These are statues of Ramses the Great. He ruled for almost seventy years. He built many temples and cities, and he fathered many, many children. In a real sense we are all his children." She paused. "He lived nearly a thousand years ago."

Reeling, Plato reconsidered his answer. "I am willing to learn," he said.

His guide smiled again. "Can you finish what you begin?" she said. "Our course of study requires quite a long time to complete."

"How long?" Plato said, less sure of himself. He thought he might be able to stay for two, maybe three years.

"Forty years," she said serenely.

Greek Cosmology

A Greek child was prepared to join the community through the *paideia*, a word meaning "education" but also including the meaning of understanding the natural order, including the stories of the gods. Everyone's first exposure to the paideia was through stories told by professionals or parents, usually at community gatherings or at home at night.

The greatest stories were those told by the poets, Homer, Hesiod, and Orpheus. The Homeric works include a collection of hymns, thirty-one song/prayers addressed to individual gods and goddesses telling stories of their origin and exploits. There are also two long stories: the *Iliad*, telling of the sack of Troy, and the *Odyssey*, the story of Odysseus's journey home after the war. The hymns of Hesiod and Orpheus describe the origin of the gods, and Hesiod's *Works and Days* gives agricultural instructions in a sacred context.

The poets Homer, Hesiod, and Orpheus were held to be historic figures. Scholars point out that the story collections qualify as bardic traditions, as they were passed forward in time through generations of retelling with each singer adding their own perspective on the tales. Even so, it is remarkable how historically accurate some of the details remain. The *Iliad* contains a long passage, the Catalogue of Ships, listing the cities that sent soldiers to the war. European scholarship treated the catalogue as colorful and metaphorical until nineteenth-century archaeology unearthed the cities listed in it, proving the catalogue was not a fantasy but a historical record. It seems that at least portions of the *Iliad* date to the Mycenaean era, about 1100 BCE, five centuries before Plato lived.

Homer was the oldest of the poets, and his stories have endured through millennia. In Plato's time, the *Iliad* and the *Odyssey* were still performed extensively. They were performed through the Byzantine era. They were performed in Renaissance Europe. They are performed today—a Google search on Homer gives a list of movies based on the Homeric works. The vivid depictions of war in the *Iliad*, and Odysseus's meandering journey through fantastic lands to reach home in the *Odyssey*, still fascinate audiences of all ages. The people in the poems act with power, pride, compassion, arrogance, and faithfulness; they laugh, they grieve, they lose, and they win. Troy falls; Odysseus makes it home, where Penelope is waiting for him. They are great stories.

The bardic traditions were not only entertaining but also educational, letting the audience know what was expected at every station of life. Homer also described what happened to the soul in the afterlife. The Greek conception of the soul was simpler than the Kemetic system; for the Greeks, soul meant breath, and when the breath flew the body, the soul went with it. Homer describes the realm of the dead as a damp and dismal plain ruled by Hades and Persephone where misty shades flit endlessly.

It was possible to speak to the dead. In Books 10 and 11 of the *Odyssey*, the sorceress Circe describes to Odysseus how to reach the mouth of the underworld. Following her instructions, Odysseus sails to that shore, digs a pit, sacrifices animals, and speaks to the spirits of the dead.

Homer's description of the underworld where wicked souls are tortured and even the happiest souls spend eternity as shades strikes us as grim today. It must have struck the ancients as grim as well. The Eleusinian Mysteries were the ritual response to this fate. The mysteries told the story of how Hades, god of the underworld, abducted Demeter's young daughter Persephone and stole her away to the underworld. Demeter responded by hiding herself in a cave. Nothing grew and the people starved. Finally Zeus entreated Demeter to come out, but she refused unless her daughter was returned to her. Zeus agreed that Persephone could return, but only if she had not eaten in the underworld. When the gods came to rescue her they found Persephone had refused all food except a few pomegranate seeds. Zeus decreed that she had to spend the same number of months in the underworld every year as seeds she had eaten. Each year Persephone returns to the underworld and winter grips the earth; when she returns to her mother, warmth and life also return.

In the Eleusinian Mysteries the initiates were introduced to Persephone, goddess of the afterlife. While the mysteries remain a secret, many ancient sources attest that after the initiation they felt they had literally been saved and no longer feared death.

In addition to the cosmologies, the bardic traditions describe the Olympian deities. There are twelve, male and female, grouped into male/ female pairs in antiquity:

- Zeus, the father of the gods, and Hera, the mother
- Aphrodite, goddess of love, and Ares, god of war
- Artemis, the virgin huntress, and Apollo, god of prophecy and healing
- Athena, goddess of wisdom, and Poseidon, god of the sea
- Hephaestus, the smith, and Hestia, goddess of the hearth
- Hermes, messenger of the gods, and Demeter, goddess of the earth

These were not the only Greek deities. Other prominent goddesses and gods had temples and stories. In later times the god of intoxication Dionysos displaced Hestia on Olympus (and ruined the gender pairing scheme). We have already met Hades and Persephone, rulers of the underworld, and the god of healing Asclepius whose temples served as centers of healing. Later theurgists honored them all, but it was the Olympians who framed the universe.

GOING HOME

"Careful with that," Plato said to his slave. It had been thirteen years since he composed his youthful writings, but he still valued the precious words of his first teacher.

Since then he had learned so much more. He had studied physical sciences no one in Athens had ever seen. He had thought he'd learned mathematics in his childhood school, but the calculations he had mastered in Egypt surpassed them. He had learned the Egyptian tongue quickly and had been accepted among the priesthood, who taught him how to purify himself and approach the gods. Above all they shared with him the philosophy which revealed and explained the mysteries of the universe, the teachings of Ma'at.

He had learned why Thales, one of the philosophers who had also studied here, had preached the principle that water was the source of life. Watching the Nile flood year after year, seeing with his own eyes the mud rising as the waters receded, later hearing in the temple the stories of how the universe was created, he knew in mind and heart that water truly was both chaotic and the nourisher of life.

Now he was called home. He was a third son and had never been critical to his family's fortunes, and his uncles and brothers had seen to the running of the estates, but his mother was ill and wanted to see him again before she died. Despite his worry, he smiled to think of her. Perictione's philosophical book "On Harmonious Women" was popular; he was coming home as the son of a famous mother.

What was that wailing? A woman hung on the neck of his faithful slave. Over the years the man had become his dearest friend from home. Plato put a hand on the man's shoulder. "I am sorry," he said. "You do not belong to me, but to my family, so I cannot free you. Do you wish your son to remain with you? I can buy him for you."

"No," the man said immediately. "He should stay with his mother in the way of Kemet. He will comfort her and care for her."

Before he left Plato went back to the temple one last time. He searched through the halls and rooms before he finally found his first teacher. She sat on the edge of the temple pool watching the sun set in the desert west over the city of the dead.

He joined her and watched the sun for a while. "I feel as if I am dying," he said softly. "I am going away from the source of life and knowledge."

She turned to him. "You take your knowledge with you," she said. "It nourishes life wherever it is planted."

"I didn't finish," he said. "I feel as if I have only just begun."

"Thales spent only a few years. Even Pythagoras only studied twenty-three years," she laughed. "No Greek has done more."

"I have learned from many wise teachers, but you were the first to accept me," he said. "Thank you for taking in an ignorant man."

She touched his hand. "You were willing to learn," she said. She smiled at him as serenely as the first day he had met her. "Are you willing to teach?"

Greek Temples and Priesthood

Temples in classical Greece served a somewhat different function than the houses of deity in Kemet. They were not houses where living deities were tended by a full-time professional priesthood. The temple grew around objects holding the sacred power of deity and acted more as a storehouse or museum. The earliest temple of Athena on the Acropolis hill overlooking Athens housed a wooden object called a *xoanon* that fell from the sky in answer to a prayer to Athena. Later the much larger Parthenon with its magnificent pillars was built on the Acropolis and a huge statue of gold and ivory was installed there. However, the eyes and mouth of the statue were not opened as in Kemet and India.

Festivals honoring the deity took place on a periodic basis. These were often funded by wealthy citizens, sometimes including *hetaera* or prostitutes. The statues were not fed and clothed daily but were given food offerings during the festivals. In the yearly festival to Athena a young girl presented a robe that had been woven by the town's women; that robe did not go to the ivory and gold statue of Athena in the main temple but to the temple of the humble xoanon. We may infer that the object itself held the power of deity the great statue lacked.

Priestesses and priests did not leave home to reside in the temple and did not study in the temples as in Kemet, serving only on special occasions. They also did not shave or bathe daily to maintain a state of purity, although they did engage in fasting or avoiding some foods in devotion to the deities. The offices involved more administrative than spiritual work, organizing the feasts, parades, and other offerings to the deity.

Priestly offices could move from person to person or be held in families. Several families in Eleusis seem to have made their primary living on the yearly Eleusinian Mysteries, serving in the offices of Hierophant, Hegemon, Hierus, Dadouchos, and Stolistes, among others. These titles are still in use among Golden Dawn magicians as well as in Neo-Pagan reconstructions of the mysteries.

THE GROVES OF ACADEME

Plato was restless. He wandered through the streets of Athens, hardly recognizing anyone. Many of the faces were so young they hadn't even been born when he was fighting in the war. It was strange to see so many men on the street; when he did see a woman she was a slave or a prostitute, a hired dancer. Of course it was the prostitutes who were the most knowledgeable women and owned their own property too, but even these women were not as free as men and certainly not as free as the women of Kemet.

He found himself wandering outside the city walls and clambering over the nearer hills. Abruptly he stopped, recognizing the place. "The grove of Akademos," he said to himself. The hero was rumored to be buried in the grove of trees sacred to Athena. "Neit," he murmured. When he was in Egypt he had traveled to Sau (or Sais), sister city of Athens, and he had paid his respects to the goddess who had invented weaving and had saved her people from war. The priestesses and priests there told him Neit had travelled to Greece, where she had become Athena, still a protective goddess of weaving and knowledge, patron of the city that bore her name.

Plato sat beneath one of the trees, glad for the shade and the relative quiet of the forest after the bustle of the city. He was still in culture shock from the transition. Waset was a city of temples and schools, a city of learning and culture. After more than a decade in the temple there, the Parthenon seemed small; Athens seemed small, too … in size as well as outlook.

"Aristocles!" a young voice called. "Uncle Aristocles!"

"Here, Speusippus," Plato said with a sigh.

His sister's son came bounding up the path. "Mother said I should follow you and make sure you're well."

"I'm well," he said. "You can go home and tell her so."

The boy plopped himself against a tree. "It's a long way and it's hot. Want some food?" He handed over a hunk of bread and a wineskin. Plato was pleased to eat Greek bread again, not so tough as the hard, flat cakes the Egyptians ate, but he'd grown accustomed to Egyptian beer, and watered wine tasted sour to him.

"Potone says you went to Egypt to learn," the boy said. Plato nodded. "What did you learn?"

Plato laughed. "I can tell you, if you want. How many years do you have?"

"As many as you can give me."

Looking into his youthful, hopeful eyes, Plato sighed. He dug into his memory for the first words his teacher had spoken. "Settle the body, still the mind, contemplate the divine." Looking forward a dozen years, he added, "so that you may encounter the divine."

Plato's Worldview

Plato's works have survived in some number. Scholars note that it is difficult to decide which of Plato's thoughts can truly be attributed to him. We can consider the corpus of his work to include the thoughts of his predecessors including his unnamed Kemetic teachers, as well as Pythagoras, Socrates, and Diotima. (Mary Ellen Waithe recovers Diotima's thought in *A History of Women Philosophers*.) There are numerous translations of Plato; Benjamin Jowett's readable translations from the early twentieth century are posted online by MIT.

Plato's works call into question the conventional wisdom about the gods, particularly the stories told by the poets. In Book 10 of the *Republic*, Socrates says there is a "quarrel" between philosophy and poetry. Even though Homer has been the educator of the youth, in the *Republic* there will be no poetry except hymns to the gods, or pleasure and pain will rule the state rather than reason. Book 2 argues that the gods do not change shape or lie to humans, and therefore any entertainment depicting them doing so must be a lie.

Plato devotes one entire dialogue, *Ion*, to a dialogue between Socrates and a Homeric performer in which Socrates demonstrates to the performer that his work is not truthful. In the dialogue *Phaedrus* Plato says the Muses inspire poets with a kind of madness, and that if anyone tries to be a poet through knowledge rather than through inspiration, that person will fail.

If Plato's cosmology did not derive from the poets, what did he teach? In the dialogue *Timaeus*, Critias recounts the story of Solon's visit to Egypt. Solon, a politician and leader of the Athens, visited Sais, ruled by the goddess Neit, whom the Greeks equated with their Athena. Critias reproduces the dialogue between Solon and the priests of the temples. They told him that the Greeks were children because they had no beliefs passed down from ancestor to ancestor as in Egypt. The priests then delivered to him the history of his people as they had kept it.

The next speaker, Timaeus himself, acknowledges the gods and goddesses in order to tell the story of the creation of the world. Timaeus starts by making a distinction between the world of being that does not change, usually referred to by Platonists as the "Forms," and the world of becoming which can be grasped by the senses. These two are often described as the "Intelligible" world and the "Sensible" world. The demiurge, the Craftsman, a being good and without jealousy, created the cosmos on the plan of the Forms. The Craftsman shaped fire, earth, air, and water into the body of the cosmos. This body was filled with the World Soul.

Plato had travelled the world to expose himself to new ideas, and he shaped those ideas in the dialogues. These core ideas have been passed forward in time through all the teachers who have studied his works.

THE MOST FAMOUS PLATO

"Stop crying," he told Potone.

"I can't help it," she said. "You're the only brother I have left."

"Go ahead, give me a kiss." She bent down and kissed his forehead. "There. You see I love you," he said. "Now go get my students."

Eventually they crowded around his bed. How had they gotten to be so many? There were even two women—Axiothea, who came dressed like a man, and Lasthenia, who didn't. Some of the boys didn't like it, but Plato had lived among the women of Kemet, and he remembered Potone's love of learning when they were both young.

"No mourning," he said, as he heard one of the younger ones sniffle. "Socrates wasn't afraid to die, and I'm not either. Now, I've called you here so I can name a successor."

Aristotle leaned forward. He was undoubtedly the most brilliant of Plato's students. More, he had ambition. He was also one of the men who didn't think much of the women students. "Aristotle," he said, and the man leaned forward eagerly. "I know you desire the position. You will go far in the world. But I think your destiny is to find your own way. You don't need to be confined to the way I do things."

Aristotle reared back. "I respect you," he said. "I have studied with you for twenty years."

Had it been that long? "I know," Plato said gently. "Now you must make your own studies. When you are ready, you will teach those." He beckoned to Speusippus. "My sister's nephew, and my closest heir," he said. "Speusippus, I wish you to guide the Academy, to continue the work I have begun."

Speusippus knelt beside the couch and kissed his hand.

No one seemed surprised that he was keeping the Academy in the family. Aristotle tried to hide his disappointment, but it was clear the decision was a blow to him. Plato was convinced he was right; Aristotle had his own path to follow, and trying to maintain Plato's legacy would only hold him down. Speusippus was better suited to carry on Plato's work. He would continue teaching the women too. Anyway, Aristotle's family could afford to support him, but Speusippus needed the teaching fees.

Plato reflected on his legacy. Whatever people said of him, he felt he owed everything to Egypt and to Socrates. A thought struck him and he started laughing. Seeing that he was distressing his grief-filled students, he explained, "When I was young one of my friends told me I was far from the most famous Plato in Athens. Now I guess I am."

Speusippus vowed passionately, "You will be the only Plato history remembers."

Plato's Afterlife

We have seen that for Homer the soul was simply breath. In her paper "Soma and Psyche in Hippocratic Medicine," Beata Gundert explores Homer's thought in a bit more detail. For Homer the human person was composed of both thoughts and works. The mind that thinks, nous, remains constant even when the body changes. The seat of thought is in the chest. The breath of life, called psyche, leaves the body at death and travels to the underworld as a shade.

The idea of reincarnation entered into Greek thought between Homer's time and Plato's. Pythagoras may have brought the doctrine of reincarnation to Greece when he returned from his travels to India, where the *Upanishads* teach that the death of the body is not the death of the soul, which goes on to be reborn in other physical bodies.

Plato's understanding of the soul is somewhat more complicated than Homer's and changes from dialogue to dialogue. In the dialogue

Phaedo, Socrates says the soul that has spent its time pursuing earthly pleasures is contaminated by the physical and is drawn back to the world, flitting about monuments and tombs. Such souls are visible to the naked eye due to their ongoing physical nature. From there they can be reborn: the wicked into animals such as asses and hawks, the good non-philosophers as bees, ants, or people. The soul that has contemplated philosophy is pure, uncontaminated by the body, and flies up to that which is "like itself," divine and immortal, to spend a happy eternity with the gods.

In the dialogue *Phaedrus*, Socrates compares the soul to a team of winged horses, one beautiful and good, one ignoble and difficult. The human charioteer has the difficult task of driving both as a team. The gods also have chariots and drive them through the heavens, Zeus at the head, followed by ten other Olympians, while Hestia remains behind on Olympus. Human charioteers strive to join that heavenly train. Those who succeed participate in a magnificent banquet with the gods; the horses enjoy ambrosia and nectar, while the charioteers enjoy beauties unknown by the human soul. This idea reminds us of the Egyptian concept of the ba of the deceased joining the gods in the stars upon their death.

Phaedrus contains a second conceptualization, wherein Socrates explains that souls have wings: when the soul loses its wings through contact with the ugly and foul, it wanders around until it settles into an earthly, mortal, body.

Critias tells us in the dialogue *Timaeus* that the Craftsman created the souls of humans. Each soul is immortal, and each is placed on a star as if being placed on a chariot. Each soul descends to earth to be incarnated in the human body in its first life. Souls that live well return to their stars on death, those that do not are born in their second lives as women (disappointingly), and if continuing to live badly, are reborn as a form of animal.

After creating the souls, the Craftsman delegated the creation of the body to the gods. The gods enclosed the three parts of the soul in the body: the rational and immortal part of the soul in the head; the higher mortal soul in the chest, seat of the passions; and the lower mortal soul in the trunk, seat of the appetite. In *Egyptian and Hermetic Doctrine* Eric Iverson draws an explicit connection between some of the Kemetic parts of the soul and this three-part division in Plato. Iverson connects the mortal soul with the ba and the rational soul with the akh.

To Plato, the human soul partook of the divine. In *Nature and Divinity in Plato's Timaeus*, Sarah Broadie notes that the demiurge creates the soul from the materials left over from creating the cosmic world. She argues that this points to the essential identity of the cosmic world and the human soul. In *Greek Religion* Walter Burkert points out that the language Plato uses to describe the soul's relationship to the cosmos is the language of the Eleusinian and Orphic mysteries. Through rational contemplation of the beauty of the good, the soul remembers its true identity, bringing the soul to the state of blessedness.

THE LESSONS OF PLATO

Neitokrity's story introduced us to a world where the gods eat and wear clothes and live in houses and speak to the priestesses and priests who serve them. While we have the ritual that invited a deity into a statue, we don't have a record of the techniques the priestesses and priests used to communicate with them.

Plato's work constructs a vision of the universe, how it was created and how it works, and how each human was created, one entity in the cosmos, a part of the whole. He rejects a simplified construction of the gods as entities with human-like appetites and instead views them as fundamental to a universe that is just and good.

The vision Plato constructs shifts in his works. Iamblichus in *Theurgia or the Mysteries of Egypt* dictates the order in which Plato's dialogues should be read by theurgists. In *Theurgy and the Soul* Gregory Shaw observes that read in this order, the grim descriptions of the afterlife in earlier works give way to the exaltation of the afterlife of the *Timaeus*. This order helps to make sense of Plato's cosmology, allowing insights to deepen over time. Reading Plato's works in this order becomes an initiation in itself.

Here is Iamblichus's order: *Alcibiades I, Gorgias, Phaedo, Cratylus, Theaetetus, Sophist, Statesman, Phaedrus, Symposium, Philebus, Timaeus,* and *Parmenides.* Interestingly, this list does not include the *Republic,* which is most widely studied in universities today.

The first study assignment for the theurgist is to read these works and allow them to spark meditations on the universal questions: what is the body, what is the soul, what made the universe, what happens when we die, what is divine? Each of us comes to our own understanding. Theurgy does not dictate dogma; it encourages questioning and experience.

Notes on the Story

We happen to know quite a bit about Plato, including the names of his parents and siblings, the origin of his nicknames, and of course his relationship with Socrates. The childhood stories here (his father's sexual assault on his mother, bees sitting on Plato's lips, and the origin of his nickname "broad") are in the historical record. Diogenes Laertius recorded the charges leveled against Socrates.

Our image of the classical philosophers portrays them as noble thinkers. When we start to think about how they lived their daily lives, some less admirable details emerge. As a member of a prominent family Plato would certainly have owned slaves. Only people who weren't doing their own housework could afford to spend so many hours teaching, writing, and contemplating.

Here I am choosing to take Plato's word that he studied in Egypt and explicitly reject the scholastic theories that call this into question. We don't know why Plato cut his studies in Egypt/Kemet short after thirteen years to return home, but it is a human experience in middle age to be called home to care for ill parents and make our peace with them.

THREE

PLOTINUS

About a hundred years after Plato's death, the academy he founded veered off into skepticism, the idea that it is not possible to know truth. By then Plato was less revered, and when the Stoic school split off from the academy his work was left behind. It was six hundred years before his work was studied seriously again. This renaissance occurred in the land of Kemet after it became a Roman colony but when the great temples still honored the gods and taught students. The Kemetic/Egyptian, Greek, and Roman worlds converged in the melting pot of the port city Alexandria.

In Alexandria philosophers once again turned to the study of Plato. Today we call them Neo-Platonists, but they called themselves Platonists. The first of these was Ammonius, who we know primarily through his most famous student and the first theurgist, Plotinus. He lived 204–270 CE and studied in Alexandria, Egypt. The life of Plotinus exemplifies why teachers were held in such high regard in the ancient world; he was a genuinely good man.

A PICKY STUDENT

Plotinus thought the Greeks in Alexandria who offered themselves as teachers mostly talked to hear their own voices. No sooner had the priest in the Museion finished his invocation to the Muses than they fell over each other to reach the steps where they began to earnestly lecture everyone passing by. Plotinus had spent days listening to first one, then another, searching for a man who actually made sense. He still hadn't found one he would care to call his teacher. He was beginning to wonder if he was being too picky.

A passing Greek bumped his shoulder. "Sorry," he said, not sounding sorry. Plotinus suppressed a spurt of rage. He got that a lot. He was Egyptian, and Alexandria was in Egypt, technically, but the cosmopolitan port town didn't honor her native residents. After all, it was a king of Greece who had built the town—Alexander, whose lavish tomb reminded everyone that this was his city.

The same lout sneered at one of the teachers as he passed. "Hey, Ammonius," he said. "Ammonius Saccas! There's a load waiting for you at the dock." The man's friends laughed with him as they strode away.

Plotinus had heard of Ammonius, a friend had mentioned him in passing. Plotinus sat on the steps next to him. "Doesn't that make you mad?" he said curiously.

Ammonius shrugged. "Why? They're right, I used to be a dock worker. I will be again too if I don't manage to attract more students."

Plotinus found himself attracted to the man's calm demeanor. "What do you teach?"

"Have you ever heard of Plato?"

"He lived so long ago," Plotinus said dismissively. "Philosophy moved on."

Ammonius laughed. "He's too old for you? You've forgotten your own history then."

"How so?" Plotinus said, irritated but intrigued.

"Have you read the *Critias*? Plato tells us when the politician Solon visited Egypt he travelled to Sais, to the city of your goddess Neit, who my people call Athena. There the priests told him that the Greeks were children because we have no beliefs passed on from ancestor to ancestor! And now you, inheritor of your ancient knowledge, are unwilling to learn from Plato because he lived too long ago. Truly Plato would be laughing."

Plotinus didn't see what was funny. "Alright, tell me one thing Plato said that is worth knowing."

The man took in a deep breath, as if he was settling himself, looking within. "There are two worlds," Ammonius said. "There is the world of being that does not change, the world of Forms. It can only be understood by the mind, so it is called the Intelligible World."

Plotinus had never heard this before. "What's the second world?"

"The world of becoming, the Sensible World, that can be grasped by the senses."

"If there are two worlds, who created them? The gods?"

"The Craftsman," Ammonius answered, "a being good and without jealousy. The Craftsman created the Cosmos on the plan of the forms, shaping fire, earth, air, and water into the body of the Cosmos; then the Craftsman filled the body with the World Soul."

"What does this have to do with me?" Plotinus said.

"When you understand the cosmos you understand how to commune with the gods, and with the highest intellect that created the cosmos," Ammonius said tranquilly. "And when you have done that, what does it matter if some lout insults you in the street?"

"Oh," Plotinus said, absorbing this. After a while he said, "You are the man I was looking for. Would you accept me as your student?"

Aristotle and Macedonia

Plato did not choose Aristotle as his successor to lead the Athenian Academy. Aristotle left Athens and veered into his own philosophical territory, today called empiricism. Aristotle believed we could only know the world through the evidence of the senses, not by meditation on the infinite. For this he is hailed as the West's first scientist. Aristotelian and Platonic thought have been at odds ever since, and scholars and philosophers have sought to reconcile them.

Aristotle wrote about anything and everything—biology, zoology, mathematics, philosophy, politics, theology, and poetry. Numerous works survive, fading out and in of Western history. His organization of subjects framed the curricula of the first universities in Europe, and his contempt for women closed them out of the academy for many centuries. His work was taken into Christian theology, and Islamic theology calls him the "first teacher." He did not recognize that the soul could separate from the body, and so doubted that consciousness could survive death.

Aristotle grew up in the area north of Greece called Macedonia (confusingly, Macedonia now names both a region of Greece and an independent country). At a critical moment in his life, he was offered the opportunity to found his own Macedonian academy. There he tutored future kings, including Ptolemy and Alexander.

Alexander forged a fierce army with a distinctly us-versus-them outlook: the band of brothers were family and everyone else they encountered were more like natural resources to be harvested. That army travelled the old Persian trade routes and extended the Greek Empire into Egypt, Persia, and as far east as India. Alexander left generals of the army in charge of each of the regions as he went.

Then he died. He died young, in his thirties, before he could finish all the invasions he planned. No one else could hold such a huge empire together, and his empire was torn apart immediately by civil war. The individual generals became the leaders of their particular territories. Today in India there are still fair-haired, blue-eyed people descended from the soldiers Alexander left behind.

Ptolemy inherited Egypt in 323 BCE. He declared himself pharaoh, and his family dynasty rapidly went native, adopting Egyptian customs and styling themselves as new emperors. The last Ptolemaic ruler, Cleopatra, learned to speak the native language and presented herself to the people in pharaonic imagery, comparing herself to Hatshepsut. She lost Egypt to the Roman Empire in 30 BCE, ending three centuries of her family's rule.

ALL ROADS LEAD TO ROME

"Tell me again," the woman said, rolling onto her side on her couch. "Tell me the story again! You wanted to learn from the Persians, so you went to war with them?"

"It worked for Alexander," Plotinus said testily. He wished the woman Gemina would stop laughing. He had spent eleven years with Ammonius before he enlisted in Emperor Gordian's army to travel to Persia to learn from the fabled teachers there. After two years in the army he felt older than forty. He was sick of walking and wanted to sit forever.

"And then the emperor went and got himself killed." Gemina kicked her feet laughing.

"Like Alexander," Plotinus agreed. "Although he didn't make it to India. I barely escaped with my life. I ran most of the way to Antioch. I had just enough coin to book passage to Italy, then I made my way overland to Rome."

Gemina sat up. "Well, I brought you home because you wear the soldier's tunic. And sandals," she said, eyeing his hobnailed soles. "You are old enough to draw a veteran's share. But you only served for two years?"

"I'm not Roman," Plotinus admitted. "I'm Egyptian. Normally we serve in the fleet, but the emperor needed volunteers, so they took me, old as I was."

"And now you have no coin to pay me for your room," she sighed.

Plotinus said, "I have no trade, other than that of teacher. I hope to make my way with that alone, as my teacher did before me."

"Well then," she said shrewdly, looking him over. "What do you teach?"

Plotinus composed himself, diving into his memory. What had Ammonius said to him on that first day? "Settle the body, still the mind, contemplate the divine."

The woman squinted at him. "The divine, what does that mean?"

"There are two worlds," he said slowly. After years on the road as a soldier it was more difficult than he had thought to bring his mind back to the way. "There is the world of Forms that can be understood by the mind, and the world that can be understood by the senses. The kind and good Craftsman fashioned the Sensible World on the plan of the Forms. Our task is to school our minds to approach the gods, so that our soul may approach the One. When we can do this, what does it matter whether the emperor dies on the road?" As he spoke a great flood of peace washed away his physical pain, washed away the fear and doubt he had experienced when the army failed, and his anxious sense of being alone in the world. He remembered finally that he was never alone.

Gemina studied his tranquil face for a moment. "I've never heard teaching like this," she said. "It makes sense of the world. It stirs my spirit." She lifted her voice. "Gemina! Gemina daughter! Come in here! You have to hear this."

Plotinus broke out of his trance, startled. "You mean there are two of you?"

The Roman Empire

Rome succeeded where Alexander did not.

The city of Rome was founded around 750 BCE. The Latin peoples conquered neighboring cities, planted colonies and a seaport, and built a small empire in central Italy. The neighboring Etruscan Empire invaded around 600 BCE and governed the Latin Romans for about a century. The Etruscans built Rome into a rich and prosperous city with roads, a sewer, and temples.

The last Etruscan king, Tarquin, was a despot, and the Latin aristocracy revolted, expelling the king and abolishing the monarchy in 509 BCE. Rome conquered Carthage, then Greece, adding Egypt in 30 BCE when Cleopatra surrendered to the Roman army.

The Celts had sacked Rome in 390 BCE. By 120 BCE, Rome had begun to push out along the roads of the Celtic peoples who they conquered as they went. Roman histories portray the Celts as barbarians and downplay their physical and cultural achievements, partly to justify the brutal Roman conquests. On the other hand, educated Romans respected Greek civilization; they studied Greek philosophy and literature and imported Greek teachers.

The success of the Roman Empire hinged on a number of factors. They were fantastic builders, laying down roads that could move soldiers and equipment rapidly across the empire. Soldiers were shipped out of their home area, served their enlistment, and then retired with a pension that allowed them a happy old age. The soldiers in turn kept civil order; it was said that a citizen could walk across the empire without being attacked by robbers. Roman law extended citizenship to the local elite who could in turn enjoy the benefits of civilization—plumbing, imported food, and entertainment.

At its height, the Roman Empire extended across Europe, North Africa, and the Caucasus Mountains into Asia. This is the exact area which we today point to as the cradle of civilization. This is not coincidental. "Western" civilization is in many ways still Roman, founded on colonialism and conquest, overwriting native cultures, dominating the world's peoples with a ruling elite, and funneling the world's resources to the homes of the elite.

THE DUTIFUL FATHER

"I thought I'd find you here," Amphiclea said. "We're ready for our Conference. And here you are doing the accounts."

Plotinus laid aside his pen and sat back in his chair, rubbing his eyes. From this room he could see through the whole house: the dining room where couches sat around a low table, the courtyard where the children played with the dogs, the garden where the slaves gathered dinner. "Who else will do them?"

Amphiclea drew up a small stool to sit next to him. "One of the slaves could take the work from you."

He waved his hand at the children. "Their parents trusted me to guide their fortunes until they are old enough to study philosophy themselves. I cannot fail them."

"I don't know how you do it all," she said. "You teach, you write treatises, and you make time for the care of all these orphans. And you meditate every day."

"Teaching is hardest," he admitted. "Finding new words for my thoughts."

Amphiclea tapped his desk. "You should teach what Ammonius taught you."

"I promised Ammonius to keep his teachings secret," he objected.

"So did Origen, and he's written about it!" she said.

"I've thought that myself," he admitted. "Perhaps it is time."

A boy bounded up the stairs. "We're ready!" he said.

Plotinus drew the boy against him. "Potamun, did you make the verse as I told you?"

The boy nodded solemnly. "It's for Plato's birthday," he said. He looked slyly up at his guardian. "I'd rather make it for your birthday."

Amphiclea laughed. "If you can get him to tell you when his birthday is you'll truly be a philosopher!"

Plotinus put the boy aside and rose stiffly. "The physical does not matter," he said. "But we should honor our great teachers, Plato and Socrates. The life of the mind is the life of the spirit."

Roman Temples and Priesthood

Children's books teach that there is a set of deities who have both Greek and Roman names, but the relationship between Greek and Roman deities is a little more complicated. The earliest Latin spirits, *numen* (the root of our word "numinous") were rooted in place, spirits of farmland and house. We recognize the twelve Olympians in their Roman counterparts: Jupiter, Juno, Venus, Mars, Diana, Apollo, Minerva, Neptune, Vulcan, Vesta, Mercury, and Ceres.

The Etruscan rule of Rome brought Etruscan deities to the city closely resembling their Greek counterparts. We don't know much about Etruscan deities except for their relationship to Roman deities, and scholars attempt to excavate the Etruscan essence by subtracting the Roman and Greek overlays. This effort is complicated by the later introduction of the Roman deities to the Etruscan pantheon. Here are the names of the deities associated with the Olympians (in the same order): Tinia, Uni, Turan, Laran, Artume, Aplu, Menvra, Nethuns, Sethlans, Ethausfa, Turms, Cels.

A thread connects these deities from Egypt to Greece, Etruria, and Rome. There is a familial association between Egyptian Thoth, Etruscan Turms, Greek Hermes, and Roman Mercury, just as there is a connection between Egyptian Hathor, Etruscan Turan, Greek Aphrodite, and Roman Venus. That said, the Greek and Roman gods are not identical. As with any family, each individual has a unique character, and it is prudent for the theurgist to consider them as separate but related deities with their own names, rites, and home pantheon.

Rome famously had seven hills, and there were temples to the gods on many of them. There were as many as four hundred temples throughout the ancient city. Auguries designated specific locations as suitable for divine presence. Within these rectangular precincts, called *templum*, spaces could be made sacred for specific deities. An area dedicated to a deity might have just an altar, or could have a statue of the deity as well. Different kinds of altars were used for animal sacrifices, libations, and incense offerings.

Priests and priestesses, called *sacerdotes*, performed the *sacra* or rites, serving the needs of the gods and their worshippers. In official state religion they were organized into groups, *collegia*, each governed by a *pontifex*. The pontifices in turn were governed by the Pontifex Maximus who set the liturgical calendar, governed the festivals, and ensured the religious leaders had been properly elected.

Politicians might add a part-time priestly office as part of their duties. These offices were usually held for a lifetime. Priests could be dedicated to a single deity or many. Some priests interpreted omens or sought to understand the future, some prepared sacred feasts, many conducted the rites particular to the deity. While most sacerdotes were men, the priestesses of Vesta served for life, and famously were killed if found to have engaged in sexual activity.

In addition to the official religion, private collegia formed around the worship of new and imported deities. The worship of Egyptian Isis rooted in women of the merchant classes, and numerous altars and temples were built for her, including one on the Capitoline hill itself. Foreign priests and magicians offered their services to Roman citizens.

SPIRIT GUIDES

"This is silly," Plotinus protested. "Amelius, I take it back. Let's go home."

Amelius slid an arm around his back. "You're just tired," he said. "Hostilius, take his other arm."

"I don't know why I let you and your son talk me into this," Plotinus grumbled, while the boy came up to support him. "And I don't know why the temple of Isis has so many steps."

"It's not every day we get an Egyptian sorcerer in town," Amelius said, grunting as Plotinus took another step. "He can conjure your guardian spirit. You can find out his name and how to command him."

"My guardian spirit should rather command me," Plotinus said. "Say again why we can't do this at home?"

Amelius said patiently, "The sorcerer says this temple is the only place in Rome pure enough to perform the rite."

Finally they reached the courtyard. The doors to the inner sanctuary were closed, but Plotinus could feel the holy radiance of Isis spilling out and filling the space. Two servant boys knelt on the tiles holding torches, while the sorcerer's young assistant held a pigeon in his hands. The sorcerer himself threw incense on a brazier. "Mighty Plotinus!" he said, darting forward to take the teacher's hand. "Thank you for coming. I'm eager to display my powers for you."

The sorcerer brought up a stool, and Amelius and Hostilius helped the teacher to sit. Plotinus said, "What do I need to do?"

"Think on your guardian spirit," the sorcerer said. "I will call him." He lifted his arms and began to proclaim in a barbarous tongue, making hissing and spitting sounds, then emitting a long eerie wailing of vowels.

In the courtyard before him a figure congealed in the incense. The sorcerer's voice rose, and the figure grew and became more solid. Hostilius elbowed his father. "Look!"

The sorcerer broke off and staggered back, throwing up his arm to shield his face. "This is no ordinary spirit. This is a god! Quick, ask him your questions, I cannot hold him!"

There was a hideous squawk. Plotinus glanced at the assistant and saw that the wild-eyed boy had strangled the pigeon and held it lifeless with his hands. The figure in the incense vanished. The sorcerer hissed, "Clumsy boy!"

Plotinus levered himself to his feet. "Terrified or jealous," he observed. "Calm your mind, child, and it will calm your spirit." He pulled coins from his money pouch and pressed them into the sorcerer's hands. "You have shown me a wonder today." He said thoughtfully, "It seems there is more than one kind of guardian spirit. I must write on this."

Hostilius said hoarsely, "Teacher, your guardian spirit is a god! You are exalted among men!"

Plotinus eyed the entrance. "This exalted teacher still has to get back down all those stairs."

Roman Spirits

The Roman house revolved around the *paterfamilias*, the father of the family. Among his duties the head of household ensured that the spirits of the house were properly honored. These included the family *Lar* or *Lares*, the spirits of the land on which the house was built and which remained with the house; the *Penates*, household deities who moved with the family; and Vesta, the goddess of the hearth. Each family also honored other deities who had been or were hoped to be helpful to the family's fortunes. Little cupboard house shrines might contain statues of Lares holding cornucopias, horns of plenty, and patera, offering plates; Fortuna figurines steering a rudder; or a figure of a Lares with a snake representing the genius of the paterfamilias.

Offerings of food, libations, and incense were made to the Lares, Penates, and Vesta, the other household deities, and to the genius of the paterfamilias that guided the man and by extension his whole family. These offerings could be made by anyone in the house, including the wife and daughter of the paterfamilias. As an example, Plautus begins his play "Aulularia" or "Pot of Gold" with a speech by the household Lar. A man of the house buried a pot of gold in the hearth and entrusted the Lar with its care. A succession of men in the family did not honor the Lar, and so the spirit hid the secret of the gold, until a daughter came who brought daily offerings to the household god. The Lar then revealed the gold to provide the daughter a dowry, kicking off a series of comic episodes until the young woman was safely married to a young man in the end.

Eventually the genius came to be the guardian spirit of every man, not just the head of the household; the *juno* was the corresponding guardian spirit of each woman. The genius or juno was the faithful companion, one for every person, providing helpful guidance throughout life. This conception reminds us of the daimonion of Socrates, and in later magical papyri we find instructions for summoning one's own daimon.

The genius/juno survived the death of the individual and could be made offerings after death. However, the genius or juno was not all of the person that survived death. The early Etruscan and Roman conception of the collective dead, *di manes*, developed into recognition of the individual dead, the manes with a name and personality. The dead could be either cremated or buried, but in both cases were placed in an underground tomb outside the city walls where the spirit could live. Etruscans and Romans decorated these tombs much like Egyptian tombs. They provided rooms and furniture for the use of the spirit, and painted the walls with toiletries and food for the use of the inhabitants. Some tombs had pipes into which food offerings could be dropped to penetrate into the house of the dead. Tomb paintings depict elaborate feasts in which the dead were given a share of the food. These food offerings imparted continuing life to the spirit of the deceased.

In this conception, the dead had returned to the friendly embrace of Mother Earth. The Homeric vision of the underworld also entered into Roman literature, and all the Greek and Hellenistic philosophical conceptions of the soul, from Aristotle's arid skepticism to Plato's confusing profusion of metaphors, became available to the educated Roman worldview.

AN UNEXPECTED VISIT

The servant threw the door open and gasped. "Plotinus!" he said. "My master did not tell me to expect you."

"He does not expect me," Plotinus said. "Will you take me to him?"

The servant led Plotinus to the study where Porphyry sat contemplating a row of bottles. The man sprang to his feet as if he had been caught. "Teacher!" he said guiltily. "Please, sit! Why have you come to see me?" A terrible thought struck him. "Is something wrong with Marcella? Or her children?"

"They are well," Plotinus said. "I came to save you. I see I am just in time."

"I don't know what you mean," Porphyry huffed.

Plotinus pointed to the bottles. "You were choosing which poison to take to end your life."

Porphyry sat down again hard. "I have reasoned that it is the only course left to me," he said stiffly.

Plotinus laid a hand on his shoulder. "Your mind is too good for that," he said gently. "I have trusted you with my innermost teachings, with my manuscripts, in fact with my entire life's work. I'm not ready to lose you now. It isn't reason guiding you, it's just melancholy."

Sighing, Porphyry said, "You may be right. But what can I do about it?"

"Leave Rome. Go to the countryside. It will revive your spirit."

Porphyry objected, "I don't want to leave you, teacher."

"I would rather see you leave Rome to save your health than leave your life because you can't stand Rome," Plotinus said reasonably.

Porphyry pressed Plotinus's hand to his forehead. "Wise teacher. As you command," he said.

Plotinian Cosmology

Plotinus is at the wellhead of Neo-Platonic cosmology. In *Heart of Plotinus*, Algis Uždavinys extensively analyzes the ways in which Plotinus draws together Heliopolitan cosmology, the worldview of the Upanishads, and Plato's conception of the good and the gods. In particular, Uždavinys says, Plotinus elevated Hellenic philosophy by relating metaphysical concepts to states of consciousness. This reminds us of the Hermetic Emerald Tablet that states: "as above, so below." The cosmos is reflected in the person, and the person is a fractal iteration of the cosmos.

For Plotinus the Intellect proceeds from the One like the scarab emerges from the waters of Nun. Once it has emerged, the Intellect contemplates its source, the One. The One is beyond any form. Intellect cannot grasp the entirety of the One. From the Intellect's fragmented vision comes a multiplicity of forms or intelligible beings, including the human soul. The soul's purpose is to make a journey back to the source, the One.

THE FINAL UNION

Porphyry knocked on the door, his hand trembling. The slave who answered recognized him and led him to Plotinus's study. It wasn't Plotinus who sat in the chair. "Eustochius," Porphyry said.

The man's face lit with pleasure. "Porphyry," he said, rising to clasp hands with his friend. "It's so good to see you. How are you? How is your new wife?"

"Marcella is well. The children too," he said. "They're all a great comfort to me. Do you see the others often?" He settled himself on one of the stools in the room.

Eustochius sat back down at the desk, shaking his head. "The school disbanded after the master died. I'm just taking care of his accounts."

"It's still hard to believe he's not here." Porphyry expected to see the old man walk through the door at any minute.

"You would believe it if you had seen him," Eustochius said. When Porphyry flinched, he said quickly, "He told me he had sent you away. He faded too fast for you to reach him in time."

Taking the stool the slave offered, Porphyry said, "It's so hard to believe. He seemed well when I left him."

"He hid it well," Eustochius said. "You know he was accustomed to taking a massage instead of a bath. After the plague carried off all his masseurs he had no more baths at all."

"No bath?" Porphyry said. "He must have—" He stopped.

"Oh, he smelled," Eustochius said, smiling wryly. "No one would come near him. I myself took him out to the country, to an estate one of his people had left him. It provided for him quite well. At any rate, it quickly became apparent that he was ill. The doctors said diphtheria."

Porphyry cleared his throat. "Did he suffer?"

"You wouldn't have recognized him, Porphyry," Eustochius said quietly. "He was hoarse, he could barely see, he had ulcers on his hands and feet. But the whole time he continued in contemplation. Things of the body never mattered to him."

"No, they didn't," Porphyry said, eyes misting. "How did he die?"

"I'd been out visiting." Eustochius paused. "I couldn't—you know ..."

Porphyry said softly, "You have to take time for yourself." He was grateful that Eustochius had taken such gentle care of an old and ill man.

Eustochius took up his story. "I came in later than I intended. Immediately I heard his voice calling for me. Here's what he said." Eustochius collected himself, and then recited the words, as if he had repeated them to himself to memorize them. "I have been a long time waiting for you; I am striving to give back the Divine in myself to the Divine in the All."

Porphyry paused, as if memorizing the words himself. "And then he died?"

"And then," Eustochius said, "a snake came out from under his bed and slithered into a hole in the wall, and his spirit followed with it."

The two men sat in silence for a moment.

Eustochius collected himself. "At any rate I'm happy to do whatever I can to help you in your work. I know you're collecting stories for his biography. Oh, and here," he rummaged around on the desk and pulled up a papyrus scroll. "Here it is, the one you asked for. *Against the Gnostics.*"

Porphyry took the scroll. "I think I have them all now. Even the secret ones."

"All fifty-four!" Eustochius said. "Well done."

As Porphyry turned to go, Eustochius said, "You heard about Amelius?" When Plotinus shook his head, he went on, "He sent to the oracle of Apollo to come to terms with the death of our teacher."

"What did the oracle say?"

"He said quite a lot. You should get it from Amelius. I remember he said, 'O Blessed One, you have fought your many fights; now, crowned with unfading life, your days are with the Ever-Holy.'" Eustochius smiled. "It comforts me."

For the first time Porphyry felt the fist of grief in his stomach loosen. "Thank you. It comforts me too."

Porphyry and Plotinus

Plotinus's student Porphyry arranged and edited six of his lectures into a form which is now called *The Enneads*. Stephen MacKenna's 1935 translation is available online through MIT. Algis Uždavinys provides a readable overview of the work in his introduction to *The Heart of Plotinus*.

Porphyry was a prolific biographer. His surviving works include *Life of Plotinus*, MacKenna's translation available online, and *Life of Pythagoras*, Guthrie's translation available online. His essay "On Abstinence from Eating Food from Animals," available in English in Thomas Taylor's 1823 edition, is cited today by animal rights activists. Uždavinys includes a translation of the "Cave of Nymphs" in *The Heart of Plotinus*.

Porphyry's letter to his wife and fellow student, Marcella, is one of the most touching Neo-Platonic texts. Alice Zimmern's translation is available online. Porphyry tells her that he is marrying her despite the many who spoke against it. He doesn't mind that she has so many children, ranging from quite young to nearly marriageable, even though he will be taking on the upkeep of a large family. He isn't looking for a nurse, in fact she is frail herself, and he isn't looking for a housekeeper. He is marrying her because she is a philosopher. He loves her for her mind and spirit. We can't help but think it must have been a fine marriage.

THE LESSONS OF PLOTINUS

Ammonius, Plotinus, and Porphyry rebooted Platonic philosophy. In the "Golden Chain" linking Plato to his successors, there's a big jump from Aristotle to Ammonius. From this we learn that Neo-Platonism is a literate tradition and it is always possible to pick up the writings left behind by the teachers and begin anew.

This new beginning rooted in a world in which many religions coexisted. Kemetic/Egyptian, Greek, Roman, Celtic, and Norse peoples each approached the gods in their own way. As Christianity spread and began to oppose each of these religious folkways in their own regions, the idea that they could be lumped together as "Pagan" emerged. Neo-Platonic philosophers were committed to the ways of the gods and fought the Christian attempts to halt their worship. Plotinus wrote against the Christians, and Porphyry remained bitterly opposed to Christianity throughout his life. The early Neo-Platonists were militantly Pagan.

While we draw a line between religion, philosophy, and magic today, Plotinus himself called on the services of a magician to understand his spirit guide, later writing a treatise on spirit guides. He did not hesitate to witness magic and learn from it.

Notes on the Story

Porphyry wrote the biography of his teacher, "On the Life of Plotinus and the Arrangement of His Work," available in MacKenna's translation of *The Enneads*.

We might be tempted to think that Porphyry was embellishing on Plotinus's last words, but the death scene rings true to me. I've seen the breath leave a body, and I can imagine that a snake leaving the room would resonate with that moment, particularly since the snake was so tied to the idea of the father of the family. Tibetan Buddhist monks prepare death meditations and enter into them consciously at the moment of death, and that seems to be exactly what Plotinus was doing.

Porphyry tells us that Plotinus, like Plato, taught several women in his circle, including Gemina and her daughter also called Gemina, and Amphiclea. He built a significant following in Rome and ended up caring for the orphans of his students.

FOUR

SOSIPATRA

Hellenistic civilization resembled the civilization in which we live today. People congregated in large urban areas—Alexandria, Athens, Rome, Ephesus—where the religious, political, and economic elite studied the world's history, built libraries and museums, spoke numerous languages, and in general behaved like citizens of the world. Outside the cities, rural populations lived in the way their ancestors had always lived: working the land, celebrating festivals, and offering rituals to deities for their own health, the health of their animals, and good harvests.

When the Roman Empire absorbed the remains of the Greek Empire, the effect was less transformative and more additive. The Greek world kept the religion of the Olympians and the mystery religions. The temples in Egypt continued to function as religious and educational centers. Roman temples were established in the major urban areas under Roman control, but in the provinces, religion continued much as it had done before. The umbrella term "Graeco-Roman" points to the compatibility of Greek and Roman religious beliefs, although it obscures regional differences and does not describe or include the longevity, sophistication, and effect of Egyptian religion in this time period.

Sosipatra lived in the fourth century of the Common Era, quite late in antiquity. She was born near the Greek city Ephesus in what is now Turkey. Ephesus boasted one of the seven wonders of the ancient world, the temple of Artemis—not the Artemis of Sparta or Athens, but a fertile goddess more closely related to the mother of the mountains, Kybele. The first temple to this goddess housed a meteorite, a gift from Jupiter. The temple was destroyed and rebuilt numerous times over the centuries. In Sosipatra's time (300–350 CE) the last magnificent temple still stood and was in use.

Eunapius recorded the life of Sosipatra among the many he documented. Many of the stories he tells read like mythology, events that happened in an ideal world. What was her life really like?

WHEN THE STUDENT IS READY, THE TEACHER APPEARS

When she was still very young, Sosipatra loved to sneak away from the house and explore the estate. The first time she met her teachers she had crept down to the apiary. She laid quietly on the grass and watched the bees busily flying in and out of the stack of clay tubes. Some of the bees were brushed with yellow pollen, some bright orange.

"Do you like bees?"

Startled, she leapt to her feet. The two men had approached so quietly she hadn't heard them. They wore the sturdy clothes of field workers, one old, the other older. She recognized them; the farm's caretaker Oikonomos had hired them, but they were strangers to her and frightened her. "Sorry, sorry," she said, turning to flee.

"Wait," one of them called. She poised on one foot, ready to run. "What did you see?"

Concern for the hives dragged at her. "That one is ill," she said, pointing to a tube in the middle.

The men squatted down to bring themselves to her eye level. "How can you tell?"

"It doesn't have many bees. And it sounds wrong," she said. "It needs help."

The men traded a look. The one who had spoken said, "We think so too. What else did you see?"

"That one on the end," she said. "It's too full." Before they could ask why, she said, "It has too many bees, and it sounds ... well, full!"

"We're here to give them some more room," the man said. "Do you want to help?" He laughed when she nodded vigorously.

The older one lit a fire while the somewhat younger one draped a net over his head. "What's your name?" she said.

"Call us Julian," the young one said. "Our teachers were called Julian."

"Is that really your name, though?" she persisted.

"Greeks can't pronounce our names," Old Julian said. He tamped burning twigs into a clay pot; smoke lifted up from the pot. He handed it to her. "Here, hold this."

She held the stick at arm's length. "Oikonomos says you're holy men. What's a holy man?"

Young Julian carefully pulled a clay plug out from the tube. Immediately bees boiled out of the clay cylinder. Julian took the clay pot from her and waved the smoke at the tube. "Anyone can be holy," he said.

"How?"

Moving carefully, Old Julian answered. "Settle the body, still the mind, contemplate the divine." He waved at the apiary, the fire in the pot, the bees. "Beekeeping is a good way to start."

She worked with them all summer. The end of the season came too soon. She was excited that she got to sit at the big table like at her father's birthday or the feast at the end of the festival of Artemis. At the same time she was sad that they were going back to Ephesus soon. She hated the crowded streets; there was no place to play, and her brothers and sisters teased her just because she was the youngest girl. Spending summers on the estate where she could run and drink in the sun and spend time alone was the great joy of her life.

She loved the view from the stone terrace, the fields and vineyards sloping down to the river. Her pater sat at the head of the table, her meter beside him, and all her brothers and sisters were arrayed beside her mother. The steward who managed the estate sat next to her father, along with all the important workers and slaves. She was down at the end next to the two Julians. They were wearing new clothes, not as fine as her father's or the steward's but nicer than the ones they wore in the fields.

"A toast!" Pater said, raising his wine cup. "To a successful harvest!" Sosipatra lifted her cup of water mixed with a bit of wine.

As the slaves laid food in front of them, Pater said to the steward, "Oikonomos, this is a very good year. The vineyard in particular is out-standing."

Oikonomos nodded. "It's these men," he said, pointing to the two old men neatly tucking into their food. "They showed up dressed in skins and gave me a taste of their wine. I trusted them with the vines and they bore beautifully." He paused. "And they coaxed more honey out of the bees this year too."

Pater's face lit with pleasure. "Thank you," he said, lifting his glass to them. "I hope you plan to stay?"

The men traded looks. Old Julian cleared his throat. "Well, we had planned to move on," he said. "We like travel."

"At your age?" Pater boomed. "I have half your years and I hate it. My city house suits me so well I hate to leave it to take on the dangers of the road." He looked down to the river and softened. "This view draws me back. You couldn't ask for a better place to settle down."

Young Julian said, "There is one thing that might interest us."

Oikonomos leapt in. "Name your price." Pater frowned at him but said nothing.

Old Julian said, "We would like to teach this child." He inclined his head to the girl next to him.

Everyone turned to look at Sosipatra. She hid her face in her arm.

"The littlest girl?" Pater said, surprised. "Why on earth?"

"She has a fine mind. It interests us," Old Julian said.

Meter said sharply, "Is that all that interests you?"

The men looked at each other and burst out laughing. "We have travelled together a long time," the older one said, squeezing his companion's hand with a loving smile. "And the passions of the blood have banked in us. Our joy is in the passions of the mind."

"Why waste education on a girl?" Pater said, earning a glare from Meter. "Keep one of the boys."

Her brothers lifted their heads in protest, babbling together about the pleasures of the city.

Young Julian shook his head, but Old Julian laid a hand on his arm. "We will teach anyone you wish," he said diplomatically. "We've grown fond of the girl. In a strictly parental way," he added quickly.

Seeing Meter's concern, Oikonomos jumped in again. "She spends time down in the apiary. I've sent a slave to watch them, she's come to no harm."

"Well, if there's nothing in particular for it, there's nothing against it either," her father decided. "If teaching the girl her letters pleases you as a hobby, I've no objection to it."

Meter turned to her Pater. "What, leave her here?"

"She'll have her nurse," he said carelessly, throwing back his wine.

"She's my daughter," her mother said. "She needs to learn the ways of the women's world."

Her father shrugged. "We have many daughters," he said. When the sisters in turn looked alarmed and started up about their friends in the city, he raised his hand. "We can spare one for a year."

"We can teach her to keep accounts," Old Julian said soothingly to Meter. At the same time Young Julian muttered under his breath, "Five years." No one else commented, but Sosipatra was sure she had heard him.

Pater shrugged. "Teach her what you like."

Meter laid a grim frown on the steward. "I trust her to you," she said firmly. "She had best be in good health when we return."

Later, Sosipatra watched her family climb into the carriage that would take them back to the city. Her nurse Tethe held her hand while Oikonomos waved at the party. Her two new teachers were there too.

Old Julian said to her, "Will you miss your meter?"

Tethe answered for her. "The woman barely knows her name," she sniffed. "I'm the mother who raised her."

Oikonomos sighed as the carriage wound out of sight. "That's that for a year," he said. "Thank all the gods."

"Five years," Young Julian said happily.

The steward fixed him with a measuring look. "You're not just Chaldean, are you? You're magi."

Before either of the Julians could answer, Sosipatra burst out, "I really get to stay?"

They all laughed. Oikonomos tousled her hair affectionately. "You really get to stay," he said. "We'll all be your family now."

The Chaldean Magi

By Sosipatra's time, the term "Chaldean" was more or less synonymous with "magician." Chaldea was a city in the ancient Babylonian Empire in what is now Iraq. The Babylonians were known throughout the ancient world for their astrological expertise. In fact, astronomers today still refer to the extensive and detailed records the Babylonian astrologers made of their observations.

The Persian Empire arose in the heartland of the old Babylonian Empire. *Magus* is an old Persian word describing Zoroastrian priests who served the Persian elite as astrologers and dream interpreters. The Greek used the borrowed "Magi" to describe the Magusseans, Aramaic speakers who left Persia and settled in what is now Turkey. They practiced a combination of heretical Zoroastrianism and Babylonian astrology, they were initiates of the religion of Mithraism, and they could summon spirits, daevas, as well as the spirits of the dead. Possibly the most famous magi in common culture today are those who show up in the New Testament to predict that the infant Jesus of Nazareth would grow up to become king of the Jews.

The Persian word *magus* became the Greek *magi*, which became the English *magician*. Our magic too deals with the planets, the elements, the gods and spirits. "Magician" is a worthy word to remind us that the Chaldeans are among our teachers.

TRUE JOURNEY IS RETURN

Pater stretched himself, drank off his wine, and waved for his cup to be refilled. "A worthy table," he said to Oikonomos. "As full of delights as your accounts. You've done wonders with the place. I should stay away another five years." His booming laugh filled the terrace.

Oikonomos nodded toward the Chaldeans. "Their aid has been without price," he said. "They are as wise as they are hard working."

Pater ignored him. "But tell me, where's my girl? I left a daughter with you, and my wife will harangue me if I don't ask after her."

"Why, here I am, Pater," Sosipatra said, surprised. How could he sit at the same table and not know her?

Pater blinked. "It's not possible! My daughter is only … ten, I believe. Not so tall and …" he searched for the right word. "Glowing," he said.

"The country air suits her," Tethe said.

Pater waved his wine glass at the Chaldeans. "Weren't they supposed to be teaching you? How are you at keeping books?"

"Ask her anything you like," Young Julian said.

Sosipatra lifted her head, composed beyond her years. "Ask me about your journey."

Pater downed half his cup in a swallow. "My journey? It was filled with trouble, as they always are."

"The horses broke out and had to be caught, so you left late, at midday," Sosipatra said. "You didn't travel as far as you planned and had to find lodging. It didn't suit you."

"True," Pater said dismissively. "As many a journey begins."

"The bed was too hard, and the blanket was thin. The chicken soup you ate tasted like water. There was no wine. The driver had to share your room, he slept on the floor, and he snored."

Pater blinked. "Lucky guesses," he said nervously, waving for more wine.

"Then the next day the wheel came off the coach. The horses had to be unhitched and everything unloaded so it could be replaced. Good thing the driver brought an extra," she said. "While you were sitting beside the road it started to rain. Then you became afraid, thinking you were all vulnerable to attack."

"Enough," Pater said. "You amaze me!" He turned to her teachers. "How can she know such things?"

Oikonomos said, "They are magi."

"Well then, keep her another five years!" Pater said enthusiastically. "In fact, I don't think you're magi at all. That's right. You're gods! Doesn't Homer say the gods walk among us in disguise? You've turned my daughter into a goddess!" He waved expansively. "I love you guys!" Then he put down his wine cup and gently slumped onto the table.

Sighing, Oikonomos stood and beckoned to the nearest slaves. "We'll get him to his bed."

Sosipatra started to follow her nurse, but to her surprise her teachers called her away. "A word with you before bed," Young Julian said. She still thought of him that way, although she knew how to say his name now. "If Tethe permits."

"She's never come to harm with you," Tethe said serenely.

They led her into their study where she had spent so many happy hours, where she had entered the trance, inhaled the perfume, and looked into the bowl. Where the gods had filled her vision and her mind. Here, she truly felt that she was holy.

"It's time we give you this," Old Julian said, handing her a fine linen robe embroidered with the symbols for the planets. "It's too big for you now, but you'll grow into it."

She gasped with pleasure, then pushed it away. "Oh, but you should give it to me when I'm old enough to wear it."

Young Julian shook his head. "There's no reason to wait. We've given you all the initiations we know. You truly have earned it." He pulled a small case toward him and opened the lid. "Here are copies of all our texts, including the oracles. They're for you alone, remember, so guard them well." He locked the lid and gave her the key.

She closed it in her fist and held it to her heart. "I will," she said, as solemn as a ten-year-old could be.

Young Julian held out his arms and closed them around her tight. "I love you, little seer," he said.

Old Julian gave her his hug in turn. "Always remember you are the daughter of our hearts." Sighing, he let her go. "Now off to bed with you."

She turned at the door. "Tomorrow we work with the bees!" she reminded them.

When she woke the next day she found to her horror that she had overslept. Dressing hurriedly she ran out onto the terrace and almost collided with her father. He grabbed her shoulders to steady her. "There you are," he said. "You can help us solve a mystery."

A slave ran up and reported to Oikonomos, "They're not on the road either."

Oikonomos said, "Sosi, where are the Juliani?"

"In the apiary," she said immediately. "I need to get down there too, I'm late."

The slave shook his head. "They're not. I checked."

Oikonomos said, "I watched everyone go out into the fields as I do every day. They weren't there. There's nothing in their room."

"They're—they're gone?" Sosipatra couldn't believe her friends would leave her.

Pater hmphed. "We'll find them. I was going to pay them this morning. I won't have it said I turn out my servants without pay."

"They're gone," Sosipatra said in a different voice. She felt the truth of it as they had taught her to do. "They always said when they left they'd journey to the western sea. That's where they've gone."

To her surprise, Pater didn't doubt her. "Then they were gods. Or at least heroes," he said. He looked her up and down. "They've left me a fine estate and a fine daughter." He waved to Tethe. "Pack your things, and Sosipatra's too. I'm taking her back to the city."

The Chaldean Oracles

In antiquity the most famous Chaldeans were the two Juliani, Julian the Chaldean and Julian the Theurgist, who lived between 160 and 180 CE, several centuries before Sosipatra.

Julian the Chaldean and his son Julian the Theurgist conducted spiritual operations that resulted in a poem titled the "Chaldean Oracles." They are presented as divinely authored; most of the oracles are spoken by a god or goddess in the first person. This poem gave the Neo-Platonic priest-philosophers a core technical methodology of theurgy. The method involved calling the gods directly into the body of another person. The receiver had direct communication with the gods, and the receiver could describe the gods and answer questions asked by the caller. The oracles talk about the sounds, sights, and sensations that will result from the calling, and distinguish between phenomena that are only phantoms and those that are genuine divine communication.

Among the Neo-Platonic philosophers, Plotinus may have read the Chaldean Oracles, while Iamblichus, Asklepigenia, and Proklos certainly did. Plethon attributed the oracles to Zoroaster, and his commentary, drawing heavily on Psellos, was published as *The Magical Oracles of the Magi descended from Zoroaster*. This is a memory or echo of the origin of the magi among the Zoroastrian priests and Magusseans. Plethon was the last Neo-Platonist to have access to the entire poem, but the existing fragments have been quoted and collected by scholars ever since.

It is noteworthy that the oracles specify using children as mediums. Julian the Chaldean employed his own son as his receiver. This practice sheds some light on why it was plausible to the ancient readers of Eunapius that Chaldean magicians would be interested in educating a small girl.

A MARRIAGE OF PHILOSOPHERS

"You told me she was wise," Eustathius said. "You didn't tell me she was beautiful."

"If I am, what does it matter?" Sosipatra said, meeting his gaze squarely.

"Child!" her mother hissed. "Demurely, please!"

Eustathius laughed. "She's right," he said. "To a philosopher, what does the beauty of the world matter? The love of pleasure is a chain dragging down the soul. Remember Porphyry married Marcella for her spirit."

"Spirit she has," Pater said heartily. "Did I tell you about her first teachers, the gods?"

"They were magi," Sosipatra said calmly.

Eustathius said curiously, "Are you a magi?"

"Yes, I am," she said. "I learned my first philosophy from them. Now that study is the meaning of my life. Is it yours?"

Eustathius and Sosipatra both ignored the protests of her father, mother, and nurse, intent only on each other. Eustathius said, "It is the only thing that matters. Only by diligent effort can we walk the road to the heavens that follows the gods."

"Study, and calming the passions," Sosipatra said. "The Divine is in everyone, but only the mind of the philosopher is the temple of the divine."

"Whatever chance may bring, the calm mind endures," Eustathius said. "The divine brings only good, evil comes from our own actions. If we continue in our prayers and labors, the divine is our reward."

"I will have you, if you will have me," Sosipatra said.

Then Tethe and Meter cried together, and Pater offered a toast, and Eustathius took her hands and looked dazed in a happy sort of way.

"Tell your fortune," Pater said.

Eustathius squeezed her hand. "It's not necessary."

"She can, you know," Pater said. "Go on, tell us. How many children will you have?"

Sosipatra held herself still until the images came. "Two … no, three." She smiled at Eustathius. "They'll all choose philosophy over fortune. Like us."

"And Eustathius? Will he live a long life?"

Of all the people at the table only Tethe saw the moment of shock on her face before she smoothed it over with a smile. "Long and happy, of course," she said.

Later, as Tethe made her ready for bed, she confided in her nurse what she had seen. "I only have five years with him."

Tethe smoothed her hair. "Oh, Sosi."

Sosipatra blinked back tears. "It isn't enough time."

"There's never enough time with the ones we love," Tethe said.

"No, I mean it isn't enough time for him to learn what he needs to know," she said. "His soul will fly to heaven, but he'll only reach the moon. I—I'll go farther, when my time comes." Her eyes looked at something far away. "I'll reach the sun."

Paideia

The paideia of the expansive Hellenistic civilization drew its nourishment from two main sources: Kemet, long the font of civilization and knowledge for the entire Mediterranean basin; and Greece, whose seafaring traders drew in wealth from around the world, and whose colonies spread the Greek language and culture to every Mediterranean shore.

Despite the cosmopolitan feel of the era, Hellenic civilization had a kind of cohesion around the idea of education. The term *paideia* describes the education of young boys and men, more rarely women and girls, which inculcated the civic values of Hellenic culture, and in particular taught Greek philosophy.

The paideia did not essentially change under Roman rule. Greeks and Romans shared similar civic values. Educated Romans and Greeks spoke both Greek and Latin and contributed to the development of philosophy. Eurocentric education still teaches both Greek and Latin to enable the educated elites to read literature in both languages.

The Hellenistic paideia meant more than education—it preserved the "peace of the gods." This peace was the compact made between humans and the forces of the divine that allowed human life to flourish. In Egypt/Kemet, Greece, and Rome, the urban temples served the gods who supported political empires and dynasties. Urban life is always supported by the abundance of the countryside, and urban Pagan religion is rooted in the gods of farm and wilderness. In the Hellenistic world outside the urban centers and the temple complexes there were shrines to the gods everywhere, on mountain peaks, beneath trees, in caves. The people who lived in those places knew the names of the spirits of these places, brought them offerings, and conducted rites for fertility of land and people. They do so still.

PERGAMON

Tethe eased herself onto a stool in the study. "They're all washed, fed, and ready for the day," she said. "The girl and I will play with them."

Sosipatra had begun thinking of the new nurse as Young Tethe. "Thank you," she said. "I couldn't manage without you."

"I never thought you'd turn into a city girl," Tethe said. "You loved the quiet of the country. Here we are in brand-new Pergamon, with all these new buildings and all the people in them."

"And the library," Sosipatra said. "We don't have one of those on the farm." A commotion at the door brought her to her feet. "Or students either."

"You don't need them," Tethe grumbled. "With your family's fortune you could afford a poor husband, you can afford not to work."

"I don't need their money," Sosipatra said. "I need their company."

They crowded into her study, bright young men and women, laughing and chattering. "We've just come from Aedesius," Chrysanthius said. "He was talking to us about the soul."

"How interesting," Sosipatra said. "That's just what I was going to talk about." As they packed themselves into the room, sitting on each other's feet, she went on, "You know that the true home of the soul is in the stars."

"Just as the Egyptians said," Maximus piped up.

"And you know that the soul descends from the stars, through the sun and the moon, and so to earth."

"So Aedesius said," Chrysanthius put in.

"I am sure he told you that the soul is immortal. Did he also tell you that the soul has parts?" She almost laughed as the students leaned forward eagerly. "Some are vulnerable to punishment, even death—" She broke off, then stiffened, looking off into space.

"Teacher?" Maximus said nervously.

She barely heard him. "Philometer!" she cried out, holding out a hand as if to catch him.

Maximus whispered, "Who's Philometer?"

Chrysanthius whispered back, "The one who was in love with her. He made her desire him."

"Desire?" Maximus whispered, incredulous. "*Our* teacher?"

Chrysanthius nodded. "She suspected magic and asked Aedesius to intervene. Aedesius discovered the spell he was making and confronted him. Since then Philometer has since left her in peace."

They stopped talking as Sosipatra shook herself. "Philometer has had an accident," she said calmly. "His carriage hit a rough patch and overturned. His legs were about to be run over, that's why I shouted at him."

One of her slaves brought her a cup of water. She drank and went on, "His slaves dragged him out of the way and scraped his arms on the rough dirt. He's being brought home in a stretcher." She waved to a slave. "Run to his house and take him this," she gave him a jar of ointment. "It will help to heal his arms."

"Divine Sosipatra," Maximus breathed.

"She sees everything, like a god," Chrysanthius said.

Laughing, she shook her head. "Only those I care about."

"You still care for him?" Maximus said, surprised.

"Of course I do," she said briskly. "He had the good sense to admire me."

Julian and Sallustius

Eunapius tells us that Sosipatra's son Antoninus travelled to Alexandria, studied at the Kemetic temples, and learned Kemetic mysteries. Students flocked to him; he offered lengthy lectures on Plato but refused to talk about theurgy, probably because it was already dangerous to do so in a world ruled by Christian emperors.

Not every emperor was Christian in late antiquity. Eunapius tells us that the emperor Julian spent time in Pergamon in his youth. He studied philosophy with Aedesius, and when he became emperor he sent for two of Aedesius's students to continue his studies. Chrysanthius declined, warned by a god in a dream not to go. Maximus scoffed at the dream, saying that educated Greeks challenged the decrees of the heavenly powers, and left to join the emperor.

As a child, Julian had been a neglected son of the emperor's family, a nephew of Constantine the Great. His early education focused on the classics and steeped him in the paideia; only later in life was he exposed to Christianity, and it did not take root.

Constantine's heirs waged a campaign to kill off rivals for the emperor's seat. As a discounted relative, Julian managed to survive the campaign. He found a place in the army and successfully defended the Roman Empire from the Persians. When the last of Constantine's other heirs died, the soldier-scholar was proclaimed emperor by his troops.

Julian ruled for only two years. In that time he declared himself Pagan, cancelled Christian tax and teaching privileges, and began the reconstruction of Pagan temples. He also acted to protect the Jewish people. He wrote prolifically and is counted as one of the philosopher emperors.

Sallustius was his great friend and probable lover. When they were separated in his youth, Julian wrote "Consolation to Himself upon the Departure of Sallustius." He dedicated his "Hymn to King Helios" to Sallustius. All these texts are extant and available online.

Julian's ambition was his downfall—he died from an arrow wound acquired in a bid to conquer the Persian Empire. Christians immediately labeled him "apostate" and did not again let the education of an emperor's heir proceed without direct Christian supervision.

The fortunes of Maximus rose and fell. When Julian died he was stripped of his wealth and tortured, then befriended by a high placed scholar and restored to his wealth. He visited Constantinople as a Pagan hero. Eunapius says mysteriously that he risked a theurgic operation there. Subsequently he once again fell out of favor and was arrested and killed.

THE LESSONS OF SOSIPATRA

Sosipatra was not only a woman philosopher, more accomplished than her husband, she was also a child when she began her studies. This confronts us with our own values about the appropriate interaction of children with magic. On the one hand, it would seem that using a child as a medium would expose the child to images her life experience would not prepare her to handle. I think it's important as theurgists to understand that children are not essential to the rites; we can use ourselves as oracles and we can partner with other adults. I strongly hold the value than any magic should benefit the operator—if a child does magic, the child should be the beneficiary.

On the other hand, we do raise our children in our own faiths, and our practice with children may include divination. Theurgists who are parents may decide to engage in theurgic ritual with their children as part of their family magic. The ancients certainly did—Julian the son was the medium for Julian the father, Asklepigenia learned theurgic magic from her father, and the author of the Mithras Liturgy wrote the ritual for his daughter. Passing the techniques within the family is a theurgic tradition.

It is interesting that two of the stories of Sosipatra's visions involved what was happening in the present but at a distance, when she saw what happened in her father's journey and when she saw the accident that befell Philometer. However, she did foresee her husband's death, so some of her visions did involve the future as well. Clearly she was an accomplished seer.

Eunapius frames the story of Sosipatra's life as a fabulous tale with mysterious magicians who vanish without a trace, knowledge of things happening and things to come, and childhood signs of future greatness. Sosipatra appears in history as a serenely beautiful philosopher who was wife, mother, student, and teacher, devout in her studies as well as a practical theurgic magician.

Notes on the Story

The biographer Eunapius included a lengthy sketch of Sosipatra's life in his collection of the "Lives of the Philosophers"; Wilmer Wright's translation is available online. Eunapius does not record the names of Sosipatra's parents, siblings, or teachers. Oikonomos, "housekeeper" or "steward" in Greek, Tethe, "nurse," and Pater and Meter for "father" and "mother," are used here in place of proper names.

The Artemis of Ephesus is connected with bees, and beekeeping is a very ancient Mediterranean tradition. In *The World History of Beekeeping* Eva Crane discusses beekeeping techniques in Sosipatra's time. These were very similar to the beekeeping techniques of today and included the use of removable frames and smoking bees while working them to keep them docile. Images from Egypt/Kemet show the use of clay tubes like the one in the story. These are still in use in Egypt today.

Eunapius records that Sosipatra's father left his daughter to the care of two men he had just met. It is difficult to imagine any parent, loving or not, doing so without fuss. Remembering that the girl would have been in the care of the servants and slaves of the estate eases the context of that decision. Whatever their sexual orientation, two men travelling together were clearly bonded to each other rather than to wives and children.

The talent of foresight can be both a gift and a burden. Sosipatra foresaw that her husband would die before her. As Neo-Platonist philosophers, both strove to send their souls into the heavens after death and rise through the moon, sun, and stars, to union with The One. Eunapius says Sosipatra saw that her husband would rise to the moon, and she would surpass him, and achieve the height of the sun.

FIVE

PROKLOS AND ASKLEPIGENIA

TOO DANGEROUS FOR PAGANS

Ulpian elbowed Proklos. "He's mumbling." Proklos hissed at his friend to be quiet. He leaned his elbow on his knee, listening raptly, while Ulpian crossed his arms on his chest and scowled.

When Olympiodoros finally wound to a stop and the students struggled to their feet, Ulpian complained, "Do you actually understand the man? He talks so fast I can't make out a word he says."

"He's perfectly clear," Proklos said mildly.

Ulpian punched his arm. "Don't be impertinent," he said. "You're too young to understand what he's saying anyway."

Proklos absorbed the blow and said mildly, "I can repeat what he said."

"Prove it."

"You know that Thales held that water is the first principle," Proklos said. As he spoke the words spooled themselves across his vision. After a while, all the students in the room sat down again, captured by his perfectly clear speech. "And so water is the source of life, offered to the gods and the dead for their continued life," he finished.

Ulpian leapt to his feet and applauded. "By all the gods, you have never drunk from the forgetful waters of Lethe!"

Olympiodoros cleared his throat said mildly, "Not too fast to hear after all?"

All the students jumped. They'd completely forgotten he was still in the room. "Your pardon," Ulpian said quickly, bowing and heading for the door, and the other students followed quickly behind. When Proklos made to join them, Olympiodoros touched his shoulder and said, "Walk with me."

The teacher and his precocious student strolled out on one of Alexandria's broad avenues, walking along the edge to keep out of the throng of people streaming in all directions. Proklos craned down the street to catch a glimpse of the harbor. "Just think," he said. "This is the exact street where Hypatia rode her horses every evening."

His teacher said, "You do have a good memory." He added tartly, "Even if you are impertinent."

Proklos laughed.

"But that's not what I want to talk about," Olympiodoros said. "You're a grown man now, old enough to think about the rest of your life. Old enough to think about marriage."

"Um," Proklos said, turning red.

Oblivious, Olympiodoros soldiered on. "You know my daughter Aedesia. Sober, and a student of philosophy too. I challenge you to make a better match."

"I don't think I'm the kind to marry," Proklos said tactfully.

Olympiodoros waved him off. "The kind of lover who attracts you has nothing to do with who keeps your house. I know you'll take good care of her, and she'll serve you well—"

A group of young men materialized out of the crowd. "Look what we've found!" one of them crowed. "Pagan philosophers, aren't you?"

"We are philosophers," Olympiodoros said mildly.

One of the youths shoved him. "That's for Mark," he said. "You filthy wretches killed him!"

"Not us," Proklos protested, stepping between his teacher and the man. "We're men of peace."

"What difference does it make?" His face was red, contorted, his eyes angry. "A Pagan killed him, a Pagan should die for it!"

Another of the youths intervened. "Gaius, give way," he said. "They said they are men of peace. So we are taught to be."

Gaius snarled and turned on him. Proklos seized the chance to grab his teacher's arm and pull him away. They both trotted rather quickly along the avenue until they reached the street where Olympiodoros lived. There the teacher paused, putting his hands on his knees to catch his breath.

Proklos said shakily, "I thought for a minute you were going to end up like Hypatia."

Straightening, Olympiodoros shook his head. "The gangs are getting worse," he said. "Since Hypatia's death it's almost become too dangerous for Pagans to live in Alexandria."

"I've been thinking of leaving," Proklos admitted. "You know Athena has always guided me. She told me to give up rhetoric and politics, to study philosophy and to love the gods. I have a great desire to see her city."

"It's safer there," Olympiodoros said. "The Christians haven't taken root there as they have here." He eyed Proklos speculatively. "Are you sure you don't want to take Aedesia with you?"

Alexandria

In the fifth century of the common era, Alexandria was one of the busiest cities in the world. The great urban center was crisscrossed with streets wide enough to allow horses and carriages to pass. Some of those streets led down to the bay, which was flooded with ships from all over the world, all guided safely into the harbor by the lighthouse on Pharos Island, one of the wonders of the ancient world.

The population of Alexandria in Proklos's time may have been as much as a million people. A million people! In the streets Proklos rubbed elbows with immigrants from Greece, Libya, Syria, Persia, and Rome, and even from as far away as India. Only Greeks and later Romans held full citizenship; native Egyptians did not, despite providing the backbone of labor that kept the city functional.

Proklos was drawn to what we know now as the Library of Alexandria. In his time, it was a school renowned for its resources. There were two main areas. The first was the Museion or Museum, a temple to the muses. It was presided over by a priest who was appointed to direct the rituals there. The second main area was the Biblion, the library, filled with papyrus and parchment scrolls and codices. The library was burned by Julius Caesar, an event still mourned by scholars today, but even after that catastrophe it continued to function as a storehouse for learning.

For students like Proklos, the real attraction was not the temple or even the library but the community where the learned population gathered to learn and to teach—people such as Hypatia, the famous philosopher/mathematician. Proklos was born about the time that Hypatia died, but learned from teachers who had learned from her, making her a critical link in the Golden Chain of Neo-Platonic philosophers from Plotinus to Damascius.

In his vivid description of Alexandria, Henri Riad notes that it was a college town, filled with the energy that students bring to a city when they have left their provincial homes and taste the freedom of the broad world for the first time. The town was lively, boisterous, and irreverent. The streets that Proklos walked were exciting but also dangerous, roamed by gangs of Christians and Pagans who often clashed, killing each other in the streets.

Like all students at the Museion, Proklos had the opportunity to meet and talk with peoples of many religions. Alexander had granted Jews the right to Greek citizenship, and the Jewish section took up one quarter of the city. In this area Jews governed themselves. For the first two centuries of the city's existence, Alexandrian Jews enjoyed a peaceful and prosperous life. They spread from the Jewish quarter to establish synagogues throughout the city. During the time of the Jewish revolt against the Romans in the first century C.E. the synagogues in Alexandria were closed and the Jewish quarter was attacked. Similar raids on the Jewish quarter would periodically recur throughout the life of the city, a template for all the attacks on Jewish neighborhoods throughout Western history.

Alexandrian students also had the opportunity to study Buddhism. The edicts of Ashoka from the second century BCE document the Indian king's efforts to spread Buddhism throughout the Hellenistic world. The edicts list Greek monarchs who had been introduced to Buddhism, including Alexander, whose army had penetrated all the way to India. Several hundred years later, in the second century CE, Clement of Alexandria mentions Buddhist temples in the city. Buddhism formed an enduring presence in Alexander's city.

Although Proklos was quite well aware of the religions around him, he remained a committed Pagan. But why was a philosopher interested in Pagan religion? Today we consider philosophy to be secular and separate from any faith. The situation was very different in the Alexandria of Proklos. In *Neoplatonism and Indian Philosophy,* Paulos Mar Gregorios notes that Alexandrian Hellenism was religious, with many philosophies flourishing side by side, while the priest of the Museion presided over the community's ceremonies, rituals, and sacrifices.

In Alexandria philosophy was not just an intellectual pursuit, it was a religious one. For Proklos, magic and Pagan religion were part of the cultural matrix that preserved the peace of the gods.

A YOUNG PHILOSOPHER

"So this is the boy prodigy?" Propped up on a couch, Plutarch peered at the room.

Syrianus slapped Proklos on the shoulder. "Fresh off the boat from Alexandria. I brought him straight to the Athenian Academy of course!"

"Oh, well, nothing so grand as the Academy," Plutarch said. "Just a school of Plato. Proklos, is it? What did you study in Alexandria?"

Proklos said calmly. "I studied Plato with Olympiodoros."

"I've heard he speaks well," Plutarch said. Proklos smothered a laugh.

"Did you also study Iamblichus?" one of the students said.

Turning toward the speaker, Plutarch said, "Let me present my daughter, Asklepigenia. She teaches along with me."

It took Proklos a moment to recognize that the speaker was a woman, with her hair tied back, wrapped in a himation identical to the men's. His face lit up. "Oh, like Hypatia!" he blurted.

"Nothing like Hypatia," Asklepigenia snapped. Hierius snickered. She cut her brother a quelling glance.

Plutarch ignored them. "Did you study with Hypatia?"

"I didn't have the honor. She died before I reached the city. I studied with some of her teachers."

Squinting at him, Plutarch said, "How old are you?"

"Nearly twenty," Proklos said. Deflecting his gaze, he said quietly, "May I hear you speak?"

"Don't steal my student," Syrianus warned.

Later, after all the students were gone, Asklepigenia settled herself on a little stool next to her aged father's couch. "You were brilliant tonight."

Plutarch stirred, turning onto his side to face her. "What do you think of Proklos?"

"He hasn't studied Iamblichus," she sniffed.

"He's said to be devout. Syrianus said he didn't hesitate to kneel and adore the moon."

Asklepigenia sighed. "I know, I know. And his friends say when he set foot outside the city his first drink was from the well of Socrates. And when he reached the city gate the watchman said 'Really, if you had not arrived, I should have closed!'"

Plutarch's lips twitched. "You don't put stock in portents?"

"He has good friends," she said wryly. "But it takes more than devotion and a year of study in Alexandria to make a philosopher. Much less a student of theurgy."

Plutarch sighed. "Some are suitable. Some are not. Time tells." He rolled over onto his back, settling in for the night. "Anyway, I like him. I'm going to teach him the Chaldean Oracles."

Asklepigenia tucked the blankets around him. "You do that," she said. Plutarch was already asleep. She said to herself, "I'll decide whether to teach him the real secrets."

Iamblichus Soter

Like Sosipatra, an aura of sainthood hung over Iamblichus. Neo-Platonists called him "divine" and "savior". Iamblichus had lived more than a century before Proklos was born. By the time Proklos moved to Athens, Iamblichus was revered as Neo-Platonic demi-god, Iamblichus Soter.

Iamblichus was born to a Syrian ruling family and travelled to Italy for his higher education. He studied Plato, and like Plato he spent time in Kemet. When he returned to Syria, he gathered a circle of students, making him another link in the Golden Chain.

At some point he also became Porphyry's student. Although he and Porphyry agreed on many points, they seem to have disagreed about the function of ritual in theurgy. Thomas Taylor's translation of Porphyry's "Letter to Anebo" is available online. In the letter Porphyry argues that the philosopher can commune with the divine through contemplation alone. In *Theurgia or the Mysteries of Egypt,* Iamblichus specifically addresses this idea and argues for the spiritual function of theurgic ritual.

In writing *Theurgia*, Iamblichus borrowed the ancient authority of Kemet by writing in the persona of an Egyptian priest, Abammon. He credited his studies in Egypt for his theurgic knowledge. The editors of the latest translation of *Theurgia*, Clarke, Dillon, and Hershbell, point to the Egyptian/Kemetic origin of many of his symbols, including the mud rising from the waters and the lotus. In *Theurgy and the Soul*, Gregory Shaw posits that Iamblichus based theurgic practices specifically on Kemetic rituals at Abydos.

The streams that nourished the river of Neo-Platonism were Egyptian/Kemetic cosmology, the Hellenic paideia, and Indian philosophy. We know that Iamblichus studied Pythagoras and wrote a biography, *Life of Pythagoras*. We can trace all these threads in Iamblichus's writings.

Iamblichus taught that the divine can be understood as being three distinct persons, or hypostases: the One, To En; Intellect, Nous; and Soul, Psyche. Although it may seem that the idea of the One validates monotheism primarily because it is ubiquitously translated as "God," the Neo-Platonic tradition also discusses the place of multiple gods, the Olympian deities in particular. The One does not cast out other gods— it encompasses them.

Writing as Abammon, Iamblichus describes the creation of the cosmos. Abammon's first cause is self-generating and the true Good. This first cause immediately generates a second, the first principle of the intelligible realm. The self-creating Good maps onto Atum, Neit, or any of the gods or goddesses who emerged from the primal waters to the first mound as well as Plato's first cause, the One.

What about the second cause, the intelligible principle? Eric Iverson compares Egyptian cosmology, notably the Shabaka stone text, with Hermetic texts in general and *Theurgia* in particular. Iverson draws attention to the dual nature of primal Egyptian deities such as Atum-Re and Ptah-Nun. These are similar to the pairing of the Neo-Platonic One and Demiurge. Iverson concludes that Egyptian sources predate the Hermetic and Neo-Platonic texts, and the Neo-Platonic texts substantially derive philosophical concepts from them, as Iamblichus clearly says.

Between the gods and humans are arrayed classes of beings who serve to connect humanity with the divine. These classes of beings include Platonic daimones and heroes.

The core of Iamblichus's teachings brings the human being participating in soul to a mystical union with the One through the ritual practice of theurgy.

A SPINNING TOP

"Now you're bragging," Asklepigenia said. "You've never been sick?"

"I enjoy a sturdy constitution," Proklos said serenely. "Although I did fall ill once, in my childhood." He peered down the street. "I think we turn right here."

"No, it's one street over," she said. "So, was it a mild illness?"

"Oh no. My mother refused to leave my side, and my father had given me up for dead."

"I see you survived," Asklepigenia said drily. "What happened?"

Proklos cast her a strangely shy glance. "Well, the way my mother tells it, a child appeared above my bed. She said he was immediately recognizable as Telesphoros."

"Asclepius's son?"

Proklos nodded. "With his little dwarf head tucked into his little cap. He spoke my name and touched my forehead. My condition turned from that moment and I recovered immediately. I've hardly been ill a day since."

"Here we are," Asklepigenia said. She watched closely as Proklos eased himself into the household, speaking gently with the young father, touching the sick girl's fevered head.

"What did the physician recommend?" he said. "Oregano tea? Have you tried peppermint?" He looked over at Asklepigenia. "What would you recommend?

"That, and lemon balm also," she said.

Proklos squeezed the father's shoulder. "I go to make sacrifices on her behalf."

Back on the street, he sighed. "I wish I could do more. Anyway, thank you for coming. I needed a second opinion. I want to make sure we've done everything we can."

"You really care about your friends," Asklepigenia said.

"I am so far from home, they are my family," he said. "And I'm not the marrying kind. Anyway, what good is all my learning if I can't help the people I love?" He stopped at the threshold of Plutarch's house. "Here you are, safely home," he said. "I'm going up to the shrine of Asklepios to sacrifice for her."

"And call on Telesphoros?" she said gently.

He brightened. "It's a good idea, thank you."

Asklepigenia thoughtfully watched him head up the street. If not him, then who? She was willing to give him a chance.

Not many days later Proklos sat at her feet in her own house. Asklepigenia dropped a thread into his hands. "Have you seen one of these?"

Proklos untangled the thread to reveal a disc in the center. "It's a toy," he said.

She took it back from him. Spinning the threads, she moved the toy so that it made a whistling sound. "Now chant the vowels over it, like this." She sang the seven vowels over the whistle.

Proklos carefully took the toy from her hands. He twisted the threads and lost control of the wheel. He looked up at Asklepigenia, but she didn't laugh. "Try again," she said. "Remember, settle the body, still the mind, contemplate the divine."

Proklos breathed deeply, relaxed, and cleared his mind. The second time he mastered the trick of getting the spin going, and dutifully chanted the vowels while he did.

Asklepigenia took the toy back from him. "My father taught us both. Me and Hierius," she said. "Hierius refused to do it. He said he wasn't interested in singing the alphabet over a child's toy." She pulled out a small chest, opened the lid, and drew out a splendid globe studded with gems. "So he never got to see this one. Have you heard of it? It's an iynx. We use it to call on the wheels, the ideas of the One."

Eyes wide, Proklos didn't reach out for it, but waited for her to gently place it in his hands. When she did, he held it reverently. Only then did he dare to voice his thought. "There are those who say that the fates write our lives. Our lot is to accept their decrees and learn to live with them."

"I've heard the Christians say so. Is that what you think?" Asklepigenia said, smiling gently.

"It isn't what my heart says, as a healer. I long to bring health back where it has been lost."

She nodded approvingly. "That's my belief too. It's our job as healers to understand the source of the suffering and to work to change it. We don't accept fate—we challenge it!" She gestured to the ball in his hand. "With this iynx," she told him, "you can heal the most serious cases. With it you can call a soul back from the shores of the river Styx."

Gods and Fate

For Asklepigenia and her student Proklos, knowledge of the gods was central to the experience of being human. The point of incarnation was to understand the gods. They saw substantial differences in Christian theology and their approach. We can see this most clearly in their understanding of *Heimarmene*, fate. As Mary Ellen Waithe reads Asklepigenia, her theurgy differed from Christianity in her approach to fate. Where the Christian accepted and was resigned to fate, Asklepigenia sought to influence fate through her knowledge of Plato and theurgic ritual.

In *Theurgy and the Soul* Gregory Shaw notes that for Plato the paideia educated the human soul in the knowledge of the cosmic order. It is the soul's task to orient to that order. Plato had criticized the stories the poets told of the gods. How could humans look up to beings who were said to behave in such self-serving and destructive ways? Plato looked to the heavenly bodies—that is, the stars and planets—and saw the beauty of their mathematical movements as divine. The planets' movements, the gods' influences shaped the course of human life.

By the mid-second century BCE, astrology was firmly established as a divinatory art. Astrologers could draw up a chart placing the planets against the circle of the zodiac as they appeared at the moment of an individual's birth. The zodiac was placed against a circle of twelve houses governing aspects of life. The horoscope was fixed by the ascendant, the zodiacal degree on the horizon at the moment of birth. Other aspects could be added, in particular the Lot of Fortune, calculated in various ways.

Astrology was among the arts suppressed by the Christian revolution. The Christian emperor Constantine counted mathematicians (that is, astrologers) as undesirable, while the Christian emperor Theodosius required astrologers to burn their books in the presence of bishops. Despite this overt opposition, the art of astrology has survived and flourished. Daily horoscopes still appear in news media and natal horoscopes are cast and interpreted not only for magicians but for the general public.

A PRUDENT DEPARTURE

It seemed like a lifetime since he had left the city. Proklos peered around anxiously for a friendly face.

"Proklos! Over here!" Archiadas waved.

Proklos lit up when he saw his friend. He raced down the plank to the dock with haste seldom seen among philosophers. Proklos drew him into a long hug and stepped back to look at him. "You haven't aged a day."

"It's only been a year," Archiadas said. His face darkened. "I resent every moment the Christian slanderers cost me with you. Vultures."

"Politics come and go," Proklos said. "They raise a man up and chase him from the city. Well, such are the habitual accidents of life!"

Laughing, Archiadas said, "You haven't changed either. Did I mention I missed you?"

"Enough to put me up for the night? I seem to be between lodgings."

Eyes sparkling, Archiadas said, "I've done better than that." He led the way along the cramped city streets. "I've secured a house for you. You know the place. You told me once it is your favorite house in the city. It's a philosopher's house; Syrianus and Plutarch both lived there in their time. It's handy to the temple of Asklepios and the temple of Dionysos. And it has a view of the Acropolis."

"That's good fortune indeed," Proklos said. "I'm overwhelmed."

"Well," his friend said, pleased, "you'll have to pay the rent."

Proklos laughed. "How's the Academy?"

"Asklepigenia is more reclusive every day. She resents time that takes her away from her meditations. She's only teaching until you return."

"And Hierius, her brother? Isn't he teaching?"

Archiadas shook his head quickly. "Even if he enjoyed teaching, which he does not, the affairs of the family keep him busy."

"The fate of the eldest son, to bear the burdens of the family," Proklos said soberly. "I'm grateful I am a younger son."

They broke out of the crowded street and came out on a little field dotted with herbs and shaded by small trees. "It's good to be home," Proklos sighed. "I can't wait to offer to Athena again on her sacred ground."

"Your letters said you learned a great deal in Lydia."

"Oh yes, it was worth the journey. I believe Athena sent me there. I'm glad she called me back."

"Well, that, and the shift of the political wind."

Proklos laughed. "Look," he said, "it's midday. Will you pray with me?"

Hypatia and Synesius

Despite a deliberate campaign to destroy her work, we know a great deal about Hypatia, largely because of her student Synesius. Hypatia was born into an aristocratic family in Alexandria, the daughter of an internationally famous mathematician.

Throughout the Hellenistic period, philosophy was a religious/spiritual pursuit open only to the upper classes. The vast majority of people living in the city and in the countryside were engaged in growing and cooking food, weaving clothing, and creating pots and jewelry for everyday use. They had little time to spend in contemplation. As we study the lives of the philosophers, we must remember that they were among the elites of their times; for every philosopher is an entire estate founded on the labor of dozens of less valued family members, servants, and slaves, providing the fortune that allowed for one of them to spend decades in study.

An upper-class student heading to Alexandria to complete his or her education would already have had primary education in reading and writing; secondary education in rhetoric, geometry, and mathematics, and sciences; and physical development in the gymnasium. Formal education was open primarily to men, with women being taught informally at home and absorbed into the support system of the family. However, women did sometimes study, and women in families of famous male philosophers were often recognized as philosophers themselves.

This is what happened with Hypatia. Biographer Maria Dzielska believes she was born in 355 and was about sixty-five when she died. She lived, taught, and died in Alexandria, a true daughter of the city. Her father, Theon, was a poet, mathematician, and a member of the

Alexandrian Museion. Hypatia's education began at home but must have included a wide array of teachers. By 380 Hypatia had students of her own, and by 404 she was the head of the Neo-Platonic Academy in Alexandria, celebrated in her home city and around the empire as a brilliant mathematician and teacher.

A few generations before Proklos travelled to Alexandria to study, another young man from the provinces stumbled wide-eyed through the great city. Synesius arrived in 393, the year Emperor Theodosius forbade public performance of Pagan rituals. Synesius had been drawn by Hypatia's reputation and was accepted into her circle.

Synesius always counted the years he spent learning from Hypatia as the finest of his life. She must have been attractive but was unimpressed with her own beauty; her sole focus was on calculating the mysteries of the cosmos. Hypatia avoided marriage and devoted her life to spiritual pursuits. As an unmarried woman surrounded by men, the subject of physical as well as spiritual love came up. Damascius reports the story of how she fended off the overtures of an amorous student by handing him a menstrual rag and saying, "this is what you love." Synesius himself appears to have been deeply attached to her, and from his descriptions of the other students in the circle this attachment seems to have been common among them.

It was Synesius's sad fortune to be drawn back home to Libya to manage his family's economic and political interests, marry, and have children, confined to the life of a householder in the country. To console himself he wrote letters to Hypatia and the other students in her circle. His sad fortune is our good fortune, as his letters form a clear picture of Hypatia and how her circle of students functioned in late Hellenistic Alexandria.

Wherever you find a philosopher, you find a circle of students who were tightly connected. We can see this at work in the students of Hypatia. Synesius tells us that he continued to meditate on his meetings with his teacher, as was part of the agreement between her and her students.

He returned to Alexandria repeatedly to spend a year or two in their company. When he was away from Alexandria, he kept in close contact with his teacher and the circle of students around her, counting them among his closest friends. Clearly the group was tightly bonded.

In *Hypatia of Alexandria,* Dzielska delves into the details of her daily life. Synesius describes Hypatia's inner circle as a family. The inner circle visited Hypatia every day. She delivered lectures according to a private schedule, with some knowledge passed on to the public, and some reserved only for her initiates. They kept this inner knowledge of the mysteries of philosophy as deep secrets. At times Synesius met with three other students in a group of four to study and preserve the knowledge they had received from her.

Hypatia's students included Pagans and Christians. This was natural, as the city itself was mixed, and she was one of its most influential people. Many attended her public lectures as a way to enter into her sphere of influence. Synesius himself became Christian and eventually a bishop; however, he continued to have more in common with his fellow Hellenistic aristocrats, both Pagan and Christian, than with Christian monks, who appeared to him unlettered and lower-class. Although Christian, he was nourished by the paideia.

Hypatia taught what Synesius called the "mysteries of philosophy." Biographer Mary Ellen Waithe notes that Hypatia discussed the works of Plato, Aristotle, Pythagoras, and others. She taught mathematics, geometry, and astrology; she taught the use of the astrolabe, an instrument used to measure the sun, moon, planets, and stars; and she taught the use of the hydroscope, used to look at objects underwater, as well as in divination.

The word "mysteries" points us to understand the kind of philosophy Hypatia taught. She was less interested in rhetoric or ethical questions and more interested in the nature of the cosmos. Mathematics was for her a spiritual pursuit. Her father composed poems on the spiritual nature of the planets. Scholars today struggle with this essential unity of scientific and spiritual knowledge in her work, as today science and spirit has been separated. Studying Hypatia's work allows us a glimpse of a world in which knowledge of the stars included love of the heavenly spheres.

While Hypatia was not trained or initiated into theurgy, her students studied the Chaldean Oracles. Synesius studied the works of theurgists, including Iamblichus, and speaks respectfully of the Hermes of the Hermetic texts. While the rituals her group performed were not theurgic, they were closely related to theurgy. Dzielska speculates that her students read and sang hymns both Pagan and Christian to prepare themselves for the silent experience of the blissful silence of the heavenly spheres.

Synesius describes his teacher as a blessed lady, a saint, and holy. He says her students always felt the presence of her spirit, and even her body was considered sacred; she bore the charisma from Plato that allowed her to teach. These terms were all used to describe Plato and Iamblichus, also teachers surrounded by students who delighted in listening to their heavenly voices.

Hypatia's work was targeted for destruction, and the prejudice against women philosophers has downplayed her contributions; retrieving her work requires discovery and detection. Mary Ellen Waithe uncovered her voice in the work of her father and students in *A History of Women Philosophers*. Bruce MacLennan cast his entire work on the philosophies of Alexandria as a set of lectures by Hypatia, *The Wisdom of Hypatia*.

ATHENA LIVES

When Proklos arrived at Asklepigenia's house panting from his run through the city, he found all the students of the Academy crowding into her biggest room, filling the floor, while she sat rigid on her stool with a face white as death. "What is it?" he said, alarmed. "What has happened?"

Archiadas said hotly, "It was the Christians. They swarmed the Acropolis last night. They moved that which should not be moved!"

"They brought down Athena," Ammonius choked out. Choked sobs echoed through the room.

"No," Proklos said, clutching his stomach as if he had been stabbed.

Archiadas said sadly, "It is true. There are those in the room who saw it with their own eyes."

Proklos breathed through the pain, managing finally to stand upright again. "A statue fell," he said strongly. "But they did not bring down Athena. A god's spirit is no more trapped in a statue than our spirit is trapped in our bodies. I know that well myself as a traveler, she has found me wherever I am, just as we can find her wherever we are."

The room took a collective breath, their tears shuddering to a halt. Asklepigenia said, "Yes, this is true."

Proklos said, "Last night in a dream I saw a divine woman. She told me to prepare my house because the Athenian lady was coming to live with me. We all have images of Athena in our homes, don't we? She lives with all of us."

Asklepigenia reached up to a shelf, pulled down a box, and brought out a ball made of lacquered blue metal studded with precious stones. Many students had never seen the iynx and held their breaths, afraid to make the slightest sound. She began to whirl it, and it began to whistle; she hummed over the whistle, making a harmony with it. "Call her, Proklos," she whispered.

"Grey-eyed lady," Proklos said. "Daughter of Zeus, lady of the shield, lady of weaving, Athenian lady, whom the Egyptians call Neit, lady of wisdom..."

His voice cut off as his vision flooded with light. Asklepigenia said, "She is here. Close your eyes and you will see her." Her voice lifted strongly over the whistling top. "She lives in our hearts."

Christianization and Triumphalism

At the turn of the millennium, Jewish peoples in Jerusalem and Alexandria revolted against Roman rule. When the great temple in Jerusalem was destroyed, the governor of Alexandria also closed the largest Alexandrian Jewish temple. Finally, in the second century a revolt against the Emperor Trajan was forcibly stopped by Roman soldiers who entered the Jewish quarter and slaughtered many of its inhabitants. Pogroms against Jewish Alexandrians would continue from that point forward.

Christianity rose up among the Jews as a response to persecution. In *Zealot, the Life and Times of Jesus of Nazareth*, Reza Aslan argues that the new religion was another instance of revolt against Roman rule. Like many other revolutionaries, Jesus preached rebellion against the Romans, and was executed for that reason. When the Jewish revolt he had led failed, the new religion moved to Alexandria and reinvented itself. The followers of Christ no longer addressed Jewish people in Hebrew; instead, they spoke to Hellenes in Greek. They recast their revolution as metaphorical, a spiritual rather than literal return of the kingdom of heaven.

At first the empire responded to the new sect by attempting to suppress Christianity as they would any other revolt. This time, however, Christian leaders made converts among the Roman noble families and eventually included the emperors themselves. Eventually, the religion of revolution overtook the empire from within.

When the Pagan emperor Julian died, his Christian successor Theodosius started a campaign of forbidding Pagan worship and closing Pagan temples. Unfortunately for religious Hellenes, from Theodosius onward Christianity became the official religion of the empire. Peoples subject to Roman rule were required to convert to Christianity and to cease their familiar religious practices and customs.

In *Hellenic Religion and Christianization* Frank Trombley traces the process by which Christian religion gradually overwrote the religion of the land. First, children were taken from their parents and inculcated in Christian religion while at the same time teachers of the paideia were forbidden to teach the ancient rites. Next, urban temples were closed and the statues destroyed. The countryside caves, springs, trees, and mountaintops that had been sacred to Pagan deities were rededicated to Christian use. The deities themselves were demoted to the status of daimones, with the status of holy deity reserved strictly for the God of the Christians. This process proceeded gradually throughout Greece, Egypt, and Syria from the fourth to the sixth centuries. Trombley notes that even though Pagan religious practice was officially banned, it was still widespread throughout this period. The very fact that emperor after emperor had to reissue the bans forbidding Pagan practices attest to their persistence.

In *Religion in Roman Egypt: Assimilation and Resistance*, David Frankfurter surveys the survival of native religious tradition in Roman Egypt. The religion of the countryside was conducted beyond the reach of the imperial mechanisms. Egyptian deities took on a distinctly Roman look, wearing armor and riding horseback, but their essential character remained unchanged. The large temples had so long been the centers of religious practice that the priesthoods serving them persisted for many centuries. The temples continued to give oracles as they had always done, drawing pilgrims from far and wide. This pattern of journey to the temple provided a template for later Christian pilgrimages to sacred sites. Frankfurter argues that the rhetoric of Christianization and the decline of Egyptian civilization require reassessment. He says, "Most of all, one must get beyond the notion that religions actually die, taking seriously the anthropology of small communities and dynamic relationship with ever-changing Greek traditions."

For Pagans seeking connection with the rituals of our ancestors, it is painful to read about the history of Christianization. When we hear that Proklos dreamed of Athena the night her temple was destroyed, he seems brave, defiant, and a little sad. It's even more difficult when the historians who write about these events celebrate them. Christian scholars in the early twentieth century framed this forced conversion as the "triumph of Christianity" and presented the process as the inevitable victory of a superior religion. From this point on, Pagan religion was "dead" and only Christianity lived in ritual or custom.

As we read these comments, it is tempting to strike out in anger, to proclaim that we are rebuilding our religion, that we are bringing back the worship of the gods, and that Christians are not welcome among us. We must remember that wars based on religious differences such as the Crusades have torn apart the world for millennia.

The Parliament of the World's Religions in 1993 included a Global Ethic signed by attendees pledging to cease to war with each other over these differences. Deborah Ann Light signed the compact as a member representative of three participating Pagan groups, Circle, EarthSpirit, and Covenant of the Goddess. The ethic outlines a course of meditation and action that continues to be vitally necessary today.

The Pagan groups present at the Parliament signed the ethic alongside Christian, Jewish, Islamic, Buddhist, Hindu, and many other groups. We have taken our place among religions on the world stage; it does not contribute to the peace of the gods to resurrect this ancient war. Hypatia taught Christians and Pagans together, and there is no reason we cannot continue to study together in peace.

However, we can and should continue to politely but firmly contest the triumphalist narrative. Until recently the study of Mediterranean history championed the grand narrative of Western progress in which human culture marched inevitably forward on a straight upward trajectory from primitive to sophisticated, from undeveloped to developed, from Pagan to Christian. Scholars seriously debated the relative definitions of magic, religion, and science, with science in its Western incarnation valorized as the pinnacle of human achievement, and religion in its Christian form as the manifestation of the most sublime human spirituality. In contrast with science, magic was described as superstition; in contrast with religion, magic was primitive. The mechanical science that gave rise to the Industrial Revolution has been framed as the crowning achievement of civilization. In the last few decades, scholars in many fields have challenged this narrative, pointing to the racist and imperialist underpinnings of the idea of "progress." It is a form of exceptionalism, the doctrine that holds that certain people—in this case white European people—deservedly dominate the world through their extraordinary accomplishments. In addition to calling European exceptionalism into question, scholars challenge the Industrial Revolution as a form of imperialism that claims the world's resources for the benefit of the privileged few.

One of the forms European exceptionalism takes is the idea that the Mediterranean region was a self-enclosed realm in which writing, cities, monumental religion, and civilization itself arose and were perfected. Scholars have gone to great lengths to prove that the Babylonians invented astrology before the Egyptians, that "foreign" artifacts discovered in the Mediterranean world signal the trading of goods but not ideas, and that there was a sort of cultural wall protecting the Mediterranean region from incursions of outside customs and beliefs. In "The Paths of the Ancient Sages," Peter Kingsley describes the scholastic idea of the "Oriental Mirage" in which scholars discount the ancients' own descriptions of their travels and the influence of other cultures on Mediterranean thought as a form of wishful thinking! Fortunately these attitudes are changing. Scholars such as Kingsley, Garth Fowden, Algis Uždavinys, Molefi Kete Asante, Maulana Karenga, Sarah Iles Johnston, and others call for researchers to take seriously what the ancients themselves wrote.

The world was as singularly small and interconnected in Proklos's time as it is now. Alexandria mixed Kemetic, Greek, Roman, Syrian, Persian, and Indian thought; Judaism, Christianity, Islam, Buddhism, and Paganism all affected the philosophies that issued from the Alexandrian schools.

A THEURGIC LIFE

It was dawn. Xanthus hung back in the door until Proklos finished his prayer to the sun and turned to go inside, falling into step with him. "Master, will you eat today, or fast? Do say you will eat, you've fasted too much this moon."

"You speak of care for the body," Proklos said, amused. "I care for my soul."

"Which depends on the body," the steward said stoutly. "Food today?"

"Very well. I will eat, but lightly. It's a holy day."

Xanthus knew the Athenian calendar, and this was not a holiday. "Which holy day? A Roman, or one of the Egyptians?"

"Lydian, if you must know."

"You must not travel again. You bring gods back from every land," Xanthus muttered. He answered the door and called out, "Archiadas!"

Archiadas joined Proklos in the study. "I see you're up before me again. If you slept at all."

"A bit, between prayers," Proklos said, laying the texts out on his desk.

"How many teaching periods do you have today?"

"Four. No, five," Proklos said. "Four today, and there's one more tonight." He smiled. "An old friend has arrived. Aedesia, the daughter of my first teacher Syrianus. She's come to study with me, and she's brought her sons Heliodorus and Ammonius to learn as well. I'm spending extra time with them."

"Ammonius?" Archiadas said, diverted. "Like the teacher of Plotinus?"

"A good name for a philosophical family," Proklos said.

Archiadas frowned. "A night lesson? Are you sure the widow doesn't have her eye on you?" Proklos laughed. Archiadas went on fussily, "Anyway you don't have time to teach at night if you're going to write."

"But I will write. Seven hundred lines, every day," Proklos said.

"You've been at it, what? Four years?" Archiadas laid a hand on his arm. "I worry about you. You drive yourself too hard."

"I've only a year until I finish the work. I think," Proklos argued. "At any rate it's important. No one else has compiled a history of the Chaldean Oracles. They taught me theurgic principles and they will teach others, too." He smiled. "Not everyone has had Asklepigenia for a teacher."

Archiadas studied his face. "There's more than that," he said shrewdly. "Something else drives you."

Proklos smiled. "I can't hide anything from you, can I? I had a dream. Plutarch came to me and predicted I'd live as many years as the pages I write about the Oracles. I mean to make seventy pages."

Whistling, Archiadas said, "That's a good, long life."

"With you beside me every year," Proklos said quietly. "but that isn't all—in the dream I saw that I am one of the links of the Hermetic chain. It's my duty to finish the work."

"Can't you cut back on your teaching periods then? Or some of the prayers?" Archiadas sighed. "I see by the set of your shoulders you won't hear of it. At least tell me how I can help."

"You can set out the stools for the students."

Studying at the Academy

In his own lifetime, learning from Proklos was a significant commitment. The course of education at the Athenian school took many years to complete. Grammar and rhetoric students formed the bread and butter of every school. Those who remained after learning those basic subjects worked their way through a curriculum that laid a foundation of logic and philosophy and gradually led into metaphysics. The curriculum covered Homer and Hesiod, then followed Iamblichus's designated order of reading Plato's dialogues. This layered education was intended to elevate the intellect from the material toward the divine.

In *Proclus, Neo-Platonic Philosophy and Science*, Lucas Siorvanes outlines the curriculum. First, the student cultivated natural physical health, then civic virtue, fulfilling individual political responsibilities. Then came purifications that prepared the student for a contemplative, philosophical, life. The student contemplated physical and theological realities. Finally the student was prepared to tackle theurgy, ritual operations bringing the philosopher into union with the divine.

Higher education was available to a very small percentage of the population, almost exclusively upper-class men. However, under Proklos as with Plato, female students were welcomed at the Academy. Unlike other schools in the late Roman world, the Neo-Platonic Academy under Proclus's leadership allowed women to pursue the same education as their male counterparts.

In her work *The Academy under Proclus,* Nina Ellis Frischmann lists the justifications Proklos offered for his decision. Women have souls just as men do and share the same virtues and pursuits. Education makes women better citizens and counterbalances their natural passions. Women in other societies took leadership positions, proving this was possible. Proklos also noted the gods possessed women as well as men. Didn't that prove women and men must share the same type of soul?

The example of the goddess Athena herself argued for women's education. Although she never married, she did not reject the traditional duties of women and fulfilled her domestic duties, while leaping to the defense of Athens in times of war. She was the epitome of the educated woman.

DEAREST FRIEND

"I can't." Frustrated, Proklos pushed away from the table. "I can't make the tops any more. My hands don't work right."

Archiadas steadied him as he stood. "You've already lived five years longer than the seventy years your dream predicted. It's no wonder your hands aren't as steady as they were."

Proklos coughed. "My health has been so bad these five years I don't think they count. Here, help me into bed."

A flash of lightning briefly lit the walls, followed by a low roll of thunder. Archiadas tucked a blanket under his chin. "Do you remember when you saved Attica from drought? You called the rains down with one of your famous tops."

"Not just the top," Proklos objected. "It's the rite that activates it, and the prayer to the gods."

Aedesius drew a stool next to the bed. "We all owe you so much. I owe you my daughter's life."

"How is she?"

"As healthy and fit as if she was never poised on the shore of the Styx. Her mother and her husband are grateful every day."

"I know. They send soup," Proklos said. "It's all I can eat these days."

"Not just my family," Archiadas said. "So many of us think of you as our own family."

"It's because I never married," Proklos said comfortably. "Did you bring it? The will?"

"I have it here," Archiadas said.

Proklos unrolled the document on his chest and peered myopically at it. "All my possessions to Archiadas, that's right. After Archiadas, to Xanthus for his care, very good. Then to Athens." He pushed the document off his chest. "Will you have it entered?"

"Tomorrow," Archiadas assured him, retrieving it and rolling it up again.

"And you've made the arrangements?"

"You have the tomb next to Syrianus, as you wanted."

"Good," he said, satisfied. "May our souls find the same abode."

Archiadas squeezed his hand. "I'm selfish. I want your soul to share this one a little longer."

Proklos fell back on the bed, his eyes distant. "I have seen immortal splendor," he said. "I have seen the supercelestial force springing from a consecrated spring, streaming with fiery light. I have been possessed by a spirit of fire lifting me to the heavens with music echoing in the starry vault."

"The starry vault," Archiadas said. "It is where our souls belong. Sleep now and dream of it." As the old teacher's breath evened into sleep, he said softly, "Go when you are ready, on the wings of my love."

Successors of Proklos

The primary source for the life of Proklos is Marinus's work *On Happiness, Life of Proclus*. Guthrie's translation is available online. Proklos was about seventy-five when he died. In his youth he walked in a city that still publicly honored the ancient gods; he worshipped his patron goddess Athena in the Parthenon, the thousand-year-old temple of Athena.

Proklos wrote prolifically; five of his commentaries on Platonic dialogues and six of his books survive, including his major works *Elements of Theology* translated by Dodds, and *Platonic Theology* translated by Thomas Taylor. Proklos also wrote many hymns; five which survive were translated by Thomas Taylor as *Proklos, Five Hymns*.

Several of Proklos's students succeeded him as head of the Academy: his biographer Marinus, Isidore who named his son Proklos, and Hegias, who inherited the knowledge of the Chaldean Oracles and the rituals of theurgy.

The last head of the Academy was born in Damascus, another philosopher steeped in Syrian religion as well as Platonism. Like Proklos, Damascius was forced to flee Athens for a time, taking refuge in Persia, but he eventually returned to Athens. In the tradition of the school, he wrote a biography of his teacher Isidore. He also wrote commentaries on Plato and the surviving work *Problems and Solutions Concerning First Principles*, elaborating on the ideas of Asklepigenia and Proklos. Damascius contemplated the first cause, that which made everything, and noted he didn't even like to use the term "To En, the One," because the human mind could not comprehend it enough even to name it.

THE LESSONS OF PROKLOS AND ASKLEPIGENIA

In his lifetime, Proklos witnessed the gradual suppression of public Pagan worship. Though not the last Pagan philosopher or the last head of the Academy, Proklos was the last of them to visit the temple of Athena while it was still a functioning Pagan place of worship. In his lifetime Pagan religion transitioned from the publically performed religion of empire to a private, home-based religion.

He seemed to feel a personal responsibility to preserve Pagan religion. He gathered information about deities wherever he travelled. He kept numerous feast days. He took on priestly offices. He wrote hymns. His patron goddess Athena spoke to him all his life and he accepted her guidance.

He learned practical magic from Asklepigenia and passed on his knowledge to his successor Hegias. Both Proklos and Asklepigenia conducted theurgic ritual as well as teaching and practicing philosophy. While they would teach philosophy to many, they only passed on knowledge of the practical rituals to a chosen few, Asklepigenia to Proklos and Proklos to Hegias. Proklos was credited with numerous successes in healing and protecting Athens.

Proklos did not hesitate to learn from any source he encountered, including the teachers of Kemet. Proklos and Asklepigenia worked together and fought to keep the Academy open to women as well as men. They stand as exemplars for Pagan conduct, preserving Pagan religion, teaching philosophy in the service of the gods, turning magic to the service of their community.

Notes on the Story

The main source for Proklos's life story is the biography written by his student Marinus, "On Happiness." Guthrie's translation is available online through the Platonic Library. Marinus specifically quotes Proklos as saying "Such are the habitual accidents of life!"

Although his teachers tried to pick out wives for him, Proklos managed to duck marriage, leaving his estate to his constant companion, Archiadas, arguing for a strong friendship if not an outright bonded relationship. Proklos was also a friend to women, forming quite a strong friendship with Asklepigenia and defending the right of women to enter his circle.

Asklepigenia was known to have a beautiful sphere to conduct theurgic ritual. The children's toy described in the story is available today and is a good tool to add a buzzing or whirring sound to vowel chanting.

SIX

BOETHIUS

We are now well into contested territory, where Christian apologists claim philosophers as converts, the history of science valorizes the nonritual aspects of philosophy, and scholastic efforts to uncover ongoing Pagan religion are challenged as biased attempts to read contemporary religion back into history. Nonetheless, where we find Neo-Platonic philosophers, we often find converts to Paganism.

This appears to be the case with Boethius. Anicius Manlius Severinus Boethius was born in or near Rome around the year 480 CE. He was orphaned early and had the good fortune to be raised by Symmachus, an aristocratic Christian who provided him with the best possible education.

PLATO AND ARISTOTLE

Boethius bent over the scroll, so intent on his reading that he didn't hear Aedesia come up behind him until she put a hand on his shoulder. Then he looked up, blinking, and accepted the water she gave him. "Are you making progress?" she asked.

He rubbed a hand over his eyes. "There is so much to learn. I don't know how much time I will have. Symmachus asks me every week when I will be returning home. A consul post is waiting for me the moment I step on shore."

"To be a consul," Aedesia mused. "Is that what you want to do?"

He shook his head so his hair flew. "I want to study philosophy. It's all that matters to me." He squinted up at the woman squeezing his shoulder. "You must understand. You're a philosopher."

"And I've raised two fine philosophers," she said. "But they inclined more to Plato, being Pagan. Your church loves Aristotle."

He tapped the scroll. "Here, Aristotle is saying exactly what Plato said. They can be reconciled, I know they can." His eyes brightened. "It's my life's work to make that clear."

"Can they?" Aedesia said doubtfully. "It's like reconciling Christians and Pagans."

"That's why I'm the man for the task," he said confidently. "I've studied both Aristotle and Plato, and I've studied with Christians and Pagans."

She sighed. "I wish you could stay. You could smooth the path between Ammonius and the magistrates. It seems every year there's a new threat to close the Academy."

"This is Alexandria," Boethius said confidently. "There will always be an Academy."

"In name only," Aedesia said tartly. "You know we're being pressured to give up our ways. If we don't, we risk being closed. If we do, we're just another Christian school."

Boethius argued, "I didn't come to you because you're Pagan. I came to you because you teach philosophy. That work will always live."

"That's not what Damascius says," Aedesia said.

Boethius waved a hand. "Damascius governs the Academy in Athens, not the Academy in Alexandria. Ammonius must do what is right for your students."

Aedesia searched the face of her student. "Are you certain you must leave? Alexandria still has the finest library in the world."

"Well," he said. "I do love to study, but my heart lives in Rome."

Aedesia nodded, resigned. "It's rare to find a Roman who can speak Greek these days. We haven't had another student like you. Your mind runs ahead so quickly, you absorb what we give you and beg for more. It won't be long before you become the teacher instead of the student." She patted his shoulder again and moved away. "I wish you all the success you dream."

"In the world? Or in the spirit?" Boethius said thoughtfully.

"In philosophy, of course," Aedesia said.

As she moved away, Boethius said to himself, "I wish for both."

Byzantion

The members of Rome's ruling class had long warred with one another over who would rule the empire. In the third century CE, Rome's administrative districts were divided into east and west. Emperor Constantine moved the empire's seat from Rome in Italy to the Greek city Byzantion, calling it the new Rome, and renaming it for himself, "Constantinople." We know the city today as Istanbul.

The last emperor to rule a united Roman empire was Theodosius, who died in 395 CE. He left the eastern and western seats to his two sons, Arcadius and Honorius, splitting the empire. The Roman world would never reunite, continuing as two distinct cultures. East and west split on more than familial and political lines, they spoke different languages— Rome spoke Latin, Byzantion spoke Greek. The Christian church divided as well. While the Roman Church developed a hierarchy ruled by a pope, Constantinople resisted the pope's authority; a patriarch ruled the Eastern Orthodox Church. While Rome sent out missionaries to make converts, the Eastern Church founded monasteries that served as refuges for contemplation, developing a unique and beautiful iconography.

The citizens of the Byzantine Empire, as we call it now, continued to think of themselves as living in the Roman Empire. Byzantion survived for a thousand years, from 474 to 1453 CE, while in the west a succession of "barbarian" peoples—Huns, Vandals, and Goths—overran Rome and fragmented her provinces.

As a Greek speaker in fifth-century Rome, Boethius was a rarity, distinguishing himself in service to the Latin-speaking rulers of Rome.

MATHEMATICS AND MAGIC

Rusticana entered the study quietly and waited until her husband looked up. "A letter from Cassiodorus," she said.

Laying aside his stylus, Boethius sighed. "More business from Theodoric?" He scanned the letter quickly. "This time he wants some presents for King Gunobad of the Burgundians. A water clock and..." Boethius squinted at the letter, "a sundial."

"Is that all?" Rusticana blew out a breath. "The time that it will take you to make them!"

"No, that's not all," Boethius said. "He wants me to pick out a harper. For Clovis, king of the Franks. To tame his savage heart! And he wants me to discover why his horse and foot guards say they're not being paid properly. Someone is shorting them; he wants me to check the reckoning."

Sliding onto a bench near the desk, Rusticana said, "He overworks you. Still, it's flattering that Theodoric thinks so well of you. It will help our family's position." She rubbed her husband's arm and smiled. "No personal word from Cassiodorus?"

"Oh yes," Boethius said. "He's full of praise for my learning, my mathematical treatises, and especially my theological tracts. He urges me to write more of those." He threw the letter down. "He worries that my mathematical skills will be confused for magic. Apparently learning from Pagans leaves me open to accusations of being Pagan myself."

"Surely not," Rusticana said, drawing herself up. "We come from a good Christian family."

"Slanderers are everywhere," Boethius said. He shook himself. "This lays more obligations on me, just when I was making progress." He tapped the pages. "Aristotle and Plato speak in harmony. I know I can make that clear."

The Costs of Empire

For centuries, Western historians have described the fall of the Roman Empire as if it was a tragedy. It might have been for the Roman elite, but was it as painful for the newly freed colonies? Rome's reach was long, and her vengeance was legendary. From Britain to Asia, Roman roads carried Roman troops to enforce the Roman census and taxes. The same road carried the resources of the territories back to the center of power, gold from Gaul, wheat from North Africa, slaves from everywhere. Roman citizens managed dozens of slaves in the household and hundreds in the fields.

Until recently Western history has glossed over the Roman destruction of Celtic civilization. The names of many Celtic deities are lost beneath the *interpretatio Romana*, which substituted the names of Roman deities for native ones. There are numerous Celtic pantheons, and they do not map neatly onto the Olympian twelve. For Jupiter we have Taranis, for Mars we have Smertrios, for Neptune we have Nodens, for Hades we have Sucellos. Various attempts have been made to map the Celtic goddesses—Matrona, Morrigan, Danu, Brigit—onto Juno, Diana, Minerva, Vesta, and Ceres. The Romans identified Lugh with Mercury but the god Cernunnos does not neatly correspond with Vulcan or Apollo. The goddess Rosmerta married Mercury, just as Celtic women married Roman soldiers; Rosmerta kept her purse and added Mercury's caduceus, surely a goddess to reckon with!

In the same way that Roman names have overlaid Celtic deities, Roman descriptions of savage "barbarians" has obscured appreciation for the complexity and sophistication of Celtic culture. The Celts traded far beyond their borders, and their mathematics were generally more sophisticated than the Roman. Celtic culture was patriarchal, but women wielded more power among the tribes than in Rome, and Celtic queens and women warriors fought Roman conquest. Celtic peoples did not find Rome's conquest a civilizing force, but an exploitive one.

Rome permitted subjugated territories to practice their native religions—to an extent. State religion upheld state political power, so temples to the Roman deities were founded everywhere, including temples to the deified emperors. Roman governors owed Rome a portion of taxes, but the governors were permitted to levy a surcharge and pocket the difference, making taxes difficult to meet. In Israel the High Priest under Roman rule was no longer elected by the people but by Roman governors who usually favored collaborators over those who advocated for the rights of the subjugated. When the Jewish people revolted in an attempt to throw off Roman rule, Rome responded by killing and enslaving Jewish people and destroying the temple in Jerusalem.

Roman conquest has been romanticized as a civilizing force in barbarian territories. Contemporary nuanced analyses of the effect of colonization notes that the benefits of Roman civilization were experienced largely by the cooperating elites. The vast majority of people experienced theft of their resources, loss of autonomy, and conscription of their labor. Some were carted off to serve as slaves to Rome.

Scholarship analyzing and mourning the demise of the Roman Empire often reflects a fear of the loss of the European and American Empires succeeding the Roman. We know that it is the fate of all far-flung exploitive regimes to fragment, to cede territory and resources, to become vulnerable to exploitation in return. Recognizing this bias in ourselves can help us become more open to alternative points of view exploring the costs of empire to those who genuinely bear it. It can open history to faces and voices that reflect experiences of peoples other than the elite.

LADY PHILOSOPHY

Why should he get out of bed? He was still in prison, days turning to weeks turning to months. In the beginning his memories had comforted him, how good Symmachus had been to him, how happy he had been with Symmachus's daughter, Rusticana, as his wife. He remembered the day that was the pinnacle of his political career: his two sons Boethius and Symmachus were appointed consuls of Rome, and he stood between them to deliver a paean of praise to the emperor Theodoric.

It only took the slanderers a year after that to bring him down. They produced a letter supposedly written by him to the Emperor Justin attacking Theodoric. Clearly a forgery! Yet it was enough to exile him to this prison cell in a tower in a backwater city far from Rome.

"Get up," Lady Philosophy said. "You have work to do."

He tried to ignore her. "Leave me alone."

The light from her face filled the room. She held out a hand. "Come, to your desk. You still have life and hope."

"Will you lecture me again?" he grumbled, swinging his legs to the floor. "I know, I know. Don't trust Fortune. The swing of her wheel takes those she favors up and then down again. Now that I'm down, do I wait for her to swing me back up?"

The lady said gravely, "Why don't you get off the wheel altogether?"

He flexed his cold hands and reached for the stylus. "How is this possible?"

"What would Proklos say? Plotinus? Plato?"

"Settle the body, still the mind, contemplate the divine," he murmured. "The life of the spirit is the true life."

"Remember," she whispered. "Remember, remember. You came from the stars. Philosophy gives you wings. Rise up! Above the air, above the sun, above the stars, rise up, rise toward the One. It is the road home! When you have walked that road, you will look down again on earth and its petty rulers, and it is they who will seem like exiles to you."

Pagan Conversion

The phenomenon of prison conversion to a religion offering comfort is quite common. This seems to have been what happened to Boethius. Arnaldo Momigliano is widely quoted as saying, "Many people have turned to Christianity for consolation. Boethius turned to Paganism. His Christianity collapsed—it collapsed so thoroughly that perhaps he did not even notice its disappearance." There is no Christianity in the work Boethius wrote in prison, *The Consolation of Philosophy*, and Lady Philosophy's final call to rise to the stars is strictly Neo-Platonic.

Despite the hope Boethius expressed that his fortunes would turn again, he was executed for treason by strangulation. His foster father Symmachus defended him to the end and was executed too. After Boethius's death, his friend Cassiodorus edited Boethius's works. Fabio Troncarelli observed drily that Boethius had known how to die, but Cassiodorus knew how to live, reinventing the works of Boethius in an acceptably Christian image.

The works of Boethius entered into the *quadrivium*, the medieval monastic teaching curriculum.

THE LESSONS OF BOETHIUS

The Alexandrian Neo-Platonists mixed Christian students with Pagans for centuries. Neo-Platonism influenced the development of Christian theology through Boethius and other sources. Yet the study of Plato and his followers focused on the contemplation of the vastness of the universe and always seemed to have a fundamentally Pagan character.

Few have had such a dizzying fall from height as Boethius. In struggling to maintain his balance in a perilous moment, Boethius found comfort in lifting his eyes above his physical to gaze steadfastly at the goal of the philosopher, to know the divine. The comfort of Lady Philosophy is always available to those who place our lives in the context of that goal.

Notes on the Story

Boethius spoke Greek and was highly educated in Neo-Platonic philosophy as well as practical mathematics and astrology. No account remains of his early education; some scholars believe he learned entirely from teachers in Rome, some think he might have visited Athens, and some speculate that he traveled to Alexandria to learn from Ammonius. I see no reason why he would not have traveled; the breadth and depth of his education argues for it. The mixed Pagan and Christian atmosphere in the Alexandrian school seems suited to the young Boethius's temperament.

Helen Barrett's biography *Boethius: Some Aspects of His Works and Times* includes the interesting details about Cassiodorus's letters and Theodoric's requests of Boethius.

Boethius's own work, *Consolation of Philosophy*, offers us the window into his prison cell during the time of his incarceration. Although his prison stay ended with his execution, his work survives to this day.

SEVEN

GEBER

When Christian persecution drove Pagan philosophers out of Alexandria, Athens, and Rome, Byzantion formed a refuge. This city continued the tradition of Greek literate culture—Homer's *Iliad* was taught in the schools—and Platonic and Neo-Platonic commentaries continued to be studied and written there.

While Paganism survived in Christian Constantinople, one Hellenistic city remained openly Pagan. Harran, a trade route crossroads in the scorching desert and one of the stops on the Silk Road, had been the city of the moon god since Akkadian rule in 2000 BCE. The last Pagan emperor Julian offered a sacrifice at the temple of the moon god in Harran. Early medieval Harran had seven gates and seven temples, each dedicated to one of the planetary deities, Mercury, Venus, Mars, Jupiter, Saturn, and the moon and sun, considered planets by the ancients.

The last Pagan city certainly included Christians, Jews, and Muslims among its population, drawn to the learned atmosphere of the city. In the eighth century, the Muslim caliph Umar II founded a Neo-Platonic academy in the city and invited persecuted Hermetic scholars from Athens and

Alexandria to move there. The Neoplatonist Simplicius, who had studied with Damascius at the Academy in Athens before it closed, wrote his treatise on physics there.

The man who is credited with founding Arabic alchemy is thought to have studied at the university in Harran. Known in Western Europe as Geber, Jabir ibn Hayyan was born about 721 CE. An alchemist and Sufi, he studied Pythagorean and Neo-Platonic texts; numerous commentaries bear his name.

SILVER FOR THE MOON GOD

Jabir finished the last line, set his pen aside on the pad, and sprinkled sand on the parchment. The script seemed to move on the page; was it his tired eyes, or did the words themselves dance with knowledge? It was done, praise be to Allah, a fair copy. He glanced over at the long-necked alembic and the small box holding a mound of powder. He had made the silver nitrate, and he had recorded how it was made.

He had been working so long the light had started to fade. He reached for the tray near his elbow to pick up a slice of cheese or a bit of flatbread. The tray was empty. He must have eaten them all, although he had no memory of having done so or how long ago that had been.

Gathering up his notes, he threw on his cloak and stepped outside. His little beehive house made of clay sat a small distance from his neighbors—no one wanted to live too close to the odors and explosions that resulted from his experiments. A few minutes of walking brought him deeper into the city where the streets were filled with people.

A passerby jostled Jabir's elbow. Automatically he clutched the manuscript close against his chest.

"Apologies," a young woman murmured, and stopped. "Jabir ibn Hayyan? It's really you! We haven't seen you in months."

"Layla," Jabir said turning to her with a smile. It always gave him a lift to see her. Today she wore a bright red robe worked with intricate embroidered designs and was scented with a floral perfume. "What's your errand?"

She lifted a basket. "I'm taking an offering to the temple of the moon god."

They both looked up reflexively to the great stone temple on the hill at the center of town. "It's an ancient thing," Jabir murmured. "Ehulhul, home of Sin, god of the moon."

"Women of my family have brought offerings there since time began," Layla said.

Jabir laughed. "Since time began? It has been destroyed and rebuilt many times."

"Just so, it still stands," she said serenely. "Will you walk with me? I would appreciate the company."

"I will walk with you as far as I can," he responded readily. "My destination is the university."

They fell into step together. She said, "How are your studies in alchemya?"

"I have created a salt of silver," he said, happy to share his discovery. "It's a white powder but it turned my hand black. It sealed a cut on that hand, too," he said. "It's a lunar caustic. I believe it will have many beneficial medical uses."

"Well then, you should make an offering at the temple," she urged him. "Since silver is the metal of the moon god."

"The work is my offering," he said piously. "And this," tapping the manuscript still tight in his hands. "I'm taking a copy for the library."

Just then his stomach growled. Layla laughed. "You devotees of Hermes always neglect your health!"

"I know Hermes as Idris," he said mildly.

Layla did not let him lead her off her point. "When did you last eat?"

"It might have been yesterday," he confessed.

Layla lifted the basket. "Here, take one."

"I'm not a god," he said uncomfortably.

"No, you're just a scholar, but you're a hungry one," she said. "And it's a long way to the university."

The scent of the honey cakes made his mouth water. Layla handed him one, and he took a bite, savoring the burst of sweetness on his tongue. "Did you make this? It's delicious!"

She laughed. "That's the hunger talking." She stopped and pointed down the street. "This is where we part company. Unless you change your mind and come to the temple with me."

He sighed. "I am anxious to deliver this to the library. My regards to your father."

"Please come to dinner soon," she said cheerfully, waved, and was swallowed up in the crowd.

It was a good omen to have a honey cake from the hand of a devotee of the moon god. He breathed a quick prayer, "May all the gods look with favor on my work." Then he pushed on toward the university. Layla was right, it really was a long walk.

Harran and Bagdad

Jabir ibn Hayyan died about 851 CE. If he did live in Harran, he witnessed the destruction of the great temple of the moon god and the construction of a mosque on the site. Even while replacing temples with mosques, for centuries successive Islamic rulers tolerated the city's Pagan ways. The city's luck finally ran out when the last functioning Pagan temple was destroyed by an ally of the Turks in 1081 CE. In 1271 Mongols deported the population and walled off the city, which was left to fill up with sand.

Contemporary theurgist Don Frew, along with Anna Korn, toured Harran's temple ruins in the late 1990s, a trip documented in "Harran: Last Refuge of Classical Paganism." Frew noted that population pressure had brought irrigation farming and permanent settlement to the area. Archaeological investigation of the ancient temple sites remains an urgent need for the study of medieval Pagan religion.

Jabir's work was so highly respected that numerous subsequent authors borrowed his name for their writings, establishing a Jabirian tradition of Hermetic alchemy in Islamic philosophy.

In *The Hermetic Link: From Secret Tradition to Modern Thought*, Jacob Slavenburg traces a connection between Harran and Baghdad. Hermetic and other scholars migrated to Baghdad when that city established its House of Wisdom in the ninth century. At its height, the city held a million people and drew multilingual intellectuals from around the Islamic world—Spain, Egypt, the Near East, Syria, Iraq and Iran, and Afghanistan.

Today, scholars refer to this time period as the Golden Age of Islam. The university in Baghdad imported printing press technology from China and preserved numerous works from the ancient Greek, Roman, and Hellenistic academies. The ready availability of texts containing the scientific and philosophic knowledge of the ancient world inspired numerous Islamic Neo-Platonists.

Jabir's work inspired a secret society that met in Baghdad, the Ikhwan al-Safa or Brethren of Purity. The Ikhwan compiled an encyclopedia of fifty-two epistles summarizing science, philosophy, metaphysics and theology. In *An Introduction to Islamic Cosmological Doctrines*, Seyyed Hossein Nasr notes the works of the Ikhwan al-Safa contain many Hermetic and Pythagorean elements. He calls them the "guardians and propagators of Hermeticism in the Islamic world," the spiritual descendants of the Harranians, heirs to the religion of the prophet Idris. They cited four sources for their knowledge: the scientific works of the ancient world; the religious texts, Torah, Gospels, and Quran; the study of nature; and divine books accessible only to angels and purified humans. They met three times a month to sing hymns to Plato, Aristotle, and Idris, the Islamic version of Hermes. In this they remind us of the theurgists of Alexandria and Rome who revered teachers as divine beings and began their meetings by singing hymns to the gods.

THE LESSONS OF GEBER

Eurocentric versions of history lament the dark ages of the West and the loss of precious knowledge in the gap between the classical world and the Renaissance. That gap did not exist in the Islamic world, where the same time period is known as a great flowering of knowledge and culture. The cities of Harran and Baghdad were impressively large and supported universities that preserved works that had been destroyed in Western Europe. While medieval monks labored to hand copy a few precious works on animal skin vellum, printing technology imported from China allowed many copies of scrolls to be struck from carved woodprints on durable linen paper. The history of civilization takes a decided detour from Athens and Rome through the great Islamic cities.

The Ikhwan al-Safa form a critical link in the transmission of Hermetic knowledge through the centuries. They are followers of Jabir ibn Hayyan within the Islamic mystic tradition, but the group also bears a resemblance to the circles that surrounded the Pagan philosophers. With their hymns to the great teachers, they form another example of the worship that surfaces whenever students commit to Neoplatonism.

Notes on the Story

While some scholars place Geber in Harran, this is purely speculative, although any history written about Jabir ibn Hayyan is at least partly fiction. The clay houses of Harran are called "beehive" houses for their conical shape, resembling medieval conical skeps.

In *A Treatise on Chemistry, Volume 2*, Henry Enfield Roscoe and Carl Schorlemmer note that Geber first made silver nitrate. They describe the process for doing so. It is still used today for numerous purposes, including cauterizing wounds.

EIGHT

PSELLOS

In the time of the Ikhwan al-Safa, Constantinople was one of the largest cities in the world. The terminus of the Silk Road leading from China through Baghdad and Harran, it carried both material wealth and the knowledge of the world into the city. The Byzantine intellectual tradition added these new sources to its deep store of Greek philosophy, with its debt to Egyptian/Kemetic knowledge in addition to newly developed Christian thought.

Michael Psellos was born in 1018. The son of an elite family, he was named Constantine at birth. He was groomed to serve the masters of the empire, studying with teacher John Mauropos alongside men who would eventually become emperors and patriarchs.

In 1047 the emperor Constantine IX appointed Constantine Psellos head of philosophy at his new University of Constantinople. Stephen Skinner notes Psellos was given the title *Hypatos,* or Consul of Philosophers. Psellos succeeded in centering the curriculum of the new university on the paideia, the Hellenic cultural classics. In 1050 he came into possession of an important manuscript.

A PRECIOUS TEXT

"Constantine, he is here."

Psellos turned away from his desk and strode across the floor to greet his visitor. "Welcome, well met," he said, placing the man's outstretched hand between his palms, a visible sign of his pleasure and an offer of protection. He waved his hand at his youthful slave. "Wine, Milosh." The young man backed away and left quickly.

"Milosh?" his visitor said.

"He's a Scyth, a Slav," Psellos said shortly. "Please, come sit by the fire." His visitor eyed the elaborately carved chairs inlaid with gold and ivory. When Psellos carelessly dropped onto the cane seat, his visitor gingerly followed suit.

"Now then," Psellos said, "what shall we call you?"

The man fiddled with his Arabic robe. "Idris Khaldun, as I have signed my letters, of course." When Psellos didn't speak, he went on, "Khaldun is of my family. Idris—"

"Is a form of Hermes, of course," Psellos said. "I thought you might call yourself Ibrahim al-Andalus, a scholar from one of the Spanish courts."

"Ah," Idris said, light dawning. "You think I should pass as Jewish. You think this will hide the fact that I am a refugee from Harran, that I will be taken for Muslim. Of course you know that I am not Muslim either. You would think of me as Pagan, like Milosh."

As if he had heard his name, the young man reappeared, balancing a tray of goblets and wine. Idris smiled at him, but Milosh avoided his eyes, carefully sat the tray on a low table, and left the room. Idris raised his eyebrow at the golden cups. "You drink well here," he commented.

Psellos filled a goblet and passed it to him. "You're in Byzantium now, my friend. All the comforts of empire are at your fingertips." He grimaced. "For as long as we can retain them."

Idris took a gulp of wine as if to give himself courage to speak. "Your people are no kinder to Jews than to Muslims. I don't speak Hebrew, and I have no idea what to do in a synagogue."

"You'll be a Jew converting to Christianity. No need to enter a synagogue, and it accounts for your accent," Psellos said. "As a Christian I can find you a position. You'll enjoy your work here at the university."

"I am ungrateful," Idris said suddenly. "It is more than I could have hoped to find refuge in a place of learning."

"As for that," Psellos said, "if a love of philosophy is Pagan…" He glanced at the door where Milosh hovered half out of sight.

Idris said, "I understand this new university has an old curriculum. I expected to find a great deal of Aristotle and Christian apologetics. Instead I hear that you are teaching Homer, Plotinus, and Iamblichus."

Psellos nodded. "Back to the wellspring of the early Church," he said piously. He leaned forward. "I'm an idealist. I have so looked forward to discussing Plato with you," he said intensely. "As a scholar from Harran you will have new insights. I hope to share many dinners with you." He laughed and shook himself. "Once you've settled in. Is that the whole of your luggage?" He gestured at the bag Idris had laid beside the chair.

Idris roused himself. "This? No, it's a gift. For you," he said, holding out the bag.

Psellos waved it off. "It isn't necessary. You can see we have everything we need here."

"I don't believe your gold will buy you this," Idris said, smiling slightly. "Please."

Taking the bag, somewhat grimy from its journey but fundamentally sturdy, Psellos lifted the flap and pulled out the scrolls tucked inside. Curious now, he unrolled one of the scrolls and sat reading for a long minute, then turned wide eyes to Idris. "What is this?"

"The Hermetica."

Psellos stopped breathing for a moment. Then he cleared his throat. "Did you say the Hermetica?"

"With my own annotations, I'm afraid. I hope you don't mind—"

Idris stopped as Psellos was crushing his ribs in a fierce embrace. "The Hermetica!" Psellos said. "I thought never to see it in my lifetime! This is a more precious gift than you can possibly know."

"I have come to the right place," Idris said with relief, relaxing for the first time since he had walked into the room.

"You were welcome as a scholar," Psellos said. "This gift makes you a friend of knowledge."

Jewish Neo-Platonists in Spain

Jews lived and studied in Alexandria, in the Islamic world, and throughout the Roman and Byzantine empires. The Jewish religious and intellectual traditions absorbed some Hellenistic thought; for example, in the first century of the Common Era the Alexandrian Jewish scholar Philo sought to reconcile the teachings of Hebrew texts with Plato and Pythagoras.

During the Golden Age of Islam, Jews were respected as "people of the book." This was especially true in Moorish Spain. At the time of the destruction of the moon temple in Harran, Islamic Spain was arguably the site of the most enlightened culture in Western Europe. Islamic leaders permitted Christians and Jews not only to practice their faiths but also enter the professions, becoming doctors, architects, and teachers. In this culture upper-class women could be literate and sometimes served as scribes in the courts.

When Harran fell, Neo-Platonists, Muslim mystics, and Jewish intellectuals fled to other parts of the world. Some may have ended up in the Spanish courts, others in Constantinople. They may have brought texts with them. We do know that from the eleventh to the fifteenth century, from the fall of Harran to the fall of Constantinople, Hermetic literature seeped back into the West.

In "Hermeticism in the Alfonsine Tradition," Henry and Renee Kahane trace Jewish translators who worked in the Spanish courts, translating Hebrew and Arabic texts into Latin and Spanish. In the thirteenth century, Arabic texts appeared in Latin, teaching Hermetic ideas such as the four elements and the ascent to the stars.

Avicebron exemplifies the Jewish intellectual in this decidedly mixed tradition. Sarah Pessin outlines his life: Solomon ben Judah Ibn Gabirol, Latinized as Avicebron, was born in Spain in the eleventh century, three years after Michael Psellos was born in Constantinople. In contrast to Psellos's patrician upbringing, Avicebron lived a brief and apparently somewhat miserable life. He described himself as an orphan with a disfiguring skin ailment. Although he did move in Jewish intellectual circles, he had difficulty procuring patrons, friends, and even servants. Pessin notes the legend that he created a golem to do his housework!

While he alienated his contemporaries in person, Avicebron impressed others with his poetry and philosophical writings. His work was influenced by Neo-Platonic and Pythagorean thought as well as Jewish, Islamic, and Christian sources. His *Fons Vitae*, "Fountain of Life," was written in Arabic and translated into Hebrew and Latin. The book takes the form of a dialogue between student and teacher similar to the form of Hermetic texts.

He died when he was only thirty-six, the year Psellos entered the monastery at Bithynia. There is no particular evidence that Psellos and Avicebron met, corresponded, or read each other's works. Their lives form separate but adjacent threads in the Neo-Platonic tapestry.

THE PHILOSOPHER POLITICIAN

Psellos had handpicked John Italos to succeed him as Hypatos. A visit from his successor provided an excuse to escape the monastery for a private conversation. Psellos walked quickly, climbing the green hill rapidly. "Every time I mention Plato those crabbed little monks bless themselves against the 'Hellenic Satan.' We must move out of earshot."

His somewhat shorter friend panted beside him. "Let us walk a little less urgently," he begged. "Remember, still the mind, calm the body."

Slowing, Psellos blew out a breath, calming himself. "It's so good to get out of there, even for an afternoon." He turned to his friend with his trademark intensity. "Now, you must tell me all about everything. How is Constantinople?"

John was used to his friend in this mood. "Well, Xiphilinos continues to rise in the church hierarchy."

"The monks approve of him," Psellos said flatly.

"He abandoned you!" Italos said. "After you defended him when he was accused of heresy. You said he had no equal in grammar and poetry."

"It was not a successful defense," Psellos said mildly. "Both of us were forced to take the tonsure. Although he took it better than I did."

"He has taken to it far too well," Italos muttered into his beard. "He has accused you of abandoning Christ to follow Plato. Constantine, he accused you of heresy!"

"Michael," Psellos corrected. "It's Michael now. I took the name when I came to this place."

Diverted, Italos said, "Will you become Constantine again when you go back to the city?"

"No. I mean to keep it," Psellos said. "After all, it's the archangel Michael who controls the demons." He waved his hand. "I've spoken with him, John. I knelt in the church, the one with a piece of the true cross, and the whole place was filled with his presence." He cut his friend a glance. "Surely that's Christian of me."

"You don't have to defend yourself to me," Italos said. They crested the hill and stopped, looking out over green fields and little houses. "It's a pretty countryside."

"It's peaceful," Psellos said. "I've thought if I could have my own cottage, I could live here for the rest of my life." He took a deep breath. Psellos said, "John, this is all old news. Get to it. What have you come to tell me?" He laughed shakily. "Will I end up like Boethius, consoled by philosophy while I await my death?"

"You're called back to court." Psellos stood very still. Italos said uncertainly, "My friend?"

Suddenly Psellos whooped and crushed Italos in a quick embrace. "Called back to court?" he said. "Music, food, conversation—books!"

"The Empress Theodora finds she has need for your counsel," Italos said, grinning now. "And, frankly, so do I. So much that I left the city for this provincial backwater to deliver the news myself."

"Theodora…" Psellos said with satisfaction. "Mark my words, John, and cultivate the women. They do have minds and they will appreciate you for knowing it."

"That's not all I've come to say," Italos said. Even though they were out in the open with no one near, he leaned close to Psellos and said quietly, "Your work on the Chaldean Oracles—"

"—does not progress in this environment," Psellos said shortly.

"It will in the city. You've talked about the use of the iynx wheel, using stones to purify the spirit, calling the gods into statues."

"Don't tell me—it's all blasphemous?" Psellos teased. "You'll call me a heretic like Xiphilinos did?"

Italos couldn't help himself. "Teach me," he cried. "That work has always passed one to one!"

"There is more," Psellos said intensely. "There is a way to … become divine. But I'm not going to write about that."

Italos's face was growing red and his nostrils flared. "Constantine Michael Psellos, I swear—"

"Of course I'll teach you," Psellos said. "I'll trust your discretion." He turned his back on the countryside and flew back down the hillside, calling over his shoulder, "Come, we can be gone before dusk!"

Panting, John Italos followed behind.

The Lessons of Psellos

Psellos was banished to the monastery at Bithynia in 1054 and returned to court in 1055. He served Empress Theodora as her prime minister and kept the post under his former student, the Emperor Michael VII Ducas. Psellos retired from public life in 1078, and most biographers believe he died shortly afterwards, although some argue that he lived for another twenty years.

Psellos's student John Italos fared less well. His Italian upbringing, his legendary temper, and his advocacy for Platonic philosophy led him in turn to face charges of "Hellenizing" and cost him his academic position. Even after losing the chair he continued to teach, educating women as well as men. The Empress Anna Comnena praised him as having bad grammar but prodigious knowledge. In *Change in Byzantine Culture*, Kazhdan and Petrovich note that Italos's successor as Hypatos, Theodore of Smyrna, was the last to hold the position. Subsequent administrators abolished the position of philosophy chair and filled the university with teachers of the Gospel and the lives of the apostles.

Psellos wrote on numerous subjects and is hailed as a Renaissance man. His effect on the transmission of Hermetic knowledge from Alexandria to the present was mixed; his version of the Hermetica is thought to be the source for subsequent copies in Greek, but his work on demons shifted the popular understanding from the Greek belief that the spirits were both helpful and malicious to the idea that demons represented only evil. Only angels identified with Christianity were entirely good to Psellos despite the fact that the Latin *angelus* described the same class of being as the Greek *daimones*. We can see in this the privileging of Latin over Greek as well as Christianity over Paganism.

While the Greek Orthodox Church exercised considerable influence in Constantinople, Byzantine culture always rested on the base of the Greek paideia, which was Pagan in origin. In Psellos's life we can see another iteration of the cycle of study of Neo-Platonism, resurgence of Pagan thought, and Christian suppression.

Notes on the Story

Like the Greek and Roman empires, the Byzantine Empire bought and sold people, trading with both Western Europe and the Islamic world. So many of these people were Slavic that they gave us the word "slave." Sewter notes that Psellos used the word "scyths" to describe the Slavs. In *Slavery from Roman Times to the Early Transatlantic Trade*, Phillips points out that the Pagan Slavs were fair game for the slave trade, while regulations sought to keep Christians out of bondage.

The figure of Idris is a fiction, standing in for the anonymous scholars who fled Harran for Spain and Constantinople. Whatever its provenance, Psellos obtained a copy of the Hermetica and passed it forward in the chain of Hermetic transmission.

In *The Argument of Psellos' Chronographia*, Anthony Kaldelis notes that Psellos's "erstwhile" friend John Xiphilinos accused him of "forsaking Christ to follow Plato." Psellos argued that he was a Platonic philosopher and that Platonism prepared the ground for Christianity. Both his contemporaries and ours view the argument as weak, calling into question his Christian convictions.

Psellos clearly resented the compulsion to take the tonsure. He championed Neo-Platonic philosophy and studied theurgic techniques. Even though he was an enormously accomplished politician, he faced charges of heresy. Psellos may have practiced the Chaldean ritual he studied; whether he did or not, he did pass on the knowledge to John Italos.

NINE

PLETHON

Psellos lived in an empire that had begun to shrink. In 1054, the year Psellos was exiled to the monastery at Bithynia, the Western pope and Eastern patriarch definitively split the Christian churches. The port cities of Italy snagged trade that once had been entirely controlled by Constantinople. Meanwhile, Seljuk Turks overran Byzantine territories. Three centuries after Psellos's death, the empire commanded a sliver of the territory it had once held, and Byzantine treasures had been carried off to enrich Western European cities. Even so, the emperor still ruled from the capitol of the Byzantine Empire and children of the elite still received a classical education.

Georgius Gemistus Plethon (commonly referred to as Pletho) was born in 1355. In the Byzantine world, the paideia once again seemed like the answer to a troubling time. As usual the Pagan underpinnings of classical Greek culture resurfaced. The scholar Demetrios Kydones tutored both Gemistus and the future Emperor Manuel II. The circles of students around philosophers had always bonded tightly, and this particular circle was no exception; the friendship between Kydones's students persisted into their adult careers, and Plethon went on to serve Manuel II when he took the helm of the empire.

AN EMPEROR'S FAVOR

The emperor was in a foul mood. Manuel Palaiologos paced the bare stone floor and threw himself into a plain wooden chair. "Do you know why I've sent for you?"

"No," Plethon said boldly, plopping onto a stool.

"It's your students," the emperor snapped. "They're wandering up and down the streets. And do you know what they're doing? Shouting hymns to the Greek gods!"

Plethon snickered.

The emperor scowled at him. "This is no laughing matter," he warned. "They say you are corrupting the youth." He waved at the brass cups on a nearby tray. "Have some wine."

"Corrupting the youth. Like Socrates?" Plethon said. He peered at the goblets. "Is there hemlock in the cups?"

"Not from my hand. But I won't be able to protect you here much longer," Manuel warned. He smiled grimly. "I see that's caught your attention. I'm sending you away."

Suddenly chilled, Plethon exclaimed, "Seriously? Where do you mean to send me?"

"To Mystras."

"*Now* I need wine," Plethon said, grabbing a cup. "I'm exiled?"

"So I'll have it said," Manuel said. Now that he had delivered his news, he seemed more relaxed. "I need a friend in Mystras. I don't hear enough about what's happening there. Anyway, you'll like it better there, it's more intellectual than Constantinople."

Taking a generous draught of wine, Plethon stared into the cup. "Constantinople is the center of the universe." He looked up. "It is where *you* live. What will I do without your friendship?"

"You always have my friendship," Manuel said gruffly. "I've no doubt that you'll have another circle of students in short order." He barked a laugh. "Mystras will complain less when those students sing Pagan hymns in the streets."

The Byzantine Empire during the Crusades

From 1095 through the 1290s, Western Europe sent armies to invade the Islamic Middle East, called to a "holy war" by popes of the Roman Church who claimed Jerusalem for Christians. Constantinople served as the jumping-off point for these invasions.

The trip to the Middle East was costly, lengthy, and not always possible to make. If a Crusade couldn't muster the resources to launch at the distant Muslim cities, there were more local targets. German leaders called to the first Crusade opted instead to target Jewish people in their own lands. The Roman pope called the Albigensian Crusade against heretical Christian Cathars in France. When the Fourth Crusade ran out of steam in 1201, crusaders settled for sacking their ally Constantinople instead, carrying off jewels and destroying Christian treasures.

Early Crusades did conquer Jerusalem and cities along the coast of Syria, Lebanon, and Palestine. These proved to be enormously difficult to maintain as Christian cities; Saladin retook Jerusalem in 1187 and Acre fell in 1291.

The Roman Church founded the Knights Templar as a band of religious warriors answering only to the Pope. These trained soldiers were pivotal to the success of the Crusades and among the last to leave or die when Islamic armies overran their positions. When the Holy Land fell, the Knights Templar came home.

It was one thing to send armed knights to do battle with Muslims; it was another to have a bored army wandering around your neighborhood. Fortunately, the Christian rulers of Spain had work to offer at home. The Muslim empires had held territory in Spain for centuries. From the eleventh to fifteenth century, Christian kings banded together to oust Muslims, inviting the Knights Templar to assist in the project.

The Templars not only gained a new source of employment, they were granted tracts of land and castles in exchange for their aid.

The order's downfall was its wealth. The Templars were the first European bankers. If you carried your money with you as you travelled, you risked losing it to highway robbers. One of the functions of the Templars was to protect pilgrims travelling from Europe to the Holy Land. Better still, you could deposit funds in one Templar stronghold and withdraw them again when you reached your destination, keeping the funds off the road altogether and making the pilgrim a much less tempting target.

The target transferred from pilgrims to the Templars themselves. All that money made a tempting prize for royalty. European kings strapped for cash to fund armies and other expensive projects borrowed money from the Templars' flush coffers. When the time came to pay back the loans, they looked for a way to avoid the debts.

King Phillip of France lobbied Pope Clement to close the order. When the pope caved in and disbanded the order, the king swiftly arrested the order's leaders in France, on Friday the 13th of October, 1307, forever marking Friday the 13th as an unlucky day. The knights were charged with spitting on the cross and worshipping a goat-headed male-female figure, Baphomet.

The Spanish kings on the other hand still had uses for the Templars and resisted the Pope's order, but ultimately did arrest the remaining free Templars. Miravet, the last Templar stronghold (originally a Muslim castle the Templars had conquered), held out until 1308. The town of Miravet today boasts that its medieval Muslim and Christian citizens coexisted peacefully even after the Templar conquest. Today the Templar castles in Spain are maintained as historical sites.

In Christian Spain some rulers were repressive, and others were tolerant of religious minorities. While Jews and Muslims were not permitted full citizenship, there were places and times where they were not persecuted. In particular, the Christian ruler Alphonso X extended protection to Jews and

Muslims in his territory. For three decades of the thirteenth century, this enlightened king in northern Spain developed a lively and literate court and caused numerous texts to be translated from Arabic into Latin languages, including Neo-Platonic texts. Spain produced texts on medieval Qabbalah that mixed Neo-Platonic ideas with Jewish mysticism.

Spain's multicultural tolerance sharply declined after the time of Alphonso X. The last Muslim kingdom was conquered in 1491. In 1492 the Spanish rulers Ferdinand and Isabella required all Jews to convert to Christianity or be expelled from the kingdom. By then, the torch of cosmopolitan European civilization had passed from Spain to Italy.

The Crusader fortresses in central Greece were absorbed into the Byzantine Empire. The town of Mystras (modern Mistra) grew up around a Crusader castle turned over to Byzantium in 1262. A second Byzantine court developed in Mystras, and the intellectual life of the empire shifted from Constantinople back to Greece.

On his arrival in Mystras, Plethon promptly founded a Pagan fraternity and settled in to revive Platonism. An unprecedented political conference offered him the opportunity to make his case on the world stage.

IRRECONCILABLE DIFFERENCES

Two long rows of tables faced each other along the dining hall. Women and men in the elaborate court dress of Florence sat along the tables, many with dogs lying at their feet; servants passed behind them, maneuvering platters of food onto the cloths. Singers, dancers, and musicians drifted in the space between the tables, plying the trade of entertainers.

Plethon was one of the entertainers. He waited with one of his students while the diners feasted on chicken and fish, grilled bread and stuffed pasta, and the flute and drum played, and the dancers twirled around the floor. When the music ended, the plates were cleared, and the diners let their food settle, and that was his moment.

Plethon stepped into the center of the room, cleared his throat, and began to talk. The first few minutes of any speech were like tuning the lyre; he gave his capsule introduction to the life of Plato, a well-memorized set of phrases allowing himself time to adjust to the spotlight and to let the diners fall quiet to listen to him.

Of course he could not fill the hall with his voice alone—that was why his student came with him. John worked the low end of the tables, learning the trade of the lecturer. Plethon himself addressed the head of the table where the city's master presided over the banquet. Cosimo de Medici ruled Florence with a tolerant but firm hand, managing the affairs of his bank and of the city with equal interest. It was his concern for trade that inspired him to host the council. The differences between the Roman and Byzantine churches threatened the city's lucrative mercantile trading system; if the churches could be brought into harmony, goods would flow through a peaceful world.

Council delegates debated matters of theology by day and feasted by night. They came from all over the known world: from Rome, Greece, Constantinople, Armenia, Russia, and even from parts of North Africa, as the Christian churches from that part of the world were included in the discussion. A small group of ebony men from Ethiopia huddled together while a Coptic delegation from Egypt spoke to each other in their own dialect.

"You all know the great works of Aristotle," Plethon said. "He framed the beginnings of our theologies. But Aristotle himself learned from the thoughts of his predecessors. His thinking was only the mirror of the thought of his teacher. It was Plato who cast the great light of knowledge Aristotle has dimly reflected to the world."

One of the delegates leaned forward. "I have read Aristotle extensively. But who has read more than a little of Plato?"

His host came to his defense. "Few have read more than Plethon," de Medici said. "His very name evokes the debt he owes to his philosophical teacher."

"Where are these texts, then, so we can read them too?" the delegate asked.

"The Byzantines have them, and the Moslems. In the Christian tongues we do not," de Medici said. "Only a few scholars have the knowledge and the language to reach him." He added offhandedly, "I'm of a mind to have them translated, if I can find the right man." He waved at Plethon. "Do continue."

Encouraged by his patron's attention, Plethon said, "Aristotle and Plato knew God, of course. You may be familiar with the *prisca theologia*, the spiritual tradition that paved the way for the coming of Christ. Hermes Trismegistus was Christ's forerunner, along with Orpheus and Pythagoras." His gaze swept the hall—this was an important point.

"So you see that the teachings of Christ are compatible with the teachings of Aristotle and Plato, and we may safely profit by their study." It seemed that this was a new idea for some, as they murmured to their neighbors.

The delegate who had spoken before addressed Plethon again. "Do you seriously mean that Plato is superior to the great Aristotle?"

"I do," Plethon said. "Moreover I can prove it. You see, Aristotle understands God as the mover of the universe. He does not recognize that God is a creator. For Plato, God is the creator of all things, of the intelligible substances. For Aristotle, God is only a force; for Plato, God is the sovereign of the universe."

The delegate leaned back in his chair. " . . . a difference indeed. Can it be reconciled?"

"It is a thorny question," Plethon said. "To my mind the differences are not possible to overcome. Aristotle simply understood less. For true wisdom, we must turn to Plato."

Privately, Plethon thought he was overstating his case; few intellectuals in Mystras or Constantinople would agree with him, seeing substantial agreement between Plato and his student. But then Byzantine education still included quite a bit of Plato, and Plethon's main purpose here was to spark interest in the philosopher's works. Anyway, the idea of "God" was only a shadow of the numinous reality of the One.

"We know a thing or two about irreconcilable differences," the delegate said, with a sly glance at de Medici. "We are wrestling with the differences between our churches. I begin to doubt that it is possible to bring us into harmony at all."

"Of course it is possible," Plethon said without thinking.

At this the delegate pounced. "Do you think so?" he said. "How would you accomplish this?"

It was the question of the century. Plethon saw the trap too late. How, indeed? Would the Eastern Church recognize the authority of the Roman pope over all Christianity or continue with her own patriarch? Would the Roman Church permit their clergy to marry as the Byzantines did? Did the Holy Spirit issue from the Father or from the Father and the Son together?

The delegate went on, "As a Byzantine, do you support the claims of your own Church? Or has the Roman Church won a convert? Which do you favor?"

"I do not favor either," Plethon said. "I turn my eyes to the source of all these traditions, to the Pagan past." He drew himself up. "If we remember our common heritage, the peace of knowledge becomes our future."

The delegate reared back. "Are you *serious*," he said, shocked. "Do you advocate that we all become ... become ... *Pagans*?"

For a long moment no one breathed, stunned. Then Cosimo de Medici's booming laugh filled the hall. "An excellent suggestion!" he said. "Tomorrow, let the hymns to the Pagan gods ring out again!" Relieved, the hall erupted in laughter, while the delegate turned away snickering. De Medici waved at his steward to bring on the next course.

While the servants laid out melon tarts flavored with cinnamon and breads soaked in sweet syrups; while the harper stepped between the tables and strummed a soothing chord; while the delegates and notables relaxed, chatted, and slipped tidbits under the tables to their dogs, Plethon and John slipped away to the kitchen where they joined the other entertainers who were finally getting their dinner.

John blew out a long breath. "That was a tricky moment."

Plethon shrugged, unconcerned. "We'll be back tomorrow to give them another little glimpse of the greatness of Plato."

"But ... the master laughed at you!"

"And saved me from another charge of heresy," Plethon said. "You must remember how this would sound to our enemies." He dipped a piece of bread. "First we bring them to study Plato. Philosophy leads to the knowledge of the gods."

His student brightened. "He said we could sing tomorrow. Can I start my lecture with a hymn to Hermes?"

Thinking about what his old friend Manuel would say, Plethon threw back his head and laughed.

The Florentine Academy

Plethon's lectures inspired Cosimo de Medici with an enduring interest in Plato. When the council ended and Plethon returned to Mystras, de Medici convinced him to leave some of his students behind. John Argyropoulos took up a teaching position giving public lectures of a general nature and exploring Platonic secrets with a few select students.

Argyropoulos's lectures increased de Medici's interest in Platonic studies. When he decided to refound the Platonic academy in 1462, he looked to Argyropoulos's students to staff it. He found two: Marsilio Ficino and Giovanni Pico della Mirandola. As Ficino spoke and wrote in Greek, de Medici set him to translate Plato's works.

Ficino may have been a friend to Hermeticism, but unusually for a Platonist, he was not a friend to women. In *A History of Women Philosophers*, Mary Ellen Waithe notes it was Ficino who first questioned whether Plato's priestess Diotima was in fact a historical personage, as women *surely* could not be philosophers!

As the Turkish Empire threatened Constantinople itself, Byzantine scholars fled the city, taking their manuscripts with them. When a Greek copy of the Hermetica surfaced in Florence, de Medici ordered Ficino to drop everything else he was doing and make a translation. The Hermetica reentered the Western intellectual world at that time; it is important to remember that the Byzantine and Arabic worlds never lost it.

While Ficino toiled as a translator, his student Pico della Mirandola took a decidedly eclectic tack: he was the first Christian to work with the concepts of Jewish Qabbalah. He lived on a substantial inheritance that allowed him to devote himself to writing new texts. His work syncretized Pagan, Christian, and Jewish mysticism with Plato, Aristotle, and Hermetic works.

By 1487 he had composed nine hundred theses on these themes and printed them as his *Conclusions*. He planned a great conference in Rome to discuss them. Unfortunately, before he could hold the conference, the pope condemned some of his theses as suspect and had della Mirandola jailed. When released, della Mirandola focused on the safer subject of reconciling Aristotle with Plato. He died in 1494 at the young age of thirty-one.

Ficino continued to be employed by his patron de Medici to translate texts and to tutor the de Medici children. He wrote many original works on Platonism, seeking out similarities between Platonic and Christian teachings. Some scholars read his work as a continuation of Plethon's work and an attempt to return Christianity to its Pagan roots. Ficino died in 1499 at the age of sixty-five.

Plethon returned to Mystras and continued to teach Pagan thought to his students. He died in the 1450s, in his nineties, just at the end of the empire. Constantinople fell to the Turks in 1452, Mystras in 1460. The Turkish conqueror Mehmed II, el-Fatih, appointed cooperative regents from the Byzantine noble families. In particular, he appointed George Scholarios, Gennadios II, to be patriarch of Constantinople.

When Plethon died, his papers were sent to Theodora. She and her husband, Demetrios, had surrendered Mystras to the Turkish conqueror. Alarmed by the contents of the papers, she called on Gennadios to advise her what to do with them.

THE ONLY COPY

"Welcome, old friend," Theodora said effusively, taking his hands. "Please, come sit with me by the fire. I've had your favorite wine brought in and your favorite honey syrup cake."

Gennadios retrieved his hands as soon as he could. "There's no need," he said, reaching for a goblet to keep his hands busy. When Theodora settled by the fire, he moved his chair out of her reach, murmuring about being too close to the heat.

"I am grateful for your friendship," Theodora said, clasping her hands in her lap. "These are perilous times. I know you have the trust of the sultan." She sighed. "It seems we are at his mercy."

"Indeed," Gennadios agreed. "If Byzantium had survived we would have power of our own. Now we must resign ourselves to being ruled."

"Byzantium would survive if the sultan returns us to Mystras." Not even a sticky sweet could lighten Theodora's angry frown.

"Mystras fell," Gennadios said carefully. Just last week the sultan had fumed to him, "Demetrios is not man enough to keep any kingdom!" He doubted that the sultan would grant the request to return Demetrios and Theodora to their province. The days of Byzantium were over and the Ottoman Empire held Constantinople now. Gennadios wasn't inclined to hazard his fragile rapport with the young sultan to stick his neck out for a woman who wanted to be empress.

Theodora squinted at him shrewdly and changed the subject. "I have more than wine and sweets for you," she said. She waved her hand at a trunk nearby. "I've brought you Plethon's writings."

Gennadios jumped to his feet and opened the trunk. "These?" he said. He grabbed a handful of papers. "I catalogued these for you and sent them back. I thought you had destroyed them."

"I can't bring myself to do it," she said, lowering her eyes. "They're the only copies."

Don't simper, lady, he thought with irritation. "They are heresy," he said. "Look at this! He talks about astrology, daemons—he has a calendar of Pagan rituals!" He shook the paper at her. "Listen to this: 'Come to us, O gods of learning, whoever and however many ye be; ye who are guardians of scientific knowledge and true belief; ye who distribute them to whomsoever you wish, in accordance with the dictates of the great father of all things, Zeus the King'. *Zeus!*"

"You were his friend. His student," Theodora said. "Can you bear to give up his work?"

Gennadios scowled at her. "These are dangerous thoughts for a perilous time. Our faith is caught between the Roman Church and the Moslem Empire. If we are not precise and pure in our public beliefs we will be lost."

"They're yours," Theodora said, licking her fingers. "Do what you want with them."

Gennadios tossed the papers in the fire.

Lessons of Plethon

Plethon died in 1452. Although Gennadios had Plethon's work *Nomoi* destroyed, he quoted from the work in order to refute it, and made a copy of the outline. Plethon's students preserved drafts of the manuscript. From this we know enough to be able to say that this could arguably be called the first work of Neo-Pagan revival written in Western Europe.

Plethon taught John Argyropoulos, who taught Marsilio Ficino, who taught Pico della Mirandola, in a direct line of succession. Pico della Mirandola syncretized four religions: Judaism, Christianity, Islam, and Paganism. From his time forward, this mix of faiths—particularly the mystic and ritual practices of these faiths—would cohere into what we now call Western esotericism and Ceremonial Magic.

Plethon sidestepped the demands of the Roman and Greek Orthodox Churches and their conflict by centering himself in Greek culture. Plethon's biographer Niketas Siniossoglou makes the point that Plethon's Paganism was the natural development of his dedication to Hellenistic philosophy. With his invocation to Zeus and his calendar of rituals, Plethon went beyond intellectual inquiry into Pagan religious practice. This should not be surprising; Plethon was Greek, and the Greeks have never forgotten the Pagan gods.

Notes on the Story
Although John Argyropoulos is known to have accompanied Plethon to Florence, he is not recorded as having lectured alongside Plethon. Michel Jeanneret describes banquet customs in some detail in *A Feast of Words: Banquets and Table Talk in the Renaissance*.

Plethon's introduction to the Nomoi is quoted by Paul Richard Blum in *Philosophy of Religion in the Renaissance*.

TEN

TULLIA D'ARAGONA

A century after Cosimo de Medici hosted the council of churches, another Cosimo de Medici ruled Florence. The great-great-grandson of his predecessor's brother, this new Cosimo was elected head of the Republic. He set about organizing public services and commissioning public buildings and artistic works. His Spanish wife, Eleanor de Toledo, produced a child nearly every year, ultimately providing the family with eleven children; her sons went on to rule or to join the church, while her daughters married into noble families.

This was the Florence where Tullia d'Aragona celebrated her greatest triumphs. Her mother, the courtesan Giulia Campana, was married to Costanzo Palmieri d'Aragona. To make the family more intriguing, Giulia and Tullia gave out the story that Tullia's father was actually Cardinal Luigi d'Aragona. Since the cardinal was the illegitimate grandson of the King of Naples, this cast Tullia as an unacknowledged royal heir—a courtesan princess.

Giulia brought her daughter up in her trade, teaching her the arts of singing, dancing, and lovemaking. Mother and daughter traveled throughout Italy and maintained a household frequented by learned men. Tullia was named for the ancient orator Marcus Tullio Cicero, and she proved to be as eloquent as her namesake, exchanging poetry with her admirers, notably her great friend and supporter Girolamo Muzio.

LOVER OF KNOWLEDGE

"Tell me again," Tullia said, laying her bare arms atop his chest. Even sated as they were, he shivered with delight when her skin touched his skin. "Which of my poems do you love the most? Tell me!"

Girolamo reached up to stroke her hair, blonde, showing a slight line of a darker color at the roots. "Your eyes," he murmured. "How they haunt me."

"The *poem*," she prompted.

"I have heard you say that the joy of love cannot be perfect if all the senses are not involved in it. And is this touch itself not perfect?"

She slapped a hand against his chest. "Muzio!"

Laughing, he said obediently:

"I will only say that following
your destiny your soul has left you
to enter into me as its true abode,

And my soul, it can truly be said,
united now with yours, as is my star,
is moved by you to change your ways."

"Have you really changed your ways?" he said, looking soft and vulnerable.

"I have changed my ways." She lifted her head to look out at the green river drifting slowly past the little tree where they had spread their blankets. "I love only you."

"No more competitions to win your hand?" he teased, wrapping her hair around his hand. "How many men did I best—five? Six? And I wasn't your first choice!"

"You are my *only* choice," she said. "Remember that I didn't choose for riches. I chose the best poet." She turned her eyes down to his face. "I chose the man who could teach me the mysteries of the universe. That the universe is made from love."

"My Diotima," he said. "My priestess of love." Surging with passion, he lifted himself up and rolled her over onto the grassy riverbank, covering her face with kisses. "Your turn. Tell me. Which of my poems do you love the most?" He propped himself up on an elbow, waiting.

Looking up into his eyes, she said:

"My soul, while you live, remember
that what is eternal glows within you,
open your breast to everlasting love

"And remember, too, that the shining light,
the sweet sound, the bright spirit
are for you the stairway to heaven"

"Lift me," she said, turning her face up for a kiss. "Rise," he said, bending down to give it.

Renaissance Humanism

Plethon brought Platonism to Florence. Marsilio Ficino made Platonic and Hermetic texts accessible to Western scholars. For the next century the Florentine courts brought together people from around the European continent; inspired by Plethon, Ficino, and Pico della Mirandola, these Italian intellectuals studied Greek and read works that had been forgotten in Western Europe. Students of the ancient texts naturally re-encountered the deities and myths of the Pagan world, and these images and themes surfaced in Renaissance paintings and writings.

Intellectuals grew more willing to challenge the authority of the Roman church. These new philosophers called themselves "humanists," and they developed the idea that the individual is the center of their own universe, focusing attention on living a beautiful and enjoyable life in the present. It was a stark contrast to the Church's emphasis on unchanging doctrine and the focus on life after death.

Throughout the sixteenth century, the Roman church's power waned. Martin Luther published his theses in 1510, and Lutheranism was well established by 1530. Henry VIII took England away from the pope in 1534. Suddenly there were alternatives to the Church as well as a dawning awareness that there was more than one religion, more than one way to view the world.

Tullia d'Aragona lived in that thin slice of secular space, newly opened and always threatening to close.

A WOMAN OF LETTERS

"It's good of you to see me," Tullia said.

Eleanor smiled warmly. "It's good to see a new face. I'm bored beyond belief." She frowned at the room. "I've been trapped in here all winter; I need a change of scenery. I have a mind to buy a summer house."

"You have an eye for color," Tullia said, admiring the blue and pur-ple velvet walls.

Eleanor beamed at her. "Do you think so? I thought when I buy the house I'll do all the rooms in a single color. A blue room, a yellow room, white..." She smiled. "How do you find the villa? Everyone tells me you have turned it into the place to be for an intellectual discussion."

"My mother adores it," Tullia said. "She walks along the river." Tullia couldn't bear to walk there herself; the river reminded her of her too-brief years with Muzio. Her pregnancy had forced her to flee from him and society, to hide and bear her child in secret.

"And your sister?" Eleanor prompted. "Does Penelope enjoy it as well?"

For an unmarried woman to bear a child would expose her to shame, and for a courtesan to have a child would make her less attractive. A little sister, on the other hand, was charming, and Giuliana already had one child, so the family bent the truth to reshape its image, as they always had. "She grows like a weed. This is a good place to raise a child." Tullia sighed. "It's so peaceful, after Siena."

"I don't even know who holds Siena this week," Eleanor said. "The French? The Spanish? Is it ours again?" She shook her head. "I am glad you are here. Florence is a much safer place for you."

Seeing her opening, Tullia drew the little books from the folds of her dress. "I've brought you a copy of my little book of poems. A small thanks."

Turning the cover, Eleanor brightened. "Why, you've dedicated it to me!" She paged eagerly through the book. "You've included the one you wrote to me! 'For such beauty and virtue shines in you...'" She trailed off. "Well, I am not beautiful, and I confess my sins like any other woman. But it is good to be thought so in public."

"You are known to be pious," Tullia said. She leaned forward slightly, striving to look earnest but not desperate. "I find that I grow more pious as I age. I wish the public to know that about me."

Eleanor cast her a shrewd look. "We are both women with a public face and a private one," she said. "My husband did not inherit his power and he fights to keep it. I fight alongside him in my own way. I wear the gowns and the jewelry; I endow the holy orders with property. So that when he leaves I rule in his stead until he returns."

Sensing she had pushed as far as she could, Tullia willed herself to relax into her chair. "It must be tedious. I wish I could be more entertaining."

"You could sing for me," Eleanor said. "I've heard that your voice would turn a marble statue to warm flesh. It's why I asked you to meet me in my music room."

"That must be what men see in me," Tullia said. "I don't have your beauty." Eleanor laughed and did not contradict her. Tullia went on, "I don't have anything prepared."

"Here's a song book," Eleanor said.

Rising, Tullia paged through it. "I haven't seen this one," she said. Humming to clear her throat, she began, "L'Amor Dona Ch'lo Te Porto. The love, my lady, that I bear for you ... "

When she finished, more than one pair of hands applauded. She turned and saw that two men had slipped into the room while she sang. "My lord," she said, dropping a curtsy to Cosimo de Medici.

"Such an angelic voice. I knew it must be you," he said. He turned to the cleric who had entered with him. "Have you met Tullia d'Aragona?"

The man scowled. "D'Aragona, you say? She's a courtesan! Why isn't she wearing the yellow scarf?"

That old charge, she thought. She'd stared it down twice in Siena, daring to live outside the designated prostitute section of town, and had only won by inventing a husband. She'd already faced the charge once in Florence, accused of wearing a cloak that only respectable women could wear.

Eleanor stood to lay a soothing hand on the man's arm. "She's a gentle woman," she said.

De Medici said, "*Fasseli gratia per poetessa*," pardon her, she is a poet.

Eleanor handed the book of poems to her husband. "Look at this book of her work. She's dedicated it to me."

"But you yourself made the law!" the cleric appealed to Cosimo.

Flipping through the book, Cosimo said absently, "And I can grant exemptions." He looked into Tullia's worldly eyes and smiled at her. "A woman of letters is an ornament of Florence."

She held his gaze frankly. "I will dedicate my next book to you."

Dialogue on the Infinity of Love

Tullia's next book was a contribution to the literature of dialogues about love. She herself had appeared as a character in one such text, Sperone Speroni's *Dialogue of Love*, where she was cast as debating her lover Bernardo Tasso, Muzio's rival. Now that she was thirty-seven, living in Florence and protected by powerful patrons, at the height of her physical and intellectual powers, Tullia dared to take center stage herself, speaking as a woman and a lover in her own voice about her own experience. In *Dialogue on the Infinity of Love* she cast herself as a main character debating her friend Benedetto Varchi. She traded love poems with Varchi as she did with many of her intellectual male admirers and lovers, but Varchi was a friend with a difference—he loved men.

In the text, Varchi enters her parlor where she is entertaining a number of men with a lively philosophical discussion. Varchi worries he has interrupted the conversation. Tullia says it was her turn to talk, but perhaps he would engage her in dialogue, unless he refuses to do this with a woman, since he holds them as philosophically inferior.

The question they have been discussing is this: can love be endless, or does one always love within bounds? There is vulgar love, based on physical desire, and honest love, including companionship. Vulgar love ends when desire is satisfied. Bodies can merge, but souls cannot, so honest love is never satisfied and thus endless.

What about the love of men for men? Tullia was greatly daring to consider this question. Plato's symposium praised love between older men and younger men and denigrated love between men and women; in fact he went so far as to question whether men could truly love women, since women are intellectually inferior. When this work was translated into a Christian culture that condemned homosexuality, Neo-Platonists struggled to understand this new view of sexuality.

Tullia dared to question why homosexuality was considered to be sinful if Plato had praised it. In her dialogue she established a justification for Varchi's affection for men, acting as his friend as well as playing to his sensibilities.

Tullia also challenged the Platonic ideal that considered women to be intellectually inferior. Who better to consider the infinity of love than a woman dedicated to love? Who better to write a Platonic dialogue on love than a Neo-Platonic courtesan?

Lessons of Tullia

The year after the publication of her poems and the dialogue, Tullia's life took a sadder turn when both her mother and her daughter died. Her looks fading, Tullia found she could no longer retain younger lovers. She left Florence for Rome. Although she had not chosen her lovers for their wealth, she had managed to save for her retirement and lived in a modest section of town. She turned her attention to writing and produced her final and largest work, *The Wretch, Otherwise Known as Guerrino*, not yet translated into English. In the introduction to this work, she complained for the first time about her mother's choice to raise her daughter as a courtesan; she wished she had not learned so much about life at such an early age.

Tullia died in 1556 at the age of forty-six. Her will surfaced a few surprises: she left her estate to a previously unknown son, Celio. She also noted that she ended her life unable to write and was being cared for by a trusted friend whom she did not name.

Tullia d'Aragona was a Neo-Platonic philosopher in the tradition of Diotima, Gemina, Hypatia, Asklepigenia, and many others. Although her mother and her society cast her as a courtesan, she sought out men who could educate her and appreciate her intellect as well as her charms. She persisted in presenting herself to the world as a writer as well as a lover, and she has left us beautiful and profound meditations on the nature of love.

Notes on the Story

The poem fragments exchanged by Girolamo and Tullia are the translations of Irma Jaffe and Gernando Colombardo in *Shining Eyes, Cruel Fortune: The Lives and Loves of Italian Renaissance Women Poets*. Jaffe and Colombardo provide many details of Tullia's life.

Giulia and Tullia presented Penelope as Tullia's sister, but many scholars point out that Giulia was over forty and Tullia was twenty-five when Penelope was born, so it is likely that Penelope was her daughter.

"Fasseli gratia per poetessa" was the phrase Cosimo de Medici wrote on the document that freed Tullia from wearing the prostitute's yellow veil.

ELEVEN

THOMAS TAYLOR

From the Renaissance onward the imperialist powers of Western Europe spread across the globe, exploiting natural resources, subjugating and enslaving non-European peoples, imposing Christianity on subject populations, and criminalizing and suppressing non-Christian religions.

Thomas Taylor was born into the British Empire in 1758, at a time when the children of wealth and privilege regarded European culture and history as the height of civilization. As a schoolchild, Thomas found his two great loves: the ancient Greek language and Mary Morton.

CHOOSING LOVE

The families planted the young couple in separate chairs on either side of the parlor. Mary's mother snarled, "How could you let your boy seduce my girl?"

Instead of defending him, Tom's father paced around his chair, shouting. "You swore to me you loved learning. You couldn't be a minister, like your father! Oh no! You couldn't take a trade either, like your uncle. Oh no! You loved *mathematics*. You loved *Latin*. You loved *Greek*. So I arrange to send you to university. And what do you do? You throw it all away! You ... you ... *marry!*"

"I love her," Thomas said quietly.

His mother snapped at him, "Be quiet!" She turned on Mary's mother. "How could you let your girl seduce my boy?"

Mary's father paced up and down the parlor floor. "You were set for life!" he howled. "I arranged a match with a man who could take care of you. More than you deserved. And you throw it all away on this—this—*child!*"

"We were going to wait until he was finished with university," Mary said. "I wouldn't have had to marry him now if you hadn't promised me to someone else while he was gone."

"You'll be penniless!" her father warned her. "Don't look to help from us!"

Tom's father said, "The same from us. Don't come home for help!"

Thomas stood, walked over to his wife and held out his hand. She took it. He led her to a loveseat under a window, where they both sat quietly together, still holding hands. "We're married," Thomas said. "That's done."

Mary lifted her chin. "We'll manage."

Everyone started shouting at once.

Neo-Platonists in the Seventeenth through Nineteenth Centuries

The church's opposition ultimately took some of the steam out of the Italian Renaissance. Nonetheless, the ideas unleashed by the influx of Platonic and Hermetic thought altered Western European philosophy and science permanently. Renaissance humanism filtered throughout Europe, paving the way for the secular revolution of the nineteenth century, and the widespread Pagan religious revival in the twentieth.

In the seventeenth century a number of theologians turned to the study of Plato, seeing themselves as carrying on in the tradition of the Alexandrine Neo-Platonists. The Cambridge Platonists grappled with the philosophies that shaped Western European thought while incorporating the discoveries of emergent scientific disciplines.

Among the Cambridge Platonists was Anne Finch, who became Viscountess Conway on her marriage. In her paper "Anne Conway's Critique of Cartesian Dualism," Louise Derksen notes that Conway challenged Cartesian dualism in her 1692 text, *The Principles of the Most Ancient and Modern Philosophy.*

Like many Neo-Platonists, Anne Conway did not only study philosophy, she investigated practice. Her search for a cure for her periodic migraines led her into esoteric studies, and she found a doctor who was Hermeticist, Kabbalist, and alchemist. In his history of the Rosicrucian orders, Christopher McKintosh notes that the circle which gathered around the Viscountess included several friends familiar with newly translated Rosicrucian treatises. She may or may not have been Rosicrucian herself—Rosicrucians do not reveal themselves—but she clearly surrounded herself with people we would recognize today as esotericists.

PATRON OF KNOWLEDGE

William Meredith stood on the doorstep of 9 Manor Place in Waltham and knocked. A boy in a Greek tunic opened the door. "Good evening," he said. "Have you come to rent the room?"

Mary hurried to the door behind him, dressed like him in ancient Greek clothing. "Master Meredith! We weren't expecting you."

"I apologize for interrupting your evening," he said. "May I come in? I'd like a word with Thomas."

Mary shepherded the boy back into the small dining room, where the dinner dishes had been pushed to one end of a simple table to make room for the children's textbooks. A tiny blur launched herself at him and grabbed his legs. "It's you!"

Laughing, he picked her up. "Good evening, Mistress Mary Meredith. How is my little namesake?"

"We're learning Greek!" she announced.

"Of course you are," he said. He sat her gently on the ground and slipped her a coin. "You must have a treat, to please me."

The coin vanished into the folds of her tunic, and the girl dashed away.

Shaking her head, Mary said, "You spoil her. This way," she said, pointing up the stairs. "His study is at the end of the hall." She smiled. "Mary Wollstonecraft called it 'the abode of peace.'" Suddenly, there was a crash in the dining room.

"It must have been because there are no children up there. Excuse me."

William tapped diffidently on the study door. After a long pause, a voice finally called out, "Come in."

Thomas was hunched over his desk, scribbling furiously, finishing one more line. When he looked up he brightened immediately. "William!" He stood and offered his hand. "I didn't realize it was you. Please forgive my lack of manners." He looked around a little wildly and cleared a stack of papers from a chair. "Please, sit."

"I'm the one who should apologize," William said. "I know I'm interrupting your precious hours of study."

"For you, I always have time," Thomas said seriously. "You have been such a good friend to the family."

"How is your health?" It wasn't an idle question; he worried about his friend.

Rubbing his right forefinger, Thomas said, "Pain is no evil." He looked down at his hand. "So long as I can write, I am content."

William nodded at the papers on the desk. "How goes the work?"

All his worries seemed to drop away; his face glowed. "I mean to finish it, you know," Thomas said. "I will bring all the works of Plato into English. So everyone can read his wisdom."

"I believe you," William replied. "You did the work for so many years at night when you were a bank clerk. How you supported your family on those wages I can't imagine."

"Mary," Thomas said briefly. "She manages."

William smiled. "Your Diotima. Is it true the two of you only speak Greek to each other?"

"It's wonderful to talk over the children's heads," Thomas said with a smile.

William laughed. "That should motivate them to study!" Playfully he added, "you should start a new Academy."

Thomas shook his head. "Don't you remember the Frenchman? He paid me every cent he had, and he didn't have many! He lived under my roof for months and finally departed for home in full military uniform saying 'I am going back to Alexander!'" The men laughed. Thomas went on, "Teaching is so much work. I can't spare the time if I'm to focus on the translations."

Leaning forward, William said, "Thomas, I wouldn't intrude if it wasn't a matter of importance. I need to speak to you in strict privacy."

"Whatever the matter, I am your man," Thomas said instantly.

His friend let out a little breath. "You're one of the ancients, do you know that? You're one of the teachers. You have that same calm, that same generosity of spirit." He waved away Thomas's instant objections. "No, hear me out. You require peace and security to do your work. The assistant secretary position you hold now is better than the clerk's job, but it takes you away from your studies. Certainly your books bring in some income—"

" ... thanks to your support in their publication," Thomas finished.

William shrugged. "But it's not enough. Not enough for your family." He laid a cheque on the desk. "I am providing you with a stipend of one hundred pounds per year."

For a moment Thomas didn't move. Finally, he cleared his throat. "I did not expect it," he said slowly. "You have been more than generous in supporting my work." His voice thickened. "But this ... this will allow me to finish it." Mastering himself, he stood and offered his hand. "My thanks to you. I would offer my eternal friendship, but you already had that."

William grasped his hand strongly and brought his other hand up in a wave of affection. "As you have mine," he said.

"Thank all the gods," Thomas said, dropping suddenly into his chair, as if his knees had given out.

Still standing, William scanned the room. "Whenever you say that, I think I'm going to find one of those Pagan altars set up in here somewhere. A little shrine to the gods."

"The gods are all around us," Thomas said.

Lessons of Thomas

Mary Morton Taylor learned both ancient Greek and philosophy from her husband. Their marriage seems to have proceeded on Pythagorean lines, requiring the commitment of the entire household. When Mary died in 1809, Thomas was in his fifties. He may have needed a lover or he may have needed a helpmate with their four children, but whatever the reason, he married again. He and his second wife, Susannah, had an additional child, Thomas Proclus Taylor.

Taylor's portrait was painted in 1812 by Sir Thomas Lawrence, commissioned by William Meredith, and it currently hangs in the National Gallery of Canada. It illustrates the description given by his friend James Jacob Welsh of a simple, modest man, frank and dignified. His right hand rests on a desk and a blank piece of paper, and one of his books sits on a table to his left.

After Susannah died in 1823 he remained unmarried until his own death in 1835 at the age of seventy-seven. He lived the whole of his life in the same modest house in Waltham. He wrote his own epitaph:

Health, strength, and ease, and manhood's active age,
Freely I gave to Plato's sacred cave. With Truth's pure joys,
with Fame my days were crown'd, Tho' Fortune adverse
on my labors frown'd.

He explained that he had learned the Greek language through the study of Greek philosophy rather than philosophy through the study of the language. He translated all of Plato's works that had not yet been translated in English, all of Aristotle's works, many Neo-Platonists and Pythagoreans, Orphic fragments, orations from the Emperor Julian, and hymns. His works are widely available. Some remain the only English versions of the texts. His translations were found in the library of Ralph Waldo Emerson, the American Transcendentalist philosopher influenced by Neo-Platonism.

Thomas Taylor exemplifies the life of a Neo-Platonist. He gave his life to his work while also maintaining the everyday life of a husband and father. His contemporaries call him a good friend. He inspired the patronage of men who had nothing to gain from it other than the work he could produce.

Taylor's formal education ended before university. He is the exemplar of the self-taught scholar, an inspiration to the many nonacademic Pagan and esoteric scholars who work diligently in their fields today.

In his biography of William Blake, Tobias Churton calls Taylor the "English Pagan." The year Mary died, Taylor anonymously published "Arguments of the Emperor Julian Against the Christians." He may or may not have kept any altars at 9 Manor Place, but he certainly kept one in his heart. He lived both the life of the spirit and the life of love.

Notes on the Story

The details of Taylor's life are recorded in only a few places. Like many Neo-Platonists, he inspired effusive praise from his contemporaries, notably James Jacob Welsh.

The story that Thomas and Mary dressed like ancient Greeks at home is repeated by several writers who note they cannot actually document this, but it's too wonderful to resist.

The feminist Mary Wollstonecraft rented a room from the Taylors for three months. Inspired by her work "A Vindication of the Rights of Women," Taylor wrote a defense of animals, "Vindication of the Rights of Brutes."

TWELVE

MODERN THEURGISTS

Taylor lived right at the beginning of the modern world. Sparked in Britain and igniting the rest of the English-speaking world, the Industrial Revolution vastly accelerated the rate of consumption of natural resources. This revolution was powered by the use of wood, then oil, coal, and other fossil fuels. In the nineteenth century, the reins of the global empire shifted from Britain, a small island nation, to America, a vast nation with great forests and significant oil and coal resources.

A century earlier, the Enlightenment brought a similar revolution to the world of belief. The European worldview reshaped around the idea that the visible universe follows laws and systems that can be measured and understood by humans. It swept away the medieval belief in divine intervention and challenged the very idea that there was any other power than the mechanisms of the universe and human reason.

European travelers encountered people around the globe who held numerous and diverse beliefs. It was possible now to talk about religion not just in the singular, but religions in the plural, calling into question the claim to hold the ultimate truth by any one of them. As the European

Empire expanded into India and China, the bureaucrats who made the empire run were exposed to Hindu and Buddhist beliefs and rituals. This encounter of West with East opened up new religious possibilities.

As the sense of the possibility of miracle dropped out of the religious and scientific realms, it resurfaced in the "magical" realms. The nineteenth and twentieth centuries saw a resurgence of interest in "occult" spirituality in Europe and the English-speaking world. Some turned to the spiritual systems of Asia—the "East" or "Orient"—seeking wisdom, while others reached back to the work of medieval natural magicians and alchemists to continue to build on their framework.

THEOSOPHY

A good example of the valorization of Oriental mysticism is Theosophy. Russian mystic Helena Petrovna Blavatsky and her friend Henry Steel Olcott founded the Theosophical Society in America in 1875. Blavatsky moved to India where she resituated the society's headquarters, accompanied by her colleague Annie Besant.

After Blavatsky's death the American branches seceded from the international organization. The American organization is still active, with headquarters in Wheaton, Illinois. This is a literate society; members can check out books from the headquarters library by mail, regional branches also have libraries, and branches maintain bookstores called Quest that feature a very wide variety of esoteric books. It is notable that the society publicly supports feminist movement that undoubtedly accounts for the very active participation of women in the society.

Of the many significant members of the society, the most notable for the history of theurgy is George Robert Stowe Mead. Born in England, he was educated in the classics in Cambridge. At the age of twenty-four he met Blavatsky and became her private secretary. He read widely, wrote a great deal, and translated gnostic and Hermetic texts. In particular he translated a collection of the fragments of the Chaldean Oracles, theurgy's core text.

TWENTIETH-CENTURY OCCULTISTS

Religions are persistent, as increasing numbers of scholars point out. Even religions subjected to a campaign of eradication tend to survive. Paul Hiebert and R. Daniel Shaw instruct a missionary audience in tactics to convert peoples to Christianity in *Understanding Folk Religion: A Christian Response to Popular Beliefs and Practices.* They warn that Christian victory has been declared prematurely:

> "Today it is clear that old ways do not die out, but remain
> largely hidden from public view."

When the factors that suppress a religion ease, the hidden can become visible again. As Christianity lost political power, Paganism began to re-emerge publicly. In Christian Europe, particularly eastern Europe, many Pagan religious practices have survived as folk customs. These survivals of European Folk Religion provided a basis and inspiration for numerous reconstructions of Greek, Egyptian, Celtic, Norse, and other Pagan practices, in their countries of origin and throughout the world.

In the late 1800s and early 1900s, the era known as *fin de siècle*, a number of esoteric societies sprang up, bringing together people with an interest not only in Neo-Platonism as a philosophy but in theurgic meditation and ritual.

Golden Dawn

In 1888 three men, all Rosicrucians and Masons, opened the first Golden Dawn Temple in Britain. Golden Dawn initiates were educated and literate, spending quite a bit of time in the British Museum and the reading room of the British Library. These women and men drew direct connections between their contemplations and rituals and ancient Hellenistic religion and magic.

Two of the temple's cofounders, Samuel Liddell Mathers and Dr. William Wynn Westcott, along with ritualists Moina Mathers and Florence Farr, contributed to the preservation and development of esoteric Neo-Platonism and theurgic ritual. In particular, Westcott contributed a translation of the collection of Chaldean Oracle fragments.

When the order fell into disarray, Israel Regardie helped to preserve the system by publishing its rituals and papers. In an appendix to his book *Ceremonial Magic*, Regardie published the Greek and English text of a fragment of the Greek magical papyri containing a prayer to the "headless one," indicating a comfort with Hellenistic ritual.

Regardie also published a form of the Golden Dawn ritual "Opening by Watchtower." This ritual uses two fragments of the Chaldean Oracles. Holding the fire wand, the operator says:

> And when, after all the phantoms have vanished, thou shalt
> see that holy and formless fire, that fire which darts and flashes
> through the hidden depths of the Universe, hear thou the
> Voice of Fire.

Later, holding the water cup the operator says:

> So therefore first, the priest who governeth the works of fire
> must sprinkle with the lustral water of the loud resounding sea.

In *Foundations of Practical Magic*, Regardie explicitly connected Ceremonial Magic to Neo-Platonic theurgy. Unfortunately he did so to contrast the "passive" meditations of the "superstitious" East with the "superior" spiritual action of the West, an assertion of European exceptionalism that mars his work.

In *The Essential Golden Dawn: An Introduction to High Magic*, Chic and Tabitha Cicero also directly equate Ceremonial Magic with theurgy.

> The magic of the Golden Dawn falls under the heading of high magic, also called Ceremonial Magic or theurgy ("divine action" or "god-working"). A Ceremonial Magician is often referred to as a theurgist.

They explicitly link the work of Iamblichus and Renaissance esotericists to the ritual work conducted in the order.

Thelema

Aleister Crowley began his magical career as a Golden Dawn initiate. He famously conducted a theurgic operation in Cairo in 1904 with his wife, Rose Kelley. During this operation, he received pronouncements from three Egyptian entities who named themselves Nuit, Hadit, and Ra-Hoor-Khuit. The result of this operation was the *Book of the Law*, the text that founded the religious philosophy *Thelema*. Crowley is also noted for his role in shaping the Thelemic fraternity Ordo Templi Orientis (O.T.O), which initiates women as well as men.

Crowley's voluminous works contain numerous theurgic operations and references, including the ritual of the Star Ruby, the essay "Energized Enthusiasm, A Note on Theurgy," and "ASTARTE vel Liber BERYLLI sub figura CLXXV, the Book of Uniting Himself to a particular Deity by devotion." The O.T.O. continues to publish his works and perform his rituals. Clearly he was an inheritor of the Neo-Platonic and Hermetic traditions as well as an accomplished theurgist.

Witchcraft

Witchcraft emerged in the twentieth century with the assertion that the religion had been practiced underground throughout the Christian era. The religion was popularized by Gerald Gardner, Doreen Valiente, and their subsequent numerous colleagues. Today many individuals and groups practice Witchcraft. Some make distinctions between Witchcraft, Traditional Witchcraft, Wicca, and Wica; definitions of these change with time and from group to group.

Some Gardnerian Wica trace a significant theurgic component. At Theurgicon 2010, Don Frew presented the paper, "Gardnerian Wica as Theurgic Ascent." After surveying the history of Neo-Platonism and Gardnerian Wica he concluded:

> There is indeed a traceable continuity of an explicit "Paganism" consisting of a body of cosmological lore and ritual practice from the Hermetic and Neo-Platonic theurgists of the Eastern Mediterranean of late antiquity down to the beginnings of Gardnerian Wica.

He connects entities in the Gardnerian Dryghton Prayer to the Neo-Platonic entities. He cites the practice of "tuning" the individual to the divine as a direct survival of theurgic practice. He also connects the three degrees of Gardnerian initiation with the three levels of theurgic ascent. It is worth noting that contemporary theurgist Bruce MacLennan presents the study of Neo-Platonic philosophy as a three-degree system in *The Wisdom of Hypatia*.

LESSONS FROM THE TEACHERS

The teachers whose lives we have studied were daughters and sons, sisters and brothers, mothers and fathers. They were scholars, householders, and lovers. They were African and European, black, brown and white; they came from Kemet, Greece, Rome, Syria, Turkey, Italy, England.

When we consider their lives as people, we learn important things immediately. Most were rich, born into privilege; some, like Tullia and

Thomas, scraped by on patronage. Many kept slaves, and when they did not, kept servants. Some teachers were women; some of the male teachers denigrated women but many taught women. Some were homophobic, some were gay. They were flawed, as all humans are flawed, but they were dearly loved in their lifetimes and admired well beyond their times.

We have learned many lessons from the teachers in reviewing their lives. Here are some of the highlights.

Theurgy Is a Literate Tradition

Knowledge is acquired through individual study and effort. Because the tradition is written, if it is not possible to find a living teacher, it can be learned through books.

Theurgy Is Rooted in Kemet

Western European esotericism and fraternal organizations have always insisted that our learning comes from Kemet. While academic skepticism scoffed at these claims in past decades, today scholars are reassessing what the teachers themselves reported, and are once again taking their reporting seriously: the Greek philosophers travelled to the great universities in Egypt to learn. In the works of Plato and Iamblichus, we can see the reflection of the wisdom of those centers of learning.

In the last century, scholars have once again translated the texts inscribed on temples and tombs recording the work of the priestesses and priests as well as the work the soul undertakes upon the end of its journey among the living. These texts assist Kemetic reconstructionists and theurgists in creating new rituals to invoke the gods.

From Kemet we learn depth of commitment. The course of study in the universities required forty years to complete. Priestesses and priests served part of the year and then returned to the community to serve among the people. The temples also sustained a full-time priesthood of women and men who dedicated their lives to this service.

The temples in Kemet created statues of deity and then invoked the deity into the statue. The priesthood served the statues daily, bringing offerings of food, clothing, incense, and their own work to maintain harmony. This operation passed into theurgy as the animated statue operation; theurgic rituals describe how to invoke a deity into a small statue that can be kept in the home. Kemetic reconstructionists and theurgists do so today.

Theurgy Owes a Debt to India

Pythagoras was said to have studied in India. The doctrine of reincarnation appears in Greece after his journey there. Scholars are analyzing similarities in Neo-Platonic philosophy and Hindu theology. This work is just beginning; the student of theurgy can profitably study the Upanishads along with the texts from Kemet, Greece, Byzantium, and Western Europe.

Pythagorean study focused on the family, bringing women into the discipline and making the practice not only a form of education but a way of life that played out in the home. This was notable enough to draw comment from the ancients. We might consider the emphasis on family in Indian culture as an influence on theurgy.

Theurgy Rests on the Work of Plato

The works of this philosopher founded the theurgic worldview. We continue to study these works today. We know that his work rested on those who came before him whose names we have lost, including his teachers in Kemet and the Pythagorean teachers he encountered on his travels. We also note the inclusion in the Platonic dialogues of the priestess Diotima, who he specifically credited with his understanding of love.

While we acknowledge his foundational contribution and study his works, we also understand that his work changed over time. Plato played with ideas, and his works contradict each other. He was a great teacher but he was human, and no human is infallible. This understanding can free us to approach his work not as a universal truth, but as a conversation aiding us in formulating our own views of the world.

Theurgy Is an Urban Tradition

There are many folk traditions that have preserved the relationship of a specific people and culture to the deities of the land. Theurgists have always acknowledged these, and Proklos in particular felt a responsibility to honor all the gods he encountered in his travels and preserve the knowledge of the gods of his homeland. Theurgy, however, is not primarily a folk tradition; it is urban, born in Alexandria from the mixing of many cultures from around the world. Theurgic ritual acknowledges holy nature without being tied to a particular place. As such it is particularly well suited to the contemporary world where we are all dealing with the worldwide effects of urban culture, whether we were born in the place our ancestors live, or have settled in a new place.

Theurgy Is a Religious Tradition

The Neo-Platonists studied philosophy. They engaged in contemplation of ideas. This is what philosophers do today. Neo-Platonists, however, also engaged in singing hymns, making this not a secular tradition but a religious tradition in our contemporary terminology. Most Neo-Platonists also engaged in a specific set of ritual, magical, practices to bring the contemplating soul into harmony with the divine.

Theurgy Meets the Challenge of Christianity

Neo-Platonic teachers took on Christian students. Many teachers wrote polemics against the Christian theologians, responding to the Christian attempt to suppress Pagan practice. From this interaction, we learn to hold our own truths. We acknowledge the spirit of nature, which is holy and universal and is not the property of any specific religion. We also tap into the spirit of renewal, which gives life to Pagan religion; despite the overwhelming efforts to repress the Pagan impulse, it remains, has budded with every opportunity, and is in full flower today.

Women Are Important to Theurgy

Despite the fact that most discussions of philosophy in the Western academy exclude women, and women are rarely included in lists of Neo-Platonic philosophers, the women in the tradition, black, brown, and white, have been as central to its development as the men. The women point to an important truth: the tradition is not only about thinking or even worship of the gods—it is about how we relate to each other. It is about love and finding the divine, not just in the universe or nature or ourselves but in the people around us. Love unites us with the divine.

THIRTEEN

THE SURVIVAL
OF THEURGIC RITUAL

Over and over we have learned that the study of Neo-Platonic texts leads to Pagan religious practice. Philosophy leads to theurgy. The lives of the teachers continually return to the path of education, knowledge of the gods; we can read the philosophical and theological thought of the teachers in surviving texts. Theurgists revered the gods in the ways of their cultures, and we can learn about Pagan religious practice from Kemetic (Egyptian) and Greek reconstructionists.

What about theurgic ritual itself? The attempt to suppress theurgy specifically excised the religious practices from the texts. Plethon's reconstruction was burned too. How can we recover the ritual aspect of theurgy?

In the last two centuries, archaeologists have collected magical texts. These instructions directly record practices that the Neo-Platonic teachers discussed in their writings. By far the largest collection has been dubbed the "Greek Magical Papyri" because many were written in Greek. Some were also written in Demotic, a Kemetic language form, so we might call them the "Greek and Kemetic Magical Papyri." While some of these texts are what we would now consider spells—actions designed to have a specific effect in the physical world—other texts describe detailed religious rituals.

There is one final story to tell. It is the story of how one particular religious ritual passed from the most ancient times to end up on our bookshelves today. That ritual is called the Mithras Liturgy. It is one of the texts in the Greek Magical Papyri. It is labelled PGM IV.475-834 (PGM stands for Papyri Graecae Magicae).

The Mithras Liturgy captures a theurgic experience of rising on the rays of the sun to the world of the gods. Sarah Iles Johnston points out in "Rising to the Occasion" that just as Plutarch taught theurgic ritual to his daughter Asklepigenia, the Mithras Liturgy is written by a father for his daughter.

THE PRIEST

He couldn't sleep. Lying rigid in the darkness, the priest battled worry until dawn lightened the room. Finally he admitted defeat. He slipped out of bed, careful not to wake his wife, and padded over to his daughter's cot. He hadn't known love could be like this: so tender, so protective, so terrified of the future. The times were chaotic. Who would protect her if he lost his life? Worse, who would teach her? His own knowledge was hard won, passed from his teachers to himself, crystalized through his own experience. It was his most cherished possession and what he most wished to preserve for her.

He glanced sideways at his scribal gear. Such things were not written, they were passed mouth to ear, reinforced through prayer and practice. But his own death seemed so real to him, so very near in the first faint light. At that moment, he understood in his heart what his teachers had always told him: writing fixes the word, it is the path to eternal life.

A rush of haste washed away his reservations. *O gods be not offended,* he breathed, and began to scribble feverishly. "Be gracious to me, O Providence and Psyche as I write these mysteries handed down not for gain but for instruction; and for an only child I request immortality, O initiates of this our power ... "

Learning from Living Teachers

Many people today study theurgic ritual as well as Platonic philosophy. These include academics, reconstructionists, Ceremonial magicians, Witches and Wiccans, Pagans and esotericists.

Although the Christian laws that prohibited the practice of Pagan ritual never succeeded in suppressing that ritual entirely and Pagan ritual is today again practiced openly, the general prejudice against Pagan practice was reflected in academic studies of theurgy until quite recently. E. R. Dodds provides an excellent example. In *The Greeks and the Irrational*, published in 1951, his "Appendix II, Theurgy" provides an indispensable survey of theurgic ritual that continues to instruct us today. However, he denigrates the subject he studies throughout the piece, labelling the practices "superstitious."

Despite this official disdain, some of the academics who studied the subject also practiced theurgic meditations and even theurgic rituals. Throughout my career as an outsider scholar, I have met academics who disclosed their practice to me while asking me not to reveal the fact to their colleagues for fear of being ostracized and even losing their university positions. That situation is changing as Pagan religion moves into the mainstream. Public Pagan scholars move into the academy, academic conferences include academics and non-academic Pagans, and academic practitioners discuss their Pagan involvement more openly. Notably, Bruce McLennan published *The Wisdom of Hypatia* under his legal name and attends Pagan conferences to interact with readers of his work.

Reconstructionists draw on academic work as well as their own travels to Africa and interactions with living traditions there to revive the ancient wisdom teachings and temple traditions. Numerous Afro-centric groups draw on the theology and philosophy of Kemet to follow the way of the neter, the gods of Kemet.

People of color are speaking out about the experience of interacting with white- and European-American-dominated Pagan groups and conferences. Pagan and magical communities are only beginning to confront the racism within the communities to meditate on how we contribute to it, and to commit ourselves to changing it. Crystal Blanton works to build community both in person and through anthologies that give space to many voices to speak, including *Shades of Faith*, *Shades of Ritual*, and *Bringing Race to the Table*. In these books, people of color discuss learning and creating rituals and personal practice. As an example, in "Paganism and the Path Back to Africa" in *Shades of Ritual*, Yvonne E. Nieves describes practicing Wiccan ritual to include Celtic, Scandinavian, and Mayan deities while being guided by orishas, and finally adding Ifá to her practice through initiation and teaching.

White European-Americans have also founded and lead Kemetic reconstructionist groups. This includes the Kemetic Temple founded by Richard Reidy, whose book *Eternal Egypt* recreates the Kemetic practices of creating a living statue as well as daily rituals to sustain the god. He has moved from the realm of the living teaches to the realm of the ancestors now, but his numerous articles and videos can be read and viewed at kemetictemple.org and the temple continues.

Egyptologist Rev. Tamara Siuda founded the Kemetic Orthodox Religion in the 1980s. In 1996, the Kemetic Orthodoxy conducted her coronation as Nisut, recognizing her as the current incarnation of the spirit of Heru, the kingly ka or spirit bridging the human world and the world of the Netjer or deities of Kemet. The Kemetic Orthodoxy offers online classes at www.kemet.org.

It is also important to acknowledge here that some black Kemetic reconstructionists and revivalists point to the legacy of colonialism in theurgic work descending through the Greco-European line. These reconstructionists challenge white Europeans and Americans to acknowledge this and join the work to counteract racism in Pagan and magical communities.

Some contemporary teachers specifically focus on recreating theurgic practice. In the 1990s, John Opsopaus's webpages brought ritual theurgy to the attention of the Pagan and magical communities. Sorita d'Este founded Avalonia Press to publish new works on theurgic practice. Avalonia published Jeffrey S. Kupperman's guide to theurgic theology and ritual, *Living Theurgy*. D'Este's own works include several books dedicated to Hekate, including *Hekate Liminal Rites*. From 2012 to 2014, she produced a Hekate Symposium in Glastonbury that included an oracular rite. This symposium drew theurgic practitioners from around the world.

Tony Mierzwicki recreates theurgic practices in *Graeco-Egyptian Magic*. From this teacher you can learn many practical techniques, including the pronunciation and theurgic use of the Greek vowels.

THE COLLECTOR

The magician looked around his little house with a burst of homecoming joy. Waset again at last! He'd had that long trip up the Nile, stopping at every major temple with a library that still functioned, sleeping every night in a different bed, before boarding a felucca for home.

He washed his face and hands with quick, economical movements, and made a quick meal of dried fruit and water. In the cool of the evening he'd go out to the market and bargain for fresh food. For now he was eager to get started. He had so many new texts to copy, so many new ideas to try!

Carefully he retrieved the precious box and unwrapped the codex inside. In this book he was copying all the works containing *heka* he could find. Magic, to use the Greek word. Some were written in Kemetic script, others in Greek. They mixed Greek and Egyptian elements, Jewish, even Christian. All of it fascinated him. His curiosity drove him, the thirst for knowledge, but there was more to his collecting than just the greed to know. More and more of his fellow citizens converted to the new faith that rejected the ways of the ancestors. These texts were harder to find. It was important, he thought, to preserve them.

He carefully turned the papyrus pages to his last entry. He'd been copying a long list of spells using the Homeric poems. He supposed he ought to finish it before adding anything else. But there was one text he'd found in his travels that captivated him. He hadn't unpacked yet but he knew just where to find it. His heart beat a little faster as he glanced through the first few lines.

" ... furthermore, it is necessary for you, O daughter, to take the juices of herbs and spices, which will be made known to you at the end of my holy treatise, which the great god Helios Mithras ordered to be revealed to me by his archangel, so that I alone may ascend into heaven as an eagle and behold the all."

Ascend as an eagle! It was the most significant work he had ever collected. Moving decisively, he pulled out his stylus and ink and began to copy it in, right where he had stopped last. Homer could wait.

Skeptical Discipleship

The stories Eunapius told of the miracles worked by theurgists strike us now as fables, and few of us today would take them for literal truth. Aleister Crowley may have been the last theurgist who could discuss the work of the ancients without irony. He stood at the beginning of the age of psychology, where "Magick is the Science and Art of causing Change to occur in conformity with Will," as he said in *Magick in Theory and Practice*.

Bringing a certain amount of skepticism to learning from teachers is probably prudent. We live in an age where the holiest of our heroes have been revealed to be flawed people. Mother Teresa is accused of validating suffering and refusing medical care, her saintly image largely an orchestrated media campaign. Mahatma Gandhi may have abused the young girls he slept with to demonstrate his purity. Revered Pagan teachers have been indicted on suspicion of sexual abuse and even murder. This is true as well of some teachers in the Hindu and Buddhist guru traditions and in Christian ministries, where some have used the veneration of students as cover for various kinds of exploitation. So we need not and probably should not expect our Neo-Platonic forebears to be beyond reproach. They were human and flawed. This frees us too to be human and flawed, accepting our own shortcomings as well as the limitations of our living teachers.

As we read the ancients, we also learn that the racism, sexism, and colonialism of the Eurocentric academy begins with the earliest academies. In *The Invention of Racism in Classical Antiquity*, Jacob Isaac notes that Hellenistic teachers devalued women as well as "foreigners" or "barbarians," kept servants and slaves, and built a classist hierarchy that valued white men. Because an attitude is old does not mean that it is venerable, nor does age make it worthy to be replicated. We can and must build justice into our systems, because justice is the foundation for peace.

The teachers we choose, whether we are invoking an ancestor or learning from a living teacher, should hold the highest human ideal that all people are equally worthy. Whatever their flaws, our teachers should strive to help the people around them as well as to reflect the goodness of the divine. When we invoke teachers from the past, we must remember that we are not learning from these teachers in their time but in our own.

Fortunately, we are not required to pledge devotion to a single teacher and pledge to keep the teachings secret as theurgists sometimes did in the past. We are free to learn from many sources and to share what we know. We can choose to learn from women as well as men, from Kemetic and Indian teachers as well as Greek, Roman, and Hellenistic. We are free to temper what we learn from the ancient sources with the knowledge gathered from the world and from our experience in the millennia since they taught. It is part of our work as links in the living chain to update teachings where the texts do not value all humans equally.

JEAN D'ANASTASI

"I hear you are paying for old things."

The dapper Armenian sized up the peasant hovering in his door, trying to keep the distaste from his face. "Only some," he said cautiously.

The man thrust a bundle at him. Dirt flaked from the wrapping. "From the tomb of a priest. It has to be worth something."

Anastasi flinched reflexively, rearing from the dust of the tomb. "Take it outside and unwrap it!"

The grave robber returned with a box. Anastasi carefully turned back the lid. He had considerable experience peddling antiquities to a European market hungry for marvels so he managed not to gasp, but his eyes widened slightly when he saw the treasure within. So many pages, an entire codex!

"You like it," the man said avariciously.

Anastasi forced himself to turn away. "It's only a book. Statues bring more money."

The grave robber took back the lid. "There are other buyers in Thebes," he said. "The Turks love books."

Clearing his throat, Anastasi said, "It does have a mild curiosity value."

Grinning, the thief sat on the floor and settled into the cadence of bargaining.

Learning from Texts

Pagan theurgy is a literate tradition. It passes from teacher to teacher but also through texts, and it can be revived through the study of those texts. Over and over again we have seen that the study of the texts fans the spark of Pagan ritual back to life.

An Alexandrian theurgist with access to the temple libraries would have been able to find the Kemetic and Greek Ritual texts, the Hermetica, the Chaldean Oracles; the works of the Neo-Platonists; the works of Plato; and Kemetic wisdom literature. Platonists through the ages have also learned from the world's cultures, and while some of those texts have vanished, some are preserved. Modern archaeology and scholarship has made available ancient texts that the Greeks did not know, and the shrinking world has brought texts from everywhere within our grasp.

Some texts can be found in local public and university libraries. Quite a few are available free online. Theurgists today build our own libraries both physical and electronic. We can read the original texts as well as commentaries written by contemporary academic and Pagan scholars.

Appendix B, Theurgic Study Course, lists the most commonly referenced source texts with annotations.

ALBRECHT DIETERICH

"Thank you, Maria." Dieterich touched her forearm affectionately.

She patted his shoulder. "Don't stay up all night," she warned him, but left the room with a smile.

Dieterich reached for a crystal glass. "Cognac, Richard?"

Wunsch took the offered glass and raised it. "May I offer a toast? To the Mithras Liturgy!"

They both drank. Dieterich raised his glass. "To Hermann Usener, our teacher!"

"And your father-in-law," Wunsch said, dropping onto a padded chair.

Dieterich said, "I am indebted to you for your close reading of my little text. There are too few of us interested in this material."

"You're too pessimistic," Wunsch protested. "The modern taste is interested in the comparison of religions."

"If only it were religion! The idea that it is 'magic' still taints it." Dieterich blew a derisive breath. "Tell me, my friend. What would you think if I were to teach a seminar on the subject?"

Wunsch coughed his brandy. "On magic?" he said. "I think it would be … brave."

"Well, perhaps not magic," Dieterich temporized. "Just on the texts. 'Selected Pieces from the Greek Papyri.'" He poured another finger of brandy in their goblets.

"I know several students who would be interested," Wunsch said, warming the glass in his hands.

Dieterich nodded cautiously. "Just so. It may be time for magic to emerge from the shadows."

Perennial Philosophy

Sooner or later students of Platonism encounter the notion of the perennial philosophy. Agostino Steuco coined the term, Marsilio Ficino popularized it. Once formulated, it became entrenched in Western European Platonism; the Cambridge Platonists relied on it, the Theosophical Society strives to embody it. But what is it?

The perennial philosophy says that for the eternal questions there are eternal answers.

In *Perennial Philosophy*, Aldous Huxley called it:

> "the metaphysic that recognizes a divine Reality substantial
> to the world of things and lives and minds; the psychology
> that finds in the soul something similar to, or even identical
> with, divine Reality; the ethic that places man's final end in
> the knowledge of the immanent and transcendent Ground
> of all being— the thing is immemorial and universal…"

Perennial philosophy claims to be accurate at all times for all people, describing a fundamental underlying, unchanging reality. It is revealed in whole or in part to humans who receive it and then teach it. Those teachers then become revered saviors.

What inspired this idea, that there is a universal truth? In some ways it is an attempt by Christian Platonists to hang onto their faith after encountering Pagan thought. The reentry of Platonic philosophy into the West presented significant challenges for the Christian Platonists, who had lost the context for the texts with the suppression of the paideia. How could church dogma be reconciled with these exciting and new ideas? One approach is to declare that there is a single underlying truth and that all religions and philosophies are fragments of this truth.

It is an attractive notion that there are no real differences between religions and that ultimately they can be reconciled. What is revealed to the sage and taught to the student is truth, and it is the student's job to learn, embody, and reteach that truth. This is convenient for the sage, but not necessarily for the student, who may find the teaching disempowering and denying the student room to grow in understanding or contribute to knowledge. The drawback is that an unchanging reality cannot change to accommodate new learning, new observations about the world, new ideas, new agreements—such as valuing all human individuals as equally worthy.

If on the other hand we approach a given teaching as a historical document, it is possible to analyze the context in which it was formulated, the effect of the life experience of the teacher formulating it, and whom the doctrine benefits and disenfranchises. Huxley goes on:

> "Rudiments of the Perennial Philosophy may be found among
> the traditionary lore of primitive peoples in every region of
> the world, and in its fully developed forms it has a place in
> every one of the higher religions."

This is undiluted racist and colonialist European exceptionalism, and this stance calls the entire perennial philosophy project into question.

Is the perennial philosophy truly ahistoric? Neo-Platonists from Ficino through to the twentieth century enthusiastically adopted the concept, but where did it originate? In *Radical Platonism in Byzantion: Illumination and Utopia in Gemistos Plethon*, Niketas Siniossoglou analyzes Plethon's idea of true doctrines and does not believe they form the source of Ficino's understanding. Plethon was Ficino's teacher's teacher, so if the idea predated Ficino's generation we would expect to see it in Plethon's work. We can pinpoint the origin of the idea in Ficino's time.

So it seems that the doctrine does have a beginning; as it has a beginning it can have an end, and we may challenge it. The similarity between various cosmologies and thoughts can be explained by the understanding that the peoples who created them were in contact. Arguably, the doctrine of the perennial philosophy constitutes an attempt to deny the influence of African and Asian peoples on European thought.

Unfortunately, Huxley and others linked the perennial philosophy with the idea that the human soul can have an experience of the divine while embodied. This is the fundamental kernel of theurgic practice—if we challenge the historicity of perennial philosophy, do we negate theurgic practice? Not necessarily; theurgic practice belongs to a moment in history before the development of the perennial philosophy concept. We can engage in contemplation and ritual practice as a contemporary iteration of Platonic theurgy. We reserve the right to challenge the philosophical tenets we encounter, noting that they are historical and benefit a privileged few. We may and should remake that philosophy into a framework of understanding that enfranchises all who wish to enter into the practice.

KARL PREISENDANZ

"There you are," Preisendanz said, waving his student to a chair. "I found a copy."

The young woman nearly grabbed the text from his hands. "It's real," she said, her hands shaking as she picked up the manuscript. "It exists."

Her teacher made a face. "In photocopies," he said. "*Papyri Graecae Magicae*. If there's any truth to magic, this thing is cursed."

Still clutching the papers, the student frowned. "Why do you say that?"

"Dieterich died just after he finished the first translation: The Mithras Liturgy, the one you're interested in. My teacher Wunsch was lost in the first war, the war to end all wars. He was working on this at the time." He sighed. "We lost so many good minds in that war. At any rate, the publisher Teubner brought me in to edit the manuscript. We decided to start over with a whole new set of translations."

"What an opportunity!"

Waving his hand to quell her excitement, Preisendanz pursed his lips. "Just as it was finished the second war broke out. So much for the war to end wars."

"War seems endless," the student said sadly.

"Teubner was bombed," he said sourly. "Fortunately I had a copy of the galleys. Since then we've been handing out photocopies to interested students. It was meant to be a study guide anyway."

"I'm glad it survived," she murmured. She started to say something else, but he had already turned his attention to another book, so she quietly slipped out the door.

Re-Paganisation

In the latter half of the twentieth century, the triumphalist narrative proclaiming that Christianity had caused the "death" of Paganism subsided. As this has occurred, subjects previously considered eccentric or fringe have become academically acceptable. Contemporary Pagan religion itself has emerged as a field of study, academics attend Pagan conferences, and a Pagan university—Cherry Hill Seminary—teaches academic courses from a Pagan viewpoint.

Anthropological studies of Eastern European villages document surviving magical customs, rites with direct lineal connections to the rituals of the paideia. In *Ritual and Structure in a Macedonian Village* Joseph Obrebski described the work of Balkan medicine women who conducted rites and spells for healing. A collection of essays edited by Dejan Ajdacic described magical customs and activities in the Balkans—rainmaking, protection against illness, spring fertility rites, and agricultural practices, including songs sung to collect swarms of bees. Recently, Avalonia Press published Georgi Mishev's *Thracian Magic Past and Present*. Mishev himself is the inheritor of the traditions of healing passed through his maternal line, a great-grandson of famous healers. Mishev directly links the extant healing rites to spells in the Greek magical papyri.

Pagan researchers and theologians also work independently, outside the academic system, drawing on academic research and their own field studies. In the last half of the twentieth century Neo-Pagan scholars have enthusiastically studied European folk religion in the library and in the field. Priests and priestesses have reconstructed and resurrected culture specific rites: Norse (Asatru), British (Celtic), Sumerian, Hittite, Roman/Etruscan, Kemetic, Greek, Byzantine, and many more. In addition to reconstructions of village folk religion, Pagan scholars re-create urban Hellenistic, Greco-Roman, and Byzantine Paganism.

This leads us back to our present work, studying Neo-Platonic philosophy and the theurgic ritual associated with it from a Pagan perspective. Contemporary theurgists act to rebuild the paideia, the pact between human and god. We act from the belief that the peace of the gods is universal, that if we approach the gods with reverence, knowledge, a willingness to learn, and the drive to share, that it is possible to create a new paideia, one that reconnects self with culture, self with land, and self with the sacred.

HANS DIETER BETZ

I brought the book home. "Check out what I found," I said.

Everyone looked at the gaudy scarab on the cover. "Another library run?" We lived within walking distance of the University of Washington, where the Suzzalo library was open until midnight on weekdays.

"Greek Magical Papyri in Translation." I beamed. "In 1978, a bunch of Claremont College people got interested in this stuff. This is a brand-new English translation, just republished in 1992."

One of my friends leafed through the pages. Stick figures scribbled with vowels crawled over the pages. "This thing feels alive!"

"Look at this. It's called the Mithras Liturgy. It's written by a man to his daughter. He asks the gods to make her immortal." I laughed. "With all this book has gone through, it was the text they made immortal!"

Linking Platonic Philosophy to Theurgic Practice

When I first picked up the *Greek Magical Papyri in Translation* it was a religious, magical, and historical revelation. Even as an outsider, a nonacademic student of history, I had imbibed the narrative that there was no historical connection between what we do today and what the ancients did. Roman Christianity killed Pagan religion dead and magic died with it.

Yet here were two-thousand-year-old texts I could immediately pick up and use. My own training as a Witch and a Ceremonial Magician had prepared me to understand many of the rituals contained in the volume. I recognized the gods. I recognized the guardians of the directions. There were angels and archangels, herbs and tools, astrological timing. There was a ritual to meet one's own daimon.

There were other ideas new to me at the time. There were protective symbols and names, vowel chanting and popping sounds, substances like wax used in new ways, substances that I hadn't heard of at all.

In *Techniques of Graeco-Egyptian Magic*, Stephen Skinner traces a direct line of descent from the operations in the papyri and nineteenth-century Ceremonial operations. He notes that when Islam conquered Egypt in the sixth century CE, Greek-Egyptian magicians fled to Constantinople, where the Byzantine emperor Heraclius welcomed them. One of these was an Alexandrian Greek Neo-Platonist, Stephanos, a student of Olympiodoros. Stephanos wrote *Hygromanteia*, a book with operations paralleling those of the Greek Magical Papyri. The *Hygromanteia* was source material for the grimoire *Clavicula Salamonis* from which many European manuscripts descend, including the *Key of Solomon* which was translated by Golden Dawn founder Samuel Liddell MacGregor Mathers, one of the Golden Dawn's founders. The *Hygromanteia* directly ties the magic of the papyri with magic practiced today.

Early studies of the papyri treated them as grimoires, collections of spells conducted for practical purposes. In recent decades scholars have approached the material more seriously and found connections between Neo-Platonic writings and the rituals in the volume. Sarah Iles Johnston has written a number of papers exploring specific rituals and ideas; Gregory Shaw finds theurgic instructions in the philosophical texts; and Eleni Pachoumi's important work explicitly links Neo-Platonic ritual references to specific operations in the papyri.

The Mithras Liturgy is a living document that can be studied and incorporated into our practice today. It forms a bridge between the practices of the past and modern Pagan theurgy.

Notes on the Story
The two quotations of the text are taken from Betz, *The Mithras Liturgy*. In the book, Betz notes that Preisendanz reviewed galleys of the Greek Magical Papyri with his friends, including Richard Wunsch.

Scholars note that this piece is inserted into a collection of Homeric verses; why the collector placed it there is a mystery.

PART TWO

THE LIVING TRADITION

Part One of this book described the lives of the Pagan teachers in context. The stories of their lives gives us back our ancestors so we can honor them and understand ourselves as their inheritors. We are their students and their successors in the theurgic tradition. We have seen them teaching in the classroom, and we have seen the results of their rituals. But what exactly was the knowledge they taught, and how did they perform their rituals?

We don't have to guess what the teachers said to their students. They wrote down what they taught and they wrote about each other, and those texts have been copied, quoted, and analyzed right to the present day. The teachers have generated a great deal of material, more than one person can understand in a lifetime. As long as we are theurgists, we will be continually learning.

As we learn from the texts, we also practice the rituals of our teachers. The proscription of ritual practice separated Pagan religion from Pagan philosophy, but despite the attempt to suppress the religious and magical rituals, they have survived, and further, they have been reconnected with the philosophical texts that describe them.

Studying the writings alone is half the journey. Only when we light incense before the images, make invocations, and invite the gods into our lives do we fully understand what the teachers were saying.

In this section of the book, we study the works and practice the rituals of the teachers. Before we can do that, there are steps we must take to prepare ourselves so we can be receptive to learning and to the direct experience of divinity.

FOURTEEN

PREPARING FOR PRACTICE

The drumbeat runs through the lives of the teachers: settle the body, still the mind, contemplate the divine. How do we accomplish these tasks?

SETTLE THE BODY

The Platonic tradition does not value the body. There are advantages and disadvantages to this approach. The advantage is that anyone can be a Platonist. The tradition doesn't care if you're male, female, or gender queer; white, black, brown, mixed; straight, gay, adventurous or celibate; young, old, able or disabled. If you are willing to learn, you can learn.

Some religious and magical traditions place emphasis on gender; in these traditions we are always struggling against the gender hierarchy that values male over female and the solidly gendered against the gender fluid. Platonism provides a welcome alternative to those who are less valued in those traditions. For the theurgist, the essential polarity is not male/female, but human/divine.

While Platonism does not value one skin color over another, theurgists must guard against cultural appropriation, incorporating key insights from other peoples out of context and without acknowledgement. It is vitally important to recognize the sources of our tradition and to respect the peoples who created that tradition, whatever their color and culture. Iamblichus points the way for us here, as he credited the Kemetic contribution to his teachings.

The disadvantage of devaluing the physical is that it does not honor the contribution of the body to our theurgic practice. We can see this pitfall in the life of Plotinus. His biographer Porphyry notes that at the end of his life he refused medication and stopped bathing. His condition forced his pupils to avoid him, whereupon he withdrew to a country house to die. We can avoid this pitfall by drawing on the Kemetic and other traditions that require bathing before practice, and make it a point to bring a clean body to the gods.

Some Platonic and Pythagorean teachers advocate vegetarianism, a time-honored practice for those who wish to participate. However, Hellenic religion involved the sacrifice of animals, and some deities prefer meat offerings. Also there are people who must eat meat. In *Animals in Translation,* Temple Grandin notes that she would prefer that people had developed as plant eaters, but we are omnivores. She finds that she requires meat to function, and suspects that this is because her autistic system is built somewhat differently than other humans. Whether to eat meat or abstain is a practitioner's personal choice, and as all humans are welcome to practice theurgy, meat eating should not be a bar to practice.

In terms of food, it is sensible for the theurgist to eat as many whole foods as possible and avoid processed foods. Recreating the offerings of our ancestors provides an interesting way to explore healthy eating. Remember that the temples of Kemet offered food to the gods that was then distributed to the temple staff. We can recreate this practice by offering our food to the deities before we eat. Now, Proklos did not offer

TV dinners to the gods; a plate of fruit, cheese, and homemade bread is a welcome offering to the gods … and a pretty good meal for ourselves.

STILL THE MIND

We chatter. The active human neocortex continually processes the input of our senses. While some people think in pictures, most of us think verbally, in words. These words create generalizations, templates of the world used to sort and screen the overwhelming influx of data.

That chatter gets in the way of spiritual practice. Almost every religion and spiritual path contains some form of exercise to still the mind. All the Platonic teachers began their practical lessons with instructions to engage in meditation or contemplation. Meditation to clear thought is helpful to the theurgist. If our minds are full, how can we make space to accept the imprint of the divine?

While we don't know exactly what priestesses like Neitokrity did in the temples of Kemet, we can learn from the many traditions surrounding us today. For example, yoga and tai chi meditations focus on breathing. Chapter 17, "Theurgic Ritual Workbook," contains a simple breathing exercise, "Meditation to Clear Thought."

Meditation can be part of ritual, but it does not have to be a ritualized activity. We don't need special clothes or a temple or a particular time of day for these activities. Actually, it's important to be able to meditate wherever we are: it is an important life tool for anyone on any spiritual path.

CONTEMPLATE THE DIVINE

To contemplate means to think deeply about a subject. As we study the teachings of our ancestors, we may find some ideas that are easy to understand, make good sense to us, and immediately enter into our worldview. Other ideas are new or contradict thoughts we already hold, challenging us to reexamine our worldview. We may find that the new idea reshapes the way we understand the world. We may also reject the idea—no one person has the ultimate truth, and not all notions are helpful to us on our own path.

Where theurgic contemplation differs from simple philosophical study is that it grounds in ritual. We not only think, we act, presenting ourselves before the gods in the way that our contemplation has revealed to us. We make ourselves available to the divine. When we speak to the gods and they answer, that illumination transforms us more than any amount of human reasoning can do. This opening of ourselves to the divine is the culmination of our work and the ultimate theurgic practice.

With these preparations in mind, we are ready to take on the study of the works of the teachers and the practice of theurgic rituals.

FIFTEEN

STUDYING THEURGIC RELIGIOUS PHILOSOPHY

A theurgic education is always self-directed. We can learn from ancient texts, from living teachers, and from our own experiences in ritual, where the entities we contact provide us with additional guidance. Even where a living teacher provides knowledge and guidance, the path is so individual that each of us charts our own way.

One place to start our studies is with the materials in Appendix B, "Theurgic Study Course." This course includes Kemetic wisdom texts and rituals, Platonic dialogues, the works of the Neo-Platonists, and Hellenistic ritual texts. Reading through these works takes some time but provides a solid foundation for our ritual work.

As a brief overview, there are two primary sources of theurgic religious philosophy. The first is the Chaldean Oracles, in which the gods, especially Hekate, describe the nature of existence. The second is the writings of Iamblichus and Proklos, understanding that the writings of Proklos also include the thought of Asklepigenia. Iamblichus, Asklepigenia, and Proklos based their religious philosophy on the theology of the oracles as well as Platonic theology. All three teachers also practiced theurgic ritual, and our ritual practice today benefits from their insights.

This chapter provides a summary view of theurgic theology based on the Chaldean Oracles and the Iamblichus/Asklepigenia/Proklos school. We begin with a discussion of the definition of philosophy and how theurgic philosophy differs from the philosophy we learn in school today. We also discuss how theurgic philosophy shapes Pagan theology. Then we dive into the discussion of the nature of the divine and the divine hierarchy.

WHAT IS PHILOSOPHY?

Although today we think of religion and philosophy as different subjects, theurgy reunites these two disciplines. In fact "philosophy" means something very different to us than it did to the ancients, so it's worth taking a moment to explore what happened to that word. Philosophy today seems to be a series of intellectual contests between elite players, mostly rich white men. People of color, women of all races and nationalities, the non-college-educated, and other outliers rarely get a chance to speak. Philosophers argue endlessly about the nature of the universe and the human experience but seldom seem to touch on what people are really doing in our daily lives. Confronted with arid mental games, most of us tune them out.

This matters because philosophy is our most sophisticated mode of thought. It is the operating system of our culture, underlying all of our assumptions about how the world actually works. Unfortunately, contemporary Western philosophy privileges reason. Philosophy today speaks to the insatiable human need to know, to understand, to press the limits of comprehension, but it does not speak to the heart—leaving that to psychology, and it does not speak to the spirit—leaving that to religion.

There was a time when philosophy, psychology, religion, and magic were not separate endeavors but part of a whole. The works of theurgists describe insights, emotions, and experiences that our mind-only philosophy does not replicate. When we call what they did "philosophy," we should remember it was a spiritual quest led by the heart as much as by the mind.

In today's definition, philosophy is separate from theology. Philosophy, which is secular, deals with the study of existence and of the human place in the cosmos. Theology, which is religious, studies deity, belief, and faith.

In the Platonic school, philosophy and theology are the same. Inquiring into the nature of existence means studying the nature of the divine. The universe was separated from deity in Western European thought in Renaissance times, when mechanical philosophy explained the manifest universe as a series of nonliving mechanisms. Platonic thought re-unites the universe with divinity and places human existence in the context of a sacred flow of life.

We can discuss theurgy as a philosophy and as a theology—both terms are appropriate. The study of theurgic theology strengthens contemporary Pagan theology, reconnecting us to the wellspring of Western religious philosophical thought.

PAGAN THEOLOGY

One of the tropes of religious studies is that Pagan theology is undeveloped. Folk religion has little need of developed theology, and sophisticated Greco-Roman Pagan religion ceased to develop with the triumph of Christianity. A few recent attempts have been made to shape a universalist Pagan theology by examining cross-cultural conceptions of polytheism and indigenous world religions (Jordan Paper and Michael York), or by cataloguing the theology of a broad spectrum of contemporary Pagans (Christine Hoff Kraemer). These are interesting and helpful efforts.

However, as we have seen, Graeco-Roman Pagan religion did not cease to develop but remained lively through the transmission of Neo-Platonic philosophy. Study of that philosophy leads to a renaissance of

Pagan religious expression, specifically reverence for deity, the keeping of festival days, and a return to attunement with the natural world.

Religious and secular scholars approach theurgic theology from the point of view of the philosophers. What did Iamblichus think? What did Proklos teach? As we engage Neo-Platonic theology, it is important to understand what the teachers themselves thought. It is also important to recognize that these teachings were not static but dynamic, building on what came before and sometimes contradicting prior ideas, adapting to the times.

Our contributions to Platonic philosophy will change it. Platonists have historically grappled with inherited ideas, sometimes adding to what we have been given and sometimes overturning the past to develop a workable system in the present. This is especially necessary for contemporary Pagan theurgists and theologians. To be useful to us in the present, our theology should reflect the values of inclusion of diversity, respect for persons and cultures, and sustainability in the natural world.

THE NATURE OF THE DIVINE

The core concepts of theurgic religious philosophy are:

- the **One**, or First God;
- the **Intellect**, or Second God, issuing from the One to manifest existence;
- the **World Soul**, or Third Goddess, bringing souls into the material realm;
- the **Empyrean, Intelligible, and Material Worlds**, which the divine triad create;
- a celestial hierarchy including **gods**, **spirits**, **heroes** (such as teachers);
- the individual human **soul**.

In this theology, the **sun** is understood as the sustaining power of the Material World and the road through which the soul returns to the spiritual world.

The First God

As Ruth Majercik and Sarah Iles Johnston explain, the oracles describe a primal triad, with three forces combining to generate the manifest universe. The first principle is called:

- the One
- Hyparxis
- Monad
- Source
- the Highest Good
- Father

What can we know about the One?

The One is.

The One is everything, and beyond everything. The One is male and female and all genders on the spectrum. The One is the consciousness of everything. The One has always been and will always be.

The limited human mind cannot hold the immensity of the One. We can think of the One as the universe, as all universes at all times, and to totality of creation and existence. These are all just shadows of understanding. Our yearning to understand is our yearning to participate in the One.

The One is sometimes translated as God. The idea of the One is not identical with God. God as we know the concept today is irrevocably conflated with Yahweh, the God of the Jews, and with the Christian God the Father, the old man in the clouds. In contrast, the One is beyond knowing. The One is the source of the visible and invisible universe. The One is the ultimate source of our souls, and returning to union with the One is the ultimate goal of theurgy.

The One has aspects of the Qabbalistic "veils of negative existence." It is not possible to comprehend the One with human minds. This makes sense from a One-as-Universe perspective too.

Most importantly, the One is good. Fundamentally, the One encompasses all living things as a nourishing matrix.

The Second God

The oracles go on to describe a second god. Ruth Majercik notes that the second god is sometimes equated in the oracles with the One, and sometimes is described as the first emanation of the One.

This god is called:

- The Demiurge
- The Intellect
- Nous
- Craftsman
- Abyss
- Father

As Intellect, the Demiurge thinks the thoughts of the One. As Craftsman, the Demiurge shapes the thoughts of the One. As Abyss, the Demiurge seems remote, but as Father the Demiurge seems close, even nurturing.

The Third Goddess

The oracles describe the third member of this triad as a goddess. She is called:

- Dynamis
- Power

- Hekate
- World Soul

Hekate is the goddess who speaks the oracles. She is the gate through which souls pass to incarnate in the Material World.

The Triple Deity

Triads are familiar to students of religion, to Witches, Pagans, Ceremonial magicians and esotericists. We can immediately call to mind the Hindu trinity of Brahma, Vishnu, and Shiva; the Christian trinity of Father, Son, and Holy Spirit; the Kemetic triads including Isis, Osiris, and Horus, Mother-Father-Son, and Khnum, Satet, and Anuket, Father-Mother-Daughter. Qabbalists will think of the Supernals: Kether, Chokmah, and Binah. Witches may think of Dryghton/Providence, Goddess, and God/Consort.

From the oracles, Ruth Majercik traces many similar phrases describing this triple deity.

First God	Second God	Third Goddess
Father	Intellect	Power
Hyparxis	Nous	Dynamis
Existence	Thought	Life

This is a little different than other trinities. For example, in the Isis-Osiris-Horus triad, Isis and Osiris mate, and Isis gives birth to Horus, their son. In the case of the Witchcraft triad, the Dryghton is the unitary spirit who gives rise to the Goddess/God pair. In the Christian trinity the Father emanates the Son and the Holy Spirit in a kind of hierarchy. The First God, Second God, and Third Goddess are not in a family relationship, but are three interlocking parts of a whole.

The vision of relationship among these three entities is not that of a linear hierarchy, but as a horizontal linking. In the horizontal image, the Third Goddess, also known as Life or Power or Hekate, is seen as mediating between the First God and the Second God.

First God	Third Goddess	Second God

The Third Goddess is always a liminal entity. Specifically, the One thinks Ideas; the Intellect projects the Ideas of the One into the World Soul's primal matter, or womb, making her the Mother to his Father. Majercik notes that this "reflects an obvious truth: that a feminine element is necessary if there is to be a process of generation at all, whether at the highest or lowest levels…"

The Three Worlds

The triad of First God, Second God, and Third Goddess together create three worlds. These are:

- The Empyrean World
- The Intelligible World
- The Material World

These worlds are arranged in a cosmic hierarchy. The Empyrean World includes the Platonic Ideas, which provide the form for the worlds below; the Ethereal World includes the sun, the fixed stars, and other planets; and the Material World includes the moon and earth.

World	Cosmic Correspondence
Empyrean World	Ideas
Ethereal World	Sun, planets, fixed stars
Material World	Moon and earth

These correspond to the Platonic worlds: the World of Forms, the Intelligible World, and the Sensible World. Qabbalists will immediately think of the four-world system of Atziluth, Briah, Yetzirah, and Assiah. Neo-Platonism predates the Qabbalistic system and formed one of the inputs to Qabbalah. However, the Platonic system sees the universe not as four, but through the lens of triplicity—everything is in threes.

How does this world creation occur? The One is filled with unbounded power that spills out like water to create the manifold cosmos. In *Proclus, Neo-Platonic Philosophy and Science*, Lucas Siorvanes describes the activity of that power as expressing itself in a threefold process: "proceeding," flowing out; "reversion," returning; and "remaining," still staying essentially itself despite going forth and returning. The universe is not static but filled with this constant movement.

The Journey

The cycle of the soul through incarnation is another example of this process of flow. The soul proceeds from the One and is impelled to make the journey of return to the One.

Everything that is exists in the One. The manifest universe is an outpouring from the One. All that pours out from the One must return to the One. Human souls partake of the One, we came forth from the One, and our entire purpose is to understand how to make the journey of return. Put another way, the theurgist seeks to move up the hierarchy from earth, to moon, to the sun, to the stars, and to the realm of the Ideas themselves.

Theurgy does not insist that theurgy itself is the only way to make the journey of return. Because the One is unknowable, so is truth. Humans often insist on a particular religion, science, or point of view as being irrefutable truth. However, we can see that human comprehension of what is true shifts over time with new understanding. In human relationships, "true" can be understood as a synonym for "right." Insistence on one truth over another leads to evil action, the source of many cruelties. It may be that Truth exists, but no human knows it.

To approach the One, to make the journey of return, we learn to be good. Among humans, this means learning to be good to one another. This is a core religious teaching as well as a core humanist value.

It is also important to note in our journey that the One and the manifest universe are good. Theurgy purports that evil derives from human imperfection; most of what we understand as evil is the action of humans. Evil exists as an error, a falling away from the understanding of the One and the processes of the universe. Coping with evil is an opportunity to learn what we need to know to return to the One.

THE DIVINE HIERARCHY

As we have seen so far, the triad deities—First God/One, Second God/Intellect, Third Goddess/World Soul—bring forth the universe in three worlds: the Empyrean World of Ideas; the Ethereal World, including the stars, planets, and sun; and the Material World, including the moon and the earth. The human soul incarnates by falling from the One, through the World Soul, through the stars, planets, sun, and moon, to a physical body on earth.

A celestial ladder links the Material World to the world of Ideas; the links include gods, spirits, heroes, and individual souls.

The Gods

For Proklos, "the God is one, the Gods are many." The myriad gods are all part of the One.

That is not to say that the individual gods do not have their own identity. The Monad, the unitary being, contains multiple other unities called henads. This is an idea akin to (but not identical) the Qabbalistic idea of the sephiroth "sphere." These henads are not gods, but they are *linked* to gods and are divine. Each henad is described by one deity, specifically one of the Greek Olympians, but may also contain multiple deities. In "On the Gods and the World," translated by Gilbert Murray, Sallustius gives several examples of how a henad can include several deities: the henad of Zeus includes Dionysos, the henad of Apollo includes Asklepios, and the henad of Aphrodite includes the Charites.

It may seem strange to equate a universal force with the Olympian deities. We're accustomed to hearing stories about the gods behaving badly—Zeus raping women, Hera punishing his victims, Hermes stealing cattle, and so on. The gods of the stories behave in ways condemned among humans. How can they be held up as examples of the highest good?

In Platonic philosophy the Olympian deities are not seen through the lens of Homer's stories about them. In fact, Plato devotes one whole dialogue, *Ion*, to a criticism of poetic license. Sallustius acknowledges that the doctrine that the gods are unchanging and good directly conflicts with the myths portraying their adultery and theft. He concludes, "Is not that perhaps a thing worthy of admiration, done so that by means of the visible absurdity the soul may immediately feel that the words are veils and believe the truth to be a mystery?" In other words, he says, it's a mystery, and the myths do not accurately describe the totality of the gods.

The task of the gods is to generate the universe. It is also the task of the gods to exercise Providence, that is, protective care. Humans participate in Providence through prayer and ritual action. We may remember that the Mithras Liturgy begins with the invocation, "Be gracious to me, O Providence ... "

In addition to the Chaldean Oracles, the works of Iamblichus, Proklos/ Asklepigenia, and Sallustius, there is another source of information about individual gods or deities. The Kemetic and Greek ritual texts known as the Greek Magical Papyri include numerous rituals invoking individual deities.

Eleni Pachoumi extensively analyses the deities in the papyri. These are not nearly so neatly organized as Sallustius's categories of the Olympians. They are Kemetic, Greek, and a Kemetic/Greek synthesis, with some survivals of Babylonian deities and additions of Jewish and Christian names and spirits. They include:

- Hermes and Hekate
- Dionysos and Aphrodite
- Apollo/Helios and Selene
- Artemis and Eros
- Tyche
- Isis and Osiris
- Horus and Typhon
- Thoth
- Nepthys
- Iao, Sabaoth, Adonai, Christos
- Aion
- Ereshkigal

New Gods

Is it possible to approach other deities than those listed here through theurgic techniques? The ancient theurgists did. Proklos added deities to his devotional list whenever he travelled. The list of deities from the papyri seems eclectic. Since this is an urban system, and a living one, there should be in theory nothing to block a theurgist from using theurgic techniques to approach deities from other pantheons than the Kemetic and Greek. For example, many Pagans who work with Hellenistic deities also work with Norse and Celtic deities.

Hinduism, Buddhism, and Santeria are living religions that honor deities with techniques similar to theurgy. Statues in Hindu temples are brought to life by the priesthood. Small Buddhist statues are sold for home use that have been consecrated with a similar technique to theurgic animation. Santeria practitioners invoke the orishas to possession.

Since these are living traditions, these deities should be approached with the devotionals from their traditions. Their devotees may use techniques similar to the work we are doing, but the deities have their own rituals, and we should honor them by learning them on their own terms, rather than incorporating what interests us out of context. The same is true for Native religious rituals from around the world.

We can begin to make reparations for European colonialist actions by forbearing to continue them in the present. Colonialism imposed a Greek and Western European overlay on many other religions. If people with ancestral heritage object to what we are doing with deities in their line, it's time to back off, listen respectfully, and meditate on correct action. Hearts committed to spiritual practice can meet through dialogue and caring.

Spirits

The oracles, the works of the philosophers, and the papyri describe numerous spirits involved in the hierarchy of being.

DAIMONES

In English today "demon" means evil or inferior spirit; "angel" means good or superior spirit. The Greek word *daimon* referred to a spirit intermediary between the gods and humans. We have also encountered the idea that an individual could have a personal daimon, as Socrates had his daimonion, an idea similar to the Christian idea of a personal guardian angel.

Each of the Olympian henads commands daimones, spirits to whom they impart their particular power. These daimones can be addressed by the names of the deities, as in, "oh daimones of Apollo." Lucas Siorvanes points out that these daimones seed the substances of the gods in the terrestrial realm, creating the symbola—plants, animals, stones, sounds—that carry the power of the gods.

In the oracles, daimones are neutral spirits who can perform both good and evil acts. Destructive daimones are sometimes called "dogs" and can be of earth, air, or water. Various oracles list either Hekate or Hades, god of the underworld, as the rulers of the negative daimones.

IYNGES AND SYNOCHES

The oracles discuss several entities unique to the theurgic system. The first of these are the Iynges or wheels. The thoughts of the One are Iynges, messages between the divine and human, magical names sent forth by the One to communicate with the theurgist.

The word *iynx* is also used to describe a ritual tool. Hellenistic magicians used magic wheels in their operations, and theurgists appropriated that magic wheel for use in their rites. They spun the wheel, iynx, to attract the divine names, Iynges. When theurgists spoke the divine names, they acquired magical powers.

Another divine force is the Synoches who harmonize and protect the universe. They establish the bonds of the universe and watch over it as guardians. An example of a Synoche is the rays of the sun.

TELETARCHES

The oracles also identify Teletarches, beings who assist the Synoches and Iynges. Majercik thinks that the Teletarches as spirits may be truly Chaldean; that is, Babylonian rather than Kemetic or Hellenic in origin. Majercik calls them the "masters of initiation" and notes that they are the rulers of the three worlds. The Teletarches are associated with three virtues: Pistis, or Trust; Aleitheia, or Truth; and Eros, or Love.

Teletarch	World
Eros	Empyrean
Aleitheia	Intelligible
Pistis	Material

The Greek word *pistis* is often translated as "faith," but faith means something different today than pistis meant to a Pagan in Hellenistic times. To a modern English speaker "faith" has a strong religious overtone, associated with the fidelity of Christian and other religious practitioners to their religions even in the face of the mechanistic or secular denial of that faith. Faith is belief despite the absence of scientific proof of something physically measurable.

Pistis is also mentioned in a few ancient sources as the personified goddess of trust. To the ancient theurgist "pistis" meant a particular kind of knowledge or gnosis. In *The Egyptian Hermes,* Garth Fowden quotes the Hermetic phrase "to have understood is to have believed and not to have understood is not to have believed." He goes on, "one could hardly wish for a more concise statement of the ancients' conviction that human and divine knowledge, reason and intuition, are interdependent." Trust, pistis, is the goal of the contemplation of the divine. Contemplation leads to intellectual knowledge but the touch of the divine itself leads to certainty.

Although the Teletarches as guiding forces may be Chaldean, Greek religious philosophy discussed Aleitheia as a concept well before Plato. Parmenides wrote the poem "On Nature" in two parts, the first named *Aleitheia,* translated "truth" (the second was *Doxa,* "opinion"). Hayim and Rivca Gordon review Heidegger's analysis of Parmenides's poem and note that the philosopher approached Aleitheia as a goddess in her own right, and as a force of "unconcealing." Understanding Aleitheia's truth as a form of unconcealing or revelation points to the importance in theurgy of learning from direct contact with divinity.

We know Eros as a Greek deity in two forms: an older form who was the cosmic force of generation, and a younger form appearing as the son of Aphrodite. Parmenides's poem described the rising of the poet to the realm of Aphrodite in a strikingly theurgic image (see John Burnett's translation). As a Teletarch, Eros inspires in us the love of philosophy and the love of the gods that drives us to seek contact and communion with them.

The Neo-Platonic Soul

The soul is the final entity in the divine hierarchy. The oracles gave specific instructions allowing the soul to approach the gods. Before we can learn these, we need to understand something about the Neo-Platonic understanding of the soul.

In the oracles, the soul descends into matter via the ether, sun, moon, and air. Each contributes to the vehicle of the soul. This descent is an intoxication from which the soul should wake up. After death, unpurified souls spend a period of time in Hades undergoing purification until they can return to earth.

The soul is purified through theurgy, the use of ritual. In his explanation of theurgy, Iamblichus was at some pains to distinguish between theurgy as god-work, and goetia or magic. Goetic magicians sought to compel the gods, while theurgists understand that the gods choose to descend and interact with humans.

Symbola and synthemata, divine objects, bear the signatures of the gods in the physical world. They are divine presence in matter. The synthemata are physical objects like herbs, plants, stones, and incense, and they can also include chants, songs, and visions of the gods. Using those sacred symbola, the soul could awaken the same signatures in the soul itself; the gods would infuse the theurgists with their power and make the theurgists themselves holy.

In *Theurgy and the Soul*, Shaw argues that theurgy's place in Platonism is to move the experience of embodiment from being imprisoned in matter to full participation in the World Soul. The soul transforms its experience of chaos into cosmic order. Iamblichus returns to the imagery of the Heliopolitan cosmology to articulate this thought, using the symbols of mud and lotus. Mud nourishes the lotus until it is ready to rise above the mound; in the same way the soul of the theurgist rises above matter, which allows its full development.

Majercik's translation of Fragment 110 of the Chaldean Oracles describes this theurgic process: "Seek out the channel of the soul, from where it descended in a certain order to serve the body, and seek how you will raise it up again to its order by combining ritual action with a sacred word …" We will discuss sacred words and passwords in the section "Rising through the Worlds" in chapter 16.

Christian Theurgy

As we encounter ideas like "One" and "Father," and "all gods are part of the One," we may be tempted to draw parallels between Platonic religious philosophy and Christian monotheism. There is, however, a difference between recognizing the unity of all things, and insisting that one conception of one God is the only correct perception of the universe.

Throughout this work, I have been making the case that the study of Platonic philosophy leads to Pagan ritual. We should note that there is such a thing as Christian theurgy. Hypatia taught Christians; her devoted student Synesius was a bishop; and the Alexandrian Academy admitted Christians until its closure. The tension between Christians and Pagans in the Alexandrian Academy is vividly portrayed in the work of Zacharias of Gaza, who would later become Bishop of the Greek city of Mytilene. In *Ammonius or On the Creation of the World*, Zacharias describes heated discussions between "the Christian" and Ammonius in which Ammonius is ultimately driven to silence. In late antiquity, committed Pagans were pressured to convert to Christianity, and Platonic philosophy was pressed to collapse the myriad forms of divinity into a single monad, God.

Christian theurgists practice today. In *Living Theurgy*, Jeffrey Kupperman analyses the theology of Dionysius alongside the theology of Iamblichus, equating Pagan entities with an angelic hierarchy. Kupperman also includes Christian practice, giving directions for animating a statue of the Christos. I am personally aware of several contemporary theurgists who primarily identify as Christian.

There are, however, fundamental differences between Christian and Pagan theurgists. We have already noted that Asklepigenia and Proklos rejected the Christian submission to fate and actively sought through magic to change the course of their lives. Pagan religion celebrates the diverse forms of deity and offers to each their particular preferred sacrifice.

These differences were emphasized by the early Christian church and continue to be emphasized by Christians today. Christian leaders issue injunctions to their followers to worship only the Christian God and not Pagan deities, and they specifically prohibit working with statues as well, requiring Christians to submit to the will of God. Christian theurgy on the other hand leads Christians into practices more congenial to Pagans. I harbor a private suspicion that non-theurgic Christians would identify the practices of Christian theurgy as Pagan in character.

I welcome Christian theurgists to the work, as Platonists have always done, but I warn that this project is not intended to alter Platonism to make it acceptable to Christianity; our emphasis here is on restoring the rich complexity of Pagan theology and practice. Readers may remain Christian if it is their will, but respect for the Pagan path is absolutely required. We congenially invite everyone to follow in the footsteps of Boethius and Plethon and fully convert to Pagan Platonism.

Updating the System

Contemporary theurgists have the responsibility to preserve Platonic philosophy and Pagan religious practice. In addition to teaching what the ancients taught, we have the responsibility to improve the system.

Platonic conceptions rely heavily on gendered imagery. While the One encompasses everything and is beyond understanding, the One is also called the Father. In "Animal Par Excellence: Soul, Body, and Gender in Plato's Timaeus," Adam Weitzenfield analyzes the ways in which Plato's dialogue *Timaeus* valorizes the male. The soul is created by the demiurge and placed in bodies by the gods. Those who succeed in contemplating the rational in their first lives are free to return to their home star, but those who do not are reincarnated as women. Here we see a denigration of the female gender as being less rational and secondary to men.

For Plato, there is a world more real than the physical, and rational contemplation puts us in touch with that world while sense experience traps the soul in a physical prison. The immortal divinely created soul is meant to contemplate the perfect world of the forms from whence it came, and to steer away from experience of the Material World. There is a devaluation of matter in this conceptualization. The world is a trap, is evil, and is the prison from which the soul is attempting to escape.

This is where the challenge to the concept of perennial philosophy becomes important. Because we know we are not looking at an eternal truth but instead ideas created within a historic context, we are free to explore the ways in which context have shaped those ideas and alter the metaphysic to fit our own needs and understanding.

Pagans are far from alone in the effort to reform aspects of this tradition. Feminist theologians challenge the gender of God as male. Contemporary feminists struggle with the historical conceptions of God as reflecting a particular people in a particular place. They seek to diversify God by acknowledging all aspects of the human in God.

It is the task of the contemporary Pagan theurgic philosopher-theologian to find terms and images that reflect an understanding of the One as not bounded by human form in ways privileging specific humans over others. We can acknowledge the historical understanding of the One as the Father while creating new language and new visions that understand the One as embodying every human form.

First, we can refer to the One as "the One" rather than "God" or "Father." The conception of the One as overflowing, giving, nurturing, creating are all beautiful images, well suited to female imagery as it is to male, arguably borrowed from language describing Goddesses.

We can engage Kemetic theology to provide us with examples of trinities that include the female. As many scholars have pointed out, Kemetic theologians routinely created new stories to reflect their own needs and changing understanding of the universe. While we create new stories we may also explore the fluidity of gender; a new trinity can include male, female, and neither/both.

In contemporary religion, there is no reason not to validate people of all genders. Some feminist philosophers point to Plato's non-gendered soul as the seed of this understanding. If a soul can be born into male or female bodies, or any kind of body, then the soul itself has no gender. Removing the value system that ranks some people as more valuable than others frees us to understand every kind of body as equally sacred. To accomplish this, we must continually challenge the default person as male, white, heterosexual, and able-bodied.

In *Witch Hunting, Magic and the New Philosophy: An Introduction to Debates of the Scientific Revolution*, Brian Easlea outlines the politics that resulted in the desacralization of the Western idea of the universe. When Platonic and Hermetic works were re-introduced into Renaissance Europe, a battle was sparked between exploratory thinkers who called themselves natural philosophers and Church clerics enforcing Christian dogma. A détente between them conceptualized the universe as a mechanism God created and then left to run itself. From there it was a simple step to ignore God altogether, bringing us to the conflict today between "religious" (Christian) and "secular" (mechanical) viewpoints. In this conceptualization, life is an artifact of a hostile universe; the only relief from the sterility of this view is belief in a distant but caring Father. The mechanical universe permitted the exploitation and destruction of the earth and its living creatures as soulless mechanisms.

New physics points to the idea that the universe is conversely an artifact of life. Similarly, deep ecology calls on conceptualizations of the earth as a single organism and all of the earth as an artifact of life. This is perhaps the most important reason to re-engage the Platonic metaphysic that conceives the universe as a living and interconnected whole. Resacralizing the world and the universe contributes to a shift in emphasis from use of dead matter to the preservation of life.

A cosmos that is sacred, in which matter is sacred, in which all genders are valued equally as both participating in embodiment and participating in spirituality is a philosophy derived from the *Timaeus* but differs from it substantially. Can it be considered to be Platonic?

Why would it not be? We honor Plato as one of the contributors to the worldview we inhabit. However, we do not worship Plato and his successors as an infallible intellect. We can test the work of our ancestors, shaping it for use in the modern era and making it our own.

SIXTEEN

CRAFTING A
THEURGIC PRACTICE

We have noted that the philosophical texts are not fully understood until we engage in ritual practice. For many Pagans today, ritual practice is the main reason we do theurgy. We study the philosophical texts to gain insight into the intended result of the ritual practice. The texts and rituals together form a whole.

In the texts, the teachers extensively discussed the religious and spiritual insights derived from their rituals. But what did they actually do? In some cases, they did not record the rituals, as it would be part of their oral teachings. In other cases, the parts of their works discussing methodology were specifically excised. How can we recover their rites?

Fortunately, texts do survive that describe religious ritual, many collected in the Greek Magical Papyri. These have been reconnected to the philosophical texts; Eleni Pachoumi directly links the rituals to discussions in the literature. Also, some rituals in contemporary Witchcraft and Ceremonial Magic are specifically theurgic and have been practiced for many decades, providing us with examples that may be useful in our own practice.

This chapter discusses both the ancient texts and the modern versions of the rituals.

HELLENISTIC OPERATIONS

The philosophers, the oracles, the papyri, and contemporary scholars list these core theurgic rituals:

- Evoke deity into a statue
- Invoke deity into someone else
- Invoke deity into yourself

In addition, there are two advanced theurgic operations:

- Meeting with one's own daimon
- Rising through the worlds

The theurgic operations can be approached as a stairway leading from the Material World through the Intelligible World to the direct experience of the Empyrean World. This retraces the journey the soul took to become embodied and brings the soul back—to the experience of the divine while still embodied—alive on earth.

In English, the words we use to describe the ritual action of bringing a deity into manifestation are "invocation" and "evocation." These words are often used interchangeably. Here I am using the term "invocation" to mean calling the deity into a human being, ourselves, or others; and "evocation" to mean inviting the deity into a statue, lamp, bowl of water, or other physical object.

Evocation into a Statue

Called "telestike" or "the technical art" by the ancients, evocation into a statue is an intense form of devotional to a particular deity. In this operation the theurgist looks in the Material World for substances that belong to the deity and uses them to call a deity to inhabit a statue. This is sometimes referred to as "animating" a statue. With this technique, the statue becomes a living form of the deity. The operator can commune with the deity and ask questions. Animating a statue allows the theurgist to literally sit in the presence of the god.

Kemet, Greece, and Mesopotamia were filled with temples. The world has been touring their ruins for thousands of years, marveling at their architectural beauty, wondering at the rites performed there. Fortunately, surviving texts describe the ritual from Kemet used to evoke deity into the statue of the deity housed in the temple. This ritual is referred to in English as the "Opening of the Mouth." When the statue was complete, the priests would take a specialized tool and touch it to the eyes and mouth of the statue so that it could see and eat. Once the statue was made to live, the deity would be offered food and other forms of worship several times a day by the temple staff. The same ritual was performed on the mummies of the pharaohs.

In "Animating Statues: A Case Study in Ritual," Sarah Iles Johnston sees the act of animating statues as an example of the way in which theurgists attempted to keep alive the knowledge of the work of the gods. As the suppression of Pagan practices forced public rituals into private homes, the living statue moved into private use as well.

Late Hellenistic theurgists and magicians worked outside the temple system. They did not have access to the skilled crafts people who created the statues, and they were not enshrining the statue to be given food and drink by a large staff every day. Without access to the staff of the temples and the tools they used, how did they bring their own statues to life?

There are numerous examples of animating statues in the Greek magical papyri and one example in the Chaldean oracles. To conduct the operation, the theurgist or magician collected physical items called synthema or symbola and applied them to the statue. These synthema and symbola were objects known to possess the power of the deity. They were the physical manifestations of the chain of being—heroes, Teletarches, Iynges, Synoches, daimones, and gods—stretching from the Material World through the Intelligible World to the Empyrean World. The statue combined with symbola was then a worthy vessel the deity could inhabit.

Johnston became interested in exactly how this operation was conducted. Did the theurgist herself create the statue? It seems that someone else could make the statue and gather the substances, so what made this a personal devotional? The magician applied the knowledge of which symbola were attached to which deities. The example Johnston gives is gold, belonging to the chain of being of the sun, Helios, not Aphrodite/Venus. It is the theurgist's knowledge and memory applied to this operation that makes it the technical art.

In the Chaldean oracle fragment 224, Hekate gives instructions for making her statue. She instructs the theurgist to use incense, myrrh, and frankincense; an herb, wild rue; and an animal, a small lizard. But how were the materials applied? They could have been inserted into a hollow statue. It was also possible to take the substances, mix them with clay or wax, and form the body of the statue.

Invocation into a Person

Invocation into a person brings the power of deity into a living human body. The term the Chaldean Oracles use for calling a deity into another is "binding and loosing." This is different and separate from the act of bringing the deity into ourselves, called "conjunction."

The operation of binding and loosing required someone to call the divine force, the caller, and another person to receive the divine force, the receiver. Julian the Chaldean and Julian the Theurgist used exactly this operation to generate the Chaldean Oracles. Not surprisingly, the oracles themselves record a lot of information about the process.

Sarah Iles Johnston cites other examples of calling and receiving from the Greek Magical Papyri. In "Charming Children: The Use of the Child in Ancient Divination," she argues that the practice of using another person as a medium is an adaptation of the processes used by the oracles at Delphi and other locations around the Hellenistic world.

The mediums used in theurgic operations were very often children, as they were considered to be closer to the gods, less likely to contaminate the speech of the gods with their own imaginings and were considered more likely to be clear channels. That was the reason magicians gave consciously, but Johnston notes that they may have had unconscious reasons as well: as children are suggestible, unconsciously the callers may have recognized that children were more likely to give the results the caller wished to get. The spells themselves indicate that the children were given suggestions as to what they should be seeing.

We suspect that the interest the Chaldean magicians took in Sosipatra as a child was connected with her use as a medium, and her biography notes that she later demonstrated the ability to see the future and to see what was happening at a distance.

Johnston also notes that the spells in the papyri don't necessarily call the deity directly into the child; the deity might be called to an oil lamp or bowl of water. The child might see visions in the fire or water, or they might directly perceive the deities. In either case the deity talked to the child who then transmitted what they said to the operator.

On the topic of child participation in theurgic ritual, it is up to parents whether their children may be involved in ritual; however, any magical act involving children should benefit the children—they are not tools but living beings shaped by their experiences. For modern practitioners, adult magicians should conduct the operation acting as seers for one another—this is effective, appropriate, and ethical.

Ruth Majercik notes that caller and receiver first purified themselves with fire and water and clothed themselves in special garments. Johnston has combed the Greek magical papyri to reconstruct the sequence of the operation. The theurgist specifically could call daimones, angels, and gods. The caller blindfolded the receiver, called the god or spirit into the receiver using incantations and synthema, removed the blindfold, and then instructed the receiver to "gaze" at a candle flame or a bowl of liquid—oil, water, or a combination. This sequence was repeated until the god or spirit appeared and communicated to the receiver, who relayed the communication of the god or spirit to the caller.

Once the channel had been established, the caller could ask questions of the receiver to relay to the god. As Proklos pointed out, this permitted divination to occur. The deity could impart an understanding of what might happen in the future. When the rite was completed, the caller could end the process. The receiver could also end the rite by turning the mind toward earthly things.

Ruth Majercik has surveyed the signs Iamblichus listed indicating success in this operation. The receiver's body could become immobile, or their body and face could move, or their body could levitate. There were visions of light that could come from the receiver's body. Visions might be seen only by the receiver or they might also be seen by the caller.

While these deities sometimes appeared in their traditional guise, in anthropomorphic (human) or theriomorphic (animal) form, they quite often appeared in their true form as fire or light. Majercik adds that the oracles list the types of fiery visions the receiver might see, including a child, a horse, a light, and a formless fire.

Invocation into Yourself

Invoking deity into yourself was a special form of "binding and loosing" called "conjunction." In this form of invocation, the ancient theurgist was both caller and receiver. The Chaldean Oracles and the Greek Magical Papyri contain examples of the ritual action of calling the deity into oneself.

Ruth Majercik describes the operation. The theurgist called on the god using "barbarous names" listed in detail in the Greek magical papyri. The theurgist also used sounds, including the Greek vowel sounds and repeated consonant sounds, also found in the papyri. The theurgist could hold or wear stones and other substances containing the power of the god, and chant the name of the god repeatedly.

CONTEMPORARY PRACTICE

Theurgic ritual is performed today. To a Witch, Ceremonial magician, or Pagan student of history, the rituals performed by Hellenistic era magicians two thousand years ago seem very familiar. The spells in the papyri are strikingly comprehensible. Our world is contiguous with the world in which these rituals were created, and there is a traceable connection through the literature of Neo-Platonic philosophy, so it should not be surprising that the rituals themselves expressing this philosophy are understandable to us.

One of the interesting things about Pagan theurgy is that it bridges contemporaneous traditions that have seemed to be at odds. Specifically, brings together the understanding of the gods from Pagan religion and the survivals of theurgy from Witchcraft and Ceremonial Magic. For those of us who work in all these traditions, theurgy is a way to explain to others why we find them to be compatible, calling attention to the shared historical substratum of English-speaking traditions, and providing a common vocabulary for trading insights and practices.

Pagans, Witches, and Ceremonial magicians may simply add theurgic ritual to our existing practice, or engage in the rituals we already perform with a deeper understanding of the meaning of theurgy. However, it is not necessary to become a Witch or take a Ceremonial initiation to practice theurgy. We can study the texts and perform the rituals to create our own practice.

Ritual Garb and Ritual Space

Theurgy is a modest discipline and starts in the home. Many Pagan and magical paths call for the dedicant to acquire special tools. These include clothing—many traditions use black robes, some call for white robes, and some call for wearing nothing at all. Many rites also involve special jewelry, for example a ring worn only during rituals, amber and jet necklaces, silver bracelets, or planetary talismans. Some rites require an altar or other equipment to be constructed or a room dedicated to the performance of the rites.

To conduct a theurgic rite, it isn't necessary to invest in elaborate tools or clothing. You are free to dedicate a room, a robe, and special jewelry to this magic. To start with, however, all you need is a simple altar. A small table decorated with a white cloth will do. You may add a white candle, flowers, greenery, or incense, as you wish.

However, it is a prudent idea to wear some sort of protective jewelry while doing this work. Witches may wear a silver pentagram, Thelemites may wear a unicursal hexagram, Pagans may wear specific stones or symbols reflecting deity. This protective jewelry doesn't have to be elaborate or expensive; I made my favorite protective lamen (pendant) from jewelry clay and inscribed the disk with an ouroboros, a snake biting its own tail, an image found frequently in the Greek Magical Papyri.

Whether we are evoking deity to a statue or invoking deity into another or ourselves, the work should be contained within a ritual space. Creating the ritual space centers our mind and energies on the work at hand. It also provides protection from influences that might seek to disrupt our work, including the "dogs" or negative daimones the Chaldean Oracles warn us about.

Witches and Ceremonial magicians have ways of creating ritual space. Witches can cast a circle. Golden Dawn magicians can do a Lesser Banishing Ritual of the Pentagram to cleanse a space. They can also do an Invoking Ritual of the Pentagram with a specific element or planet in mind.

Thelemites have Crowley's wonderful ritual of the Star Ruby, drawing specifically on the entities from the Chaldean Oracles. The ritualist says in Greek:

"Before me the Iynges, Behind me the Teletarches, on my right hand the Synoches, on my left hand the Daemones."

Chapter 17, "Theurgic Ritual Workbook," contains a ritual to create sacred space, "Ritual of the Theurgist."

Devotional to a Deity

Whether we evoke deity into a statue or invoke deity into another person or ourselves, theurgic practice centers on devotional to a deity. But which deity?

Plato talked about the soul choosing a guide for its life on earth, a personal deity. Some Pagans identify themselves as primarily guided by a specific deity. Some theurgists may immediately gravitate toward this idea but it is not necessary. We can offer devotion to any deity, and we may stop offering devotionals when it makes sense to us as well.

Devotionals can be offered both to individual deities and groups of deities. Most deities have an identity as part of a pantheon; for the sake of balance, it is important to offer a devotional to the entire set of deities as well as the individual deity, however minimal the recognition might be.

Devotional to a particular deity or set of deities begins by learning everything we can about the deity. In the case of the Olympians, groups of theurgists in the Athenian and Alexandrian Academies sometimes began their study and practice by reciting the Homeric and Orphic hymns for the deity. The theurgist can make an altar for the deity, or a pantheon of deities. Offerings can be made daily or on specific feast days.

Aleister Crowley gives a complete description of theurgic devotion in "ASTARTE vel Liber BERYLLI sub figura CLXXV," subtitled "the Book of Uniting Himself to a particular Deity by devotion." This work is deceptively short; it is profound and well worth study. In the first few lines the work covers: choosing a deity, creating a shrine, placing an image of the deity in the shrine, writing a prayer, and making an offering.

Among other recommendations, Crowley lists the attitudes the devotee may take toward the deity, approaching the god as a slave, vassal, child, priest (we may add priestess), brother (we may add sister), friend, and lover.

Noting that some deities require blood sacrifice, Crowley advises "let these sacrifices be replaced by the true sacrifices in thine own heart. Yet if thou must symbolize them outwardly for the hardness of thine heart, let thine own blood, and not another's, be spilt before that altar." This is a lovely re-conceptualization of sacrifice and a worthy approach to take in the modern world.

Evocation into a Statue

The process of evoking deity into statues exists in other cultures today, notably in Hindu and Buddhist religion. However, until recently the rite of animating statues had fallen out of use in Western esotericism, and with good reason: the Christian suppression of Pagan religion specifically targeted statues of deity, and Islam also objects to anthropomorphized images of deity. The use of a statue to represent deity and to act as a vessel for deity is one of the definitive forms of Western Pagan devotional and is newly returned to the practice of theurgy.

This operation involves these steps:

- Collect synthema
- Obtain image

- Evoke deity
- Make offerings

First, how do we choose a deity to animate? This should be a god/goddess who you work with every day, one to whom you have offered devotion over a period of time. You can begin with one operation, live with the animated statue for some time, and decide whether you wish to engage in the operation again with another deity. How many statues you choose to animate will depend on the frequency and depth of your interaction with the living god.

Which pantheons are appropriate to animate? Certainly any of the Greek, Kemetic, and Mesopotamian deities were all accustomed to inhabiting statues. Hindu and Buddhist deities still inhabit statues. Deities outside these pantheons have also been evoked by contemporary theurgists.

It is most important to follow the instructions of the deities themselves, as recorded in the Chaldean Oracles or magical texts, or in invocations to the deity. In devotional to the deity, ask the goddess or god what is appropriate as an offering and whether this operation will be appropriate. Listen carefully to the answer. You could also conduct a divination—do a tarot reading or ask the deity to send you a dream.

COLLECT SYNTHEMA

What substances are associated with the deity? From the point of view of Neo-Platonism, the gods are woven through the world like threads in a tapestry. Each deity has correspondences in the animal, vegetable, and mineral worlds. Qabbalah assembled these correspondences and attached them to the planets, making a handy reference system for looking up substances associated with deities of the planets. For example, appropriate substances for a statue of Hermes include carnelian and citrine, lavender and lemon, the color orange, and the caduceus wand.

We will need to research every deity individually to find specific substances historically associated with them. As we have seen, in the Chaldean oracle fragment 224, Hekate gives myrrh, frankincense, wild rue, and a lizard as her specific materials. In *Practical Magic for Beginners,* I give a list of correspondences with the planets.

This association of physical object to specific deities is not incidental, something we do on the way to evoking the gods. The search for synthema is the treasure hunt to find the gods in the world. We see the sun in everything colored gold: in the metal gold, in sunflowers, in all flowers that turn their face to the sun, in the smoke of frankincense, in a topaz, in the sweetness of honey and the movements of bees. We find the moon in the scent of night-blooming jasmine, in silver, in stones colored with the moon's milky brilliance, in the sound of the owl. We find the earth as we walk through the woods, the deep green of pine needles, the red of autumn leaves and spring buds, the flash of light-colored bark, the darkness of the deep earth beneath our feet. A moss agate held in the hand, a white stone streaked with green veins, seems to trace the characters of the earth in the stone itself.

We look for the signs of the gods and the world seems to be filled with them. This finding is not simply a matter of learning lists of correspondences and memorizing them, of the rational mind learning what the gods mean. It is in the walk in the woods itself, keeping ourselves open to the mysteries, the flash of insight that teaches us where the gods live. Theurgists collect these things and bring them back to our altars in order to coalesce the essence of the gods that we seek.

OBTAIN IMAGE

Where can we obtain statues? Representations of Hermes and other statues of the gods commercially available today are generally sold as museum replicas that rarely include a hollow space for inserting objects.

One option is to create a statue of the chosen deity. The Greek Magical Papyri give instructions for using wax to form images. If making your own image, wax or clay will allow you to add substances to the material.

Purchasing a commercially made deity figurine or image is another possibility. In this case, personal touches can be added: consider painting the statue or attaching a clay symbol such as a caduceus for Hermes or a shield for Athena. In particular, we can paint the eyes and mouth of the deity to make them distinct.

Where will we put the synthema? If we are using a commercially made statue, we can construct a custom base with a hollow that can accommodate the physical items, and then place the statue on that base. We can also construct a small shrine and place the items and statue together in the shrine. We can sew, knit or glue clothing that incorporates the colors, stones, and herbs to be placed on the statue. It is also possible to place all of these objects in water and then paint or bathe the statue with that water so the essence of those materials is placed on the statue.

We will also need to decide where we will keep the deity. Some theurgists simply keep animated statues on a shelf where they can watch over the theurgist every day. Others construct shrines that can be opened to work with the deity and then closed again to protect the living god. Prepare this place before conducting the ritual to animate the statue.

EVOKE DEITY

Our situation today is analogous to the Hellenistic magician. There are no large Pagan temples enshrining deities where we can go to contact the deity, or to obtain advice or tools from the staff. However, we do have the text of the "Opening of the Mouth," which can be adapted for personal use. Richard Reidy in his excellent book *Eternal Egypt* gives an example of that adaptation. His work is well worth reading for all contemporary theurgists and in particular those working with the deities of Kemet. We can also study the magical papyri for examples of animating small statues.

We will need to create our own tools to open the eyes and mouth of the statue. The Metropolitan Museum has an image of a model of these tools called "Model of the 'Opening of the Mouth'" ritual equipment: www.metmuseum.org/collections/search-the-collections/543920. The main tool is a v-shaped tool that could touch to the eyes and mouth of the statue. This tool can be constructed from clay, carved from wood, or even cut from cardboard and painted.

MAKE OFFERINGS

Offerings to the deity may take a number of forms. They may be offered daily or on special feast days.

- **Prayers and hymns:** you can make a collection of hymns and prayers to the deity. You can also write your own prayers. Some deities prefer to be offered prayers rather than any more physical substance.

- **Chants:** You may find a chant for your deity or create one.

- **Incense:** this is almost always appropriate to any deity. Some deities prefer to be offered incense rather than any other substance. The type of incense should reflect the deity's preferences as well.

- **Drink:** Liquid offerings can include water, milk, wine, olive oil, or honey. Some deities such as Bona Dea require milk and reject wine; for Dionysos, wine is the required offering. Know your deity!

- **Food:** Cheese, meat, bread, and sweets can all be part of the offerings. Some deities require meat, others will reject it.

Richard Reidy cautions against offering modern food prepared with preservatives such as candy, cereal, canned foods. I agree that these are not suitable. These items often contain non-food substances and are not particularly healthy for humans. In general, if your great-grandmother wouldn't have recognized it as food, it's not food and not a good offering. Stick with fresh food for the gods. (Fresh food for ourselves is a good idea, too!)

Once the offering has been made to the deity, what next? Temple priestesses and priests ate the offerings once the deity had had an opportunity to consume it; food offered to deity was made sacred and the benefit returned to the person eating it. In practice, you may either eat the food, or place it outdoors for animals such as birds to eat. It is quite practical to prepare your own breakfast, offer it to deities, and after a period of time, consume it yourself.

The exception is salt—it poisons earth and makes it impossible for plants to grow where it is placed. Salt should be eaten, used in ritual, or disposed of in running water.

Customs regarding how to manage the statue once it has been animated vary widely from practitioner to practitioner. The operator should already know what items the deity normally requires – incense, water, wine, milk, cheese, or any other substance. How often should they be offered? Richard Reidy requires his students to commit to reanimating the statue and feeding and worshiping it daily, even while traveling. I am aware of practitioners who animate statues and leave them in the open, or close them in shrines to protect them but do not interact with them every day. Each operator will experiment, and results will vary depending on both the nature of the deity and the ability and predilection of the operator.

In any event, this operation should be done after considerable time has been spent in devotional to that deity. It is meant to be a deepening of relationship with that deity, a more intimate connection of human and divine.

Over the course of time, the deity will communicate preferences to the practitioner. Reconstructionists tend to value this information quite a bit less than academic information, calling it unverifiable personal gnosis (UPG). However, groups of priestesses and priests working with the same deity can trade notes and bring new information about the deity. What is important in your relationship to deity is how well you feel that you yourself are connecting with that deity.

A note on animal sacrifice: spells in the Greek papyri call for sacrificing animals for a statue to be brought to life. First, if the idea is to capture the life force of the animal in the statue, this is contraindicated for theurgists, who are attempting to call a deity into the statue. Next, few of us today have the experience or skill to do so humanely. Do you keep chickens? Have you ever tried to butcher one for dinner? It is an apprenticeship skill best learned from someone who already knows how to do it. We owe the animals we keep a quick and painless death.

Some contemporary theurgists are vegetarian and cite Pythagoras and other ancients who ate little or no meat. Each of us individually must decide what we eat and what we offer our deities, but sacrifice of live animals is not necessary to the operation. As we have seen, if you feel such a sacrifice is necessary, theurgist Aleister Crowley suggested substituting your own blood for that of another living creature.

Invocation into a Person

In Witchcraft, deity invocation is performed by a paired priestess and priest. Janet and Stewart Farrar describe the priest evoking a goddess into the priestess as "Drawing Down the Moon" and the priestess evoking a god into the priest as "Drawing Down the Sun." They describe this operation in *The Witches' Goddess*. During a coven ritual, the priest invokes the goddess into the priestess, for example the goddess Aphrodite; then the priestess calls the god Pan or Eros into the priest. The rest of the coven leaves, and the priest and goddess proceed "as Aphrodite inspires them."

When we combine our knowledge of the Hellenistic tradition and contemporary practice such as drawing down the moon and sun, we can detect these common patterns:

- The ritual should proceed in a purified space.
- The receiver must be purified.
- The caller must also be purified.
- The receiver must signify in some way their receptivity.
- Invoking is accompanied by sounds, including chanting, singing, and drumming.
- The caller should understand how to release the deity at the end of the ritual.
- The operation can be conducted by one person who both calls and receives deity; by two people, one of whom calls and one of whom receives; or in a group context, with multiple people witnessing and/or receiving the spirit.

A note on gender: although "Drawing Down the Moon" and "Drawing Down the Sun" as described in *The Witches' Goddess* is a heterosexual rite, this operation need not be limited to the male-female heterosexual polarity. Today people of all genders invoke deity of all genders into people of all genders. The original Chaldean operation involved two men, probably a father and son. We know that Hellenistic women also engaged in binding and loosing and conjunction—Proklos argued that women's souls were divine because the gods entered them. The ancients were experimental and practical; why shouldn't our contemporary practice be experimental and practical too?

The advantage of binding and loosing, working with a partner, is that there is a separation between the person who is asking questions and the person who is communicating with the deity. A lone operator can be lost in the ineffable experience of touching the divine and forget to finish the operation. When two people conduct the operation, the receiver is free to sink into the experience while the caller provides the focus—asking the questions or charging the talisman—making sure the work gets done.

Invocation into Yourself

Assumption of God Form is an example of invocation into yourself in the Golden Dawn tradition. Golden Dawn writers frequently note that the operation called Assumption of God Form was considered to be an advanced operation and was not taught until a student had done significant work.

Interestingly, the founders of the Golden Dawn were at pains to distinguish this operation from Spiritualist mediumship. In a blog post about spiritualist channeling, "Astral Masters and the Golden Dawn," contemporary Imperator of the Golden Dawn David Griffin says: "Unlike today's New Age community, the Golden Dawn, from its very inception in 1888, always has been very clear in its condemnation of these kind of practices as potentially dangerous for the human spirit. The Golden Dawn tradition has always scorned passive mediumship and idealized active seership as the only true alternative for a Magician." Griffin quotes the 1888 form of the oath taken by the Neophyte: "I will not suffer myself to be hypnotized, or mesmerized, nor will I place myself in such a passive state that any uninitiated person, power, or being may cause me to lose control of my thoughts, words or actions."

We should note that Spiritualists themselves may not characterize what they do as passive or as losing control of their own thoughts or actions. Whatever the reasons for the Golden Dawn rejection of Spiritualist mediumship, the contemporary theurgist may profit from a study of all forms of spirit possession.

There are several occasions calling for Assumption of God Form. In *Ceremonial Magic: A Guide to the Mechanisms of Ritual*, Israel Regardie describes the Neophyte Initiation of the Golden Dawn as a re-enactment of the judgment of the deceased of the Egyptian Book of the Dead. In this ritual the initiate takes the part of the deceased, while the officers take on the identities of the deities who undertake the judgment, striking the characteristic physical pose of the deity. In *Self-Initiation into the*

Golden Dawn Tradition, Chic and Sandra Tabitha Cicero note that this representation of the force of the deity they call an "officer-form" is a less advanced operation than a full assumption of god-form.

The Ciceros further describe the operation of god-form assumption. The operator builds up a mental image of the form of the deity, traces a sigil of the deity, and vibrates the name of the deity. (Vibration is a Ceremonial Magic vocal technique in which the magician chants a name or word in a way that causes the body to "vibrate" energetically.) The operator then steps into the form of the deity that has been astrally energized, literally assuming the form of the deity. The Ciceros note that the operator is meant to temporarily inhabit the deity form, not become possessed by the deity.

Once the god-form has been assumed, the magician can consecrate a talisman, banish spirits, or act as an officer in initiation while acting within the form of the deity. Or, the operation may be conducted simply to learn more about the deity.

ADVANTAGES AND DISADVANTAGES

The advantage of conjunction, invoking deity into yourself, is that the operator need not find another person to work with, but can proceed with the operation at any time.

In an age when we use gods as psychological constructs, it is important to note that theurgy presumes that the gods are not metaphors or psychological archetypes but are real entities. When we invoke them into our bodies, they are energic presences sharing our bodies with us. While this form of body-sharing has many benefits, it also comes with risks.

The benefits of this operation are manifold. For the person who is inhabited by deity, this is an extraordinary experience resulting in an influx of knowledge, and a sense of having been truly in contact with the divine. People who share this experience can become very close as a consequence.

There are also risks. For example, the operation might get the wrong spirit. The oracles themselves note that the spirit who comes to the call might or might not be the deity actually called. The spirit might in fact be the soul of a deceased person or a mischievous or malicious daemon masquerading as the deity. The oracles enjoined the practitioners to ignore any phantom such as these. In "Homo Fictor Deorum Est" Johnston notes that Hellenistic practitioners spent a great deal of time learning the signs to recognize genuine deities and detect intruding spirit. The same is true today for Ceremonial magicians, who are taught to challenge spirits whose form does not fit what was expected from the invocation; for example, an invocation to Mars should not result in a form dressed in white wearing a crescent moon crown, attributes suitable to the moon.

Another risk is thinking too much of ourselves. The Greeks called the act of identifying ourselves with the powers the gods loan to us as "hubris" and warned that a mighty rise can bring on a mighty fall. The operator who frequently engages in carrying a particular deity is in danger of identifying with the powers of that deity. Ceremonial magicians warn about this possibility in nearly every discussion of assumption of god-form. One term for this is "god inflation." A god-inflated person may become irascible, arrogant, make decrees from consciousness as if they were coming from deity, and expect in general to be adored and worshiped. Another form god inflation can take is to believe that one's personal deity is the supreme deity exalted above all others and publicly proclaim this. While this is common in monotheistic religion, in polytheistic religion this is generally unwelcome.

It is important in these cases to deflate the individual. It is helpful if someone who the medium trusts can be persuaded to talk to that person and let them know it has been detected. Sometimes the operator will themselves identify this issue and ask for assistance. Once the operator is aware of the issue and is actively working to resolve it, the first step is to cease contacting the deity or working as a receiver for some period of time.

To prevent god inflation from occurring, it is advisable to ground the energy of the deity at the conclusion of each operation. Grounding is a word that means connecting the earth. We use this in electrical terms to mean taking electricity and putting it in the ground so that it becomes harmless. Exactly the same thing is meant when we use this to discuss grounding deity and magical energy – the power is placed into the earth itself, removed from the body of the operator, and made harmless.

The magical communities have evolved a number of mechanisms for grounding. One way is to dedicate a piece of jewelry, such as a necklace or a lamen with the sigil of the deity, for exclusive usage while engaged in work with that deity. The receiver puts on the object, engages in the activity, and removes the item as soon as the activity is completed.

Witchcraft groups often touch the ground at the conclusion of the ceremony, sending any excess energy into the earth. This literal grounding can also be done as a form of loosing. Many groups eat immediately after such operations as this has an immediate grounding effect. Some people find sexual activity to be grounding as well. By the way, it is a hoary chestnut for the unscrupulous to insist this is necessary ("you have to ground with sex!") to a person who sexually interests them. It is not.

The oracles themselves recommend turning the mind toward earthly things. This might include visualizing beautiful scenes of the earth and getting in touch with the feelings of the physical body.

Practicing good magical technique is the best form of prevention. We can use magical protection such as talismans; pay attention to eating, sleeping, and maintaining our personal lives; keep a magical diary to pinpoint whatever happens; and work with others who will let us know when we are overreaching.

ADVANCED THEURGIC OPERATIONS

There are two more operations that are important to theurgic practice, performed by theurgists in the past and today.

These are:

- Meeting with one's own daimon
- Rising through the worlds

The operation calling one's personal guiding spirit is performed by Ceremonial magicians today, although the spirit is now called "angel" rather than "daimon."

Meeting with One's Own Daimon

What is a personal daimon? Scholars differ about when exactly this idea arose in Greek religion. Daimones were understood to be beings between humans and gods who could be both beneficial and malicious. How did they come to be associated with the individual?

The "daimonion" of Socrates was famous. In numerous dialogues, Plato mentions the action of this guardian spirit who said no whenever Socrates was about to take an action that would harm him. Most famously, since the daimonion did not warn him against the trial that resulted in his death, Socrates accepted the verdict.

In *Greek Popular Religion in Greek Philosophy*, Jon Mikalson argues that this understanding of the daimonion differed from the popular understanding of *daimones* and that this was one of the things that made Socrates a target for his enemies. Socrates was specifically accused of creating new gods, the daimonion being an example. Mikalson makes the case that this daimonion of Socrates led Plato to create the idea that daimones acted as intermediaries between gods and humans.

One defense offered for Socrates's daimonion is that it was not a new god but a form of divination. The Greek Magical Papyri seem to treat speaking with daimones as a type of divination, as in spell PGM VII. 505-28, "Meeting with your own daimon." This spell begins with an invocation to Tyche, the deity of fate.

The personal daimon is a separate being who is in charge of the fate of the individual human and can be conjured to answer questions. Porphyry told the story of the magician who offered to evoke the personal daimon of Plotinus. They did so in the temple of Isis, the only pure place in Rome the magician could find. When the personal guide of Plotinus turned out to be not a daimon but a god, the operation fell apart before Plotinus had a chance to ask questions.

Later Platonic tradition understood the personal daimon in the sense of being a guide. Marinus, the biographer of Proklos, noted that Proklos journeyed to Asia to his profit, "for his guardian spirit (daimonion) furnished him the occasion of this departure in order that he might not remain ignorant of the ancient religious institutions which had been there preserved."

To later Neo-Platonists, the personal daimon was more than just a spirit to conjure for divination or a guide. The personal daimon was a direct connection to deity. In her work *Neoplatonism,* Paulina Remes points to passages in Plato indicating the goal of an individual life is to become godlike. The human strives to be good and to focus on spiritual rather than material gain. But exactly how godlike are we to attempt to be? If we succeed, aren't we becoming other-than-human? Is it possible to identify with the intellectual or Empyrean realm, Nous or the One, and remain embodied?

The answer lies with the personal daimon. Moving from the experience of human individuality directly to connection with the source of all is a big leap. When the theurgist first seeks communion with the daimon, and only then with a deity, the daimon acts as a stepping-stone to the world of the divine. The union proceeds in steps, a gradual perfection of the human spirit.

Shaw reads Iamblichus as saying that the guardian deity of an individual human soul assigns a daimon to the soul. Through theurgic operations the daimon appears to the soul and reveals the daimon's name. The soul identifies with the daimon through the use of this name. The daimon eventually merges with the soul. Then the united daimon/soul is guided by the deity.

In "The Delphic Maxim," Betz detects a similar formula in the Mithras Liturgy. The magician invokes the deity through a secret name the deity has provided to her. Next, the magician identifies herself with the deity through a series of steps:

"Your name is mine and mine is yours," then "I am your image," then "you are I and I am you."

Christian theology lost the idea of personal deity and altered the understanding of daimones: every human being connects directly with the single monad, and daimones are no longer understood to be both good and evil; instead, demons are wholly evil, and only angels are good. Now instead of "meeting with one's own daimon," we meet with our "holy guardian angel" assigned to us at birth.

The name of the operation shifted as well. In medieval magic we no longer sought our own daimones, but our personal angel. In contemporary Ceremonial Magic the operations is called "Knowledge and Conversation of the Holy Guardian Angel." A medieval form of this ritual is found in a German manuscript translated by Golden Dawn founder Samuel Liddell MacGregor Mathers as *The Sacred Magic of Abra-Melin the Mage*. The manuscript describes a lengthy retreat with elaborate preparations to accomplish the operation of meeting one's own angel.

Many Ceremonial orders have some form of this operation. "Knowledge and Conversation of the Holy Guardian Angel" is a central Thelemic operation. Works of the Aurum Solis order discuss the operation. In Louis Culling's book *Complete Magick Curriculum of the Secret Order G.B.G.*, the first chapter heading is "The Ultimate Aim of Magick, the Knowledge and Conversation of One's Holy Guardian Angel."

Ceremonial Magic's operation can be complicated, requiring years of preparation. Further, the operation does not have a specific ritual. Instead, each individual magician creates her or his own methodology for accomplishing this. In *Book Four* Crowley comments, "It is impossible to lay down precise rules by which a man may attain to the knowledge and conversation of His Holy Guardian Angel; for that is the particular secret of each one of us; a secret not to be told or even divined by any other, whatever his grade. It is the Holy of Holies, whereof each man is his own High Priest, and none knoweth the Name of his brother's God, or the Rite that invokes Him."

We must note here that both the monotheistic overtones of the term "holy guardian angel" and the male-centric language in which it is described have constituted a bar for Pagans, especially Pagan women and people of other genders to approach this operation. Returning to the Mithras Liturgy, addressed to a woman in Hellenistic Pagan language, provides us with a new perspective allowing Pagans of all genders easier access to the ritual.

Theurgists may engage in this operation whenever they feel drawn to it. The sense of longing for connection is the most important prerequisite. Certainly, it is prudent to engage in a great deal of meditation and contemplation as well as ritual practice. All of the practices of invoking and evoking deity will help prepare for this moment. In all the chain of being, from the One to the many deities, daimones, guides, and teachers, this operation is unique in that the personal daimon is specific to the individual. It is literally the most intimate relationship the operator can have with any entity.

It is love that compels this operation. Metaphors of erotic union and marriage are not out of place here. The personal daimon will manifest to the individual in the way in which the individual feels most appropriate. Heterosexist language presumes a male operator and female daimon, but the actual epiphany is unique. A woman who loves women may find that her daimon manifests to her as a woman, the man who loves men may experience a male daimon, the gender of the daimon may shift from occasion to occasion or be irrelevant, or the daimon may come in the form of light, heat, or another sensation. As Crowley expressed so poetically, magicians almost never speak of their experience not only because it is so personal, but because it is ineffable, difficult to express in words.

Rising through the Worlds

Communion is the culminating operation of the theurgic system. It is the fulfilment of the promise of the system to make the soul immortal, to return the soul to its true home in the stars, to return the soul to the state of being a star.

The ancients used the term "anagoge" to describe the operation. This is often translated as "ascent" and seems to have been used in that way by the ancients. But how are we rising, and what are we rising to?

In "Rising to the Occasion, Theurgic Ascent in its Cultural Milieu," Sarah Iles Johnston analyzes the Chaldean Oracles and the Mithras liturgy from the Greek Magical Papyri to reconstruct the rite of ascent or communion. In the oracles and in the Mithras Liturgy, the operator sought an experience of particular deities. In the case of the oracles, the deities were Hekate and Apollo, while the Mithras Liturgy identifies the practitioner with Hermes as the personal deity, continuing to a vision of Helios, god of the sun. The soul then passes through the gate of the sun, with Helios as a guide, the ultimate result of which is a visionary revelation.

We can find many examples of mystic visions revealing the hierarchies of the cosmos. Although the Mithras Liturgy specifies the exact deities to be experienced, we may take this as an example rather than a precise guide to what we ourselves will experience. The key here is to invoke our own personal daimon to guide the soul in this experience.

The Mithras Liturgy and the Chaldean Oracles note as the soul rises the theurgist casts a symbola in the mind. In this case, Johnston believes the symbola is a password. These passwords were not recorded, probably by design. In the Mithras Liturgy, the soul is instructed to say "I am a star, wandering about with you." However this phrase itself is probably not the actual password.

These passwords were transmitted orally, and we don't seem to have a written example of one, so what password can we use? There are several possible approaches to finding our own particular passwords: as Johnston notes, a guardian spirit may protect the journey, so calling the personal daimon to aid in the ascent would certainly be appropriate. The password may also include the secret name the personal deity has given to the theurgist.

Johnston notes that the theurgist may encounter more than one challenge during the journey and pass through multiple gates. This association suggests that the ascent may be constructed not as a single working but as a series of workings where the operator travels each time farther along the path in successive ascents.

SEVENTEEN

THEURGIC RITUAL WORKBOOK

This chapter contains rituals to accomplish the theurgic operations:

- Evoke deity into statue
- Invoke deity into another
- Invoke deity into yourself
- Meeting with your own daimon
- Rising through the worlds

MEDITATION TO CLEAR THOUGHT

This meditation can be performed at any time on its own, or as the first step in any of the rituals in this chapter.

Stand, sit, or lie down. Take a deep breath and exhale completely. Pay attention to your breathing. You can count your breaths; you can focus on the breath as it enters and leaves your nostrils;

you can notice your breath moving deep into your abdomen. The important thing is to work to empty your mind of thought. If a thought arises and brings you away from noticing your breath, let it go and return to watching your breath.

If you want, you can time this activity. Set a timer for five minutes, adding time in ten-minute increments, up to half an hour, then an hour. You could also count breaths up to a certain number.

RITUAL OF HONORING THE ANCESTORS

There is no definitive or authoritative list of Neo-Platonic teachers, saints, or ancestors. Each of us is free to create our own list of teachers, adding those who speak to us. The ritual below is an example of a rite to honor our teachers; each theurgist will modify this with our own choices, invocations, and offerings.

The teachers we turn to for understanding theurgic theology are Iamblichus, Asklepigenia, and Proklos. While we do not have any writings bearing Asklepigenia's name, we may see her teachings in the writings of Proklos. In the context of invocation, we should remember that it was Asklepigenia who taught theurgic ritual to Proklos. It is appropriate to begin theurgic practice with an invocation to these teachers to guide us. As the ancients did, it is also helpful to invoke the spirit of memory, Mnemosyne, to start the ritual.

Create the Altar

We may set aside a small shelf or table for representations of the teachers. This could be an artist's depiction of the teacher, a photograph of an ancient bust, or an object that represents the teacher for you, such as a flower, a stone, or a book. In a more modern vein, a theurgist working today can pull up an image of a teacher and keep it as wallpaper on a computer, tablet, or phone.

In addition to the Neo-Platonic teachers, we can add the names and images of personal teachers and our families to our ancestor altar as it feels appropriate.

We may also use a small table for offerings. The offerings may be as simple as a bit of incense, or as elaborate as a meal including water, wine, and food.

Light the Ancestor Candle

Light a white candle. Take a few deep breaths and clear your mind.

Speak the invocations. You may use any of these or create invocations of your own.

CALL TO THE ANCESTORS

I call on those who have come before me,
Ancestors of my body and spirit.
I walk in the world now,
The link between the future and the past.
As I walk in my day
Grant me the support that ancestors can give
And welcome me into your number when
my living journey is done.

INVOCATION TO MNEMOSYNE

I invoke Mnemosyne, Memory, mother of the Muses.
I call on you to assist me.
All the humans who came before me are my ancestors.
All human heritage is mine to honor, learn from, challenge, and grow.
I am a child of earth and of all the gods.
Send me the Muses to aid me,
Guide me to the knowledge I seek,
Help me remember that I am divine.

HYMN TO IAMBLICHUS

Iamblichus Soter, save me!
Divine Iamblichus, guide me.
Show me the unfolding of the cosmos,
Teach me the harmonies of the stars,
Help me remember I am divine.

HYMN TO ASKLEPIGENIA

Asklepigenia Triumphant!
Daughter of the Academy, Priestess of the gods
You who married divine contemplation with human action,
Teach me the rites, the words and gestures,
Lead me through the mysteries,
Make for me a shining path
That fills all my days with grace
And leads me to my blessed home.

HYMN TO PROKLOS

Proklos, great teacher,
Magician and healer,
Philosopher, priest, writer and leader,
Who gathered rites from every quarter
And carefully nurtured the knowledge I seek,
Guide me as I follow in your footsteps,
Show me the way that you have left for me,
The way of the Pagan, the way of the gods.

SPEAKING THE NAMES

The people of Kemet recited names to keep the spirit of the individual alive. You may recite the names of the teachers you wish to honor. Here are the names of teachers we have learned about:

Ptahotep, Imhotep, Shepenupet, Amenirdis, Neitokrity, Ankhesneferibre, Irtyru, Orpheus, Pythagoras, Plato, Perictione, Diotima, Speusippus, Axiothea, Lasthenia, Aristotle, Ammonius, Plotinus, Gemina and Gemina, Amphiclea, Potamun, Amelius, Porphyry, Marcella, Sosipatra, Eustochius, Julian the Theurgist and Julian the Chaldean, Eustathius, Aedesius, Maximus, Philometer, Julian the Emperor, Sallustius, Hypatia, Synesius, Theon, Iamblichus, Olympiodoros, Ulpian, Proklos, Asklepigenia, Plutarch, Syrianus, Archiadas, Aedesia, Heliodorus, Ammonius, Marinus, Isidore, Hegias, Proklos, Damascius, Simplicius, Boethius, Jabir ibn Hayyan, Idris, Solomon ben Judah Ibn Gabirol, Psellos, John Italos, Plethon, John Argyropoulos, Cosimo de Medici, Marsilio Ficino, Pico della Mirandola, Anne Conway, Mary Morton, Tullia d'Aragona, Thomas Taylor, Helena Petrovna Blavatsky, Henry Steel Olcott, Annie Besant, George Robert Stowe Mead, Samuel Liddell MacGregor Mathers, William Westcott, Moina Mathers, Florence Farr, Israel Regardie, Aleister Crowley, Gerald Gardner, Doreen Valiente, Deborah Ann Light, Richard Reidy.

Offering and Petition

When we have finished the invocations, we may make any offerings we have prepared. We may also speak or think any petition we have specifically in mind. Sit quietly, contemplating the candle, allowing the ancestors time to respond.

Conclusion

At the end of the rite, snuff the candle and dispose of any offerings. Make a record of the rite and record your impressions.

RITUAL OF THE THEURGIST

We may choose to begin the rite with honoring the ancestors, including the Invocation to Mnemosyne, Hymn to Iamblichus, Hymn to Asklepigenia, Hymn to Proklos, and speaking the names of the ancestors.

Set Up Altar

On a small table, set a candle. We may choose to add incense. The altar may be decorated with the symbola we have collected. We may also make a simple offering, such as water, milk, or wine, or a small amount of fresh food such as cheese, homemade bread, and fruit.

Dedication

Say:

> I dedicate this practice to Hyparxis, Hekate, Nous, and to my personal daimon who connects me with the ineffable.
>
> I call on the chain of beings connecting the material to the Intelligible World and the Empyrean World. I call on the gods and goddesses, the angels and daimones, the heroes and teachers.
>
> I call on the gods to guide me: Hera and Zeus, Athena and Poseidon, Demeter and Hermes, Aphrodite and Ares, Artemis and Apollo, Hestia and Hephaestus. I call on you that I may understand your true nature.

I call on the Iynges to bring me what I need to complete this task. I call on the Synoches to help me in my rites. I call on the Teletarches to guide me.

Pistis, Teletarch of the Material and Sensible World, fill me with the trust of theourigikes dynameos, the power of theurgy.

Aleitheia, Teletarch of the Intelligible World, fill me with the truth of divine philosophy, theias philosophias.

Eros, Teletarch of the Empyrean World of Forms, fill me with love, erotikes manias, so that I may experience the divine.

Working
At this point the theurgist may engage in any theurgic working.

Conclusion
When the rite is concluded, say:

I honor all the gods. I thank you for the gifts you have given me.

Close down the altar—blow out the candle, extinguish incense, dispose of offerings either by eating or donating to the birds. Record the working.

RITUAL OF DEVOTIONAL TO A DEITY
In this practice, we make a connection with a specific deity.

Choose Deity
In your journal, list the gods that you have worked with. What pantheon did they come from? Which do you continue to honor, which will remain in your past? Next, make a list of deities that you would like to understand better. Are there deities or cultures that call to you?

Next, choose one deity to offer a devotional. This may be a deity you consider your personal deity or one that you wish to establish a relationship with. You may decide to offer a devotional to one of the deities specific to theurgy, for example Hekate, Hermes, or Athena.

Create Altar

On the altar you have set aside for your contemplation and practice, set an image of your deity. It can be either a statue or a picture, but it should be an object that reflects the physical form of the deity. While substances like stones, herbs and other plants, candles, and other objects attract the power of the deity, they do not in themselves constitute a vessel for the deity. A statue is best, but a picture will do for this operation.

Conduct the Ritual of the Theurgist

Cast a circle, conduct a banishing ritual, do the Star Ruby, or perform the Ritual of the Theurgist to the Conduct Working section.

Read Names of Deities

As part of the rite, you may choose to read the names of all the deities in the pantheon you are working with. For example, for a rite of Hera, you might say, "I call on the Olympians: on Zeus and Hera, Aphrodite and Ares, Hermes and Demeter, Apollo and Artemis, Poseidon and Athena, Hestia and Hephaestus."

Evoke the Deity

Next, evoke the deity. For example, after you have called on the Olympians, you can begin the specific evocation by saying "I call on Hera."

Read Prayers and Hymns

If there is an ancient hymn or prayer your research has provided, you can use this. A web search will turn up other devotees of the deity—there are very, very few deities who have no other worshipers! It is also an offering to create your own prayer to evoke the deity.

Make Offering

Offer something physical to the deity. Incense is always appropriate. Each deity generally has preferences for offerings. For example, there are deities who wish to have animals or meat or blood, some deities ask for wine, and some require no blood offerings but instead ask for milk. Research into the preferences of your given deity is part of the devotional.

Once you have made your devotional, you can spend some time meditating in the presence of the deity. You may choose to end the rite with the meditation.

If you wish, this is also the moment to ask for what you need. Humans have been asking the gods/spirits for help, love, comfort, and peace throughout our history as a species. You can bring a problem to the deity, give it to the deity, and then release negative emotions around the problem, or you can ask for something to come into your life.

Once you have made the request, spend time with a quiet mind receptive to the responses of the deity. This response may come in the form of a vision, feeling, words spoken in your mind, or insight. The deity may not respond immediately, but you may then see the effects of the prayer in your life. The deity may also speak in a dream. All these are historically attested as well as experienced by contemporary practitioners.

Give Thanks

Most importantly, end the rite with a prayer of thanks to the deity for the gifts they bring to your life. If it is appropriate to the culture and deity, you may also consume the food offered to the deity.

Conclusion

Close the circle or banish, or perform the conclusion from Ritual of the Theurgist. Record the working.

Devotionals can be complicated and lengthy, or brief but effective. It is also possible to make an offering to more than one deity at the same time, for example in the morning, as part of a daily practice of theurgy.

1. Create altar.

2. Perform Ritual of the Theurgist to the Working section.

3. Read names of deities (optional).

4. Evoke deity.

5. Read prayers and hymns.

6. Make offering.

7. Give thanks.

8. Perform Conclusion from Ritual of the Theurgist.

RITUAL TO DISCOVER SYNTHEMA

Conduct the Ritual of the Theurgist

Cast a circle, conduct a banishing ritual, do the Star Ruby, or perform the Ritual of the Theurgist to the Working section.

Honor the Deity

Recite a prayer or hymn to the deity.

Invoke Iynges

Say:

> Oh (deity name), reveal to me how you are revealed in the world. Iynges, wheels of the gods, bring to me the knowledge

of the synthema of (insert deity name). Let me know the colors, stones, herbs, flowers, metals, sounds, incense, and other substances appropriate for (deity name).

Meditate

Meditate, sitting quietly, letting your mind become quiet to receive the images or sounds or impressions brought by the Iynges. Keep a pad of paper nearby to record impressions as they arise, or dictate into a portable recorder.

Conclusion

When the impressions subside, turn your mind back to the earth. Thank the deity. Close the circle or banish, or perform the conclusion from Ritual of the Theurgist. Record the working.

Outline

1. Perform Ritual of the Theurgist to the Conduct Working section.

2. Honor the deity.

3. Invoke iynges.

4. Meditate.

5. Perform Conclusion from Ritual of the Theurgist.

RITUAL TO ANIMATE A STATUE

Conduct the Ritual of the Theurgist

Cast a circle, conduct a banishing ritual, do the Star Ruby, or perform the Ritual of the Theurgist to the Conduct Working section.

Purify and Consecrate the Statue

Sprinkle salt water on the statue and say, "I purify this with the waters of the sea." Lift the censer and say, "I consecrate this with fire."

If the synthema were not incorporated into the creation of the statue, add them now. Place clothing on the statue, or place objects in the base, or place synthema in a dish of water and brush water onto the statue. Say: "As like calls to like, so these synthema call (deity name) into this image."

Honor the Deity

Recite a prayer or hymn to the deity.

Animate the Statue

Call the deity into the statue. Say: "I call on you, (deity name), to inhabit the body of this statue. Come to the house which has been prepared for you." Use the tools you have created to open the eyes of the statue. Say, "I open your eyes that you may see." Use the tools to open the mouth of the statue. Say, "I open your mouth that you may have sustenance."

Make Offering

Make an offering to the deity of food, drink, incense, or whatever your research and work with the deity have revealed as appropriate.

Meditate

Meditate, sitting quietly, letting your mind become quiet to receive the images or sounds or impressions brought by the deity. Keep a pad of paper nearby to record impressions as they arise or dictate into a portable recorder.

Conclusion

Give thanks. If the deity is in a shrine, close the shrine. Take the offerings and consume or dispose of them. Record the working.

Outline

1. Perform Ritual of the Theurgist to the Working section.

2. Purify and consecrate the statue.

3. Honor the deity.

4. Animate the statue.

5. Make offering.

6. Meditate.

7. Perform Conclusion from Ritual of the Theurgist.

RITUAL OF DAILY DEVOTIONAL TO ANIMATED STATUE

Outline

1. Perform Ritual of the Theurgist to the Working section

2. Open the shrine.

3. Honor the deity.

4. Make offering.

5. Meditate.

6. Close the shrine.

7. Perform Conclusion from Ritual of the Theurgist.

RITUAL TO CALL THE PERSONAL DAIMON

The ritual in this section is deceptively simple. The success of the ritual depends entirely on the preparation for it. To be able to hear our own daimon, we will need to be able to quiet the mind so the daimon can speak. Once we have established contact with our own daimon, the daimon can provide us with further instructions about how to work with the daimon, how to work with our personal deity, and how to rise through the worlds.

Outline

1. Perform Ritual of the Theurgist to the Working section.

2. Ask daimon to appear; ask daimon for name.

3. Commune.

4. Perform Conclusion from Ritual of the Theurgist.

RITUAL OF INVOKING DEITY INTO ANOTHER

This ritual involves two people, one caller and one receiver. Both should purify themselves by bathing before the ritual.

As the ancients did, we may choose to invoke a deity into a candle flame, oil lamp, or bowl of water. We may also choose to invoke the deity directly into the body of our partner.

Invoking deity in the theurgic system is not simply a visualization practice or a metaphor; it is a genuine experience of the gods. As Golden Dawn writers warn, it leads to psychological as well as spiritual changes with physical manifestations. The theurgist will prepare for this operation by engaging in meditation and contemplation and will have spent substantial time in devotional to the deity, possibly including animating a statue of the deity.

Deities invoked in the ancient rituals include Hecate, Hermes, Eros, and Aion. Many other deities can be invoked in this way as well. Appropriate theurgic deities include Hermes, Hecate, and Athena. As with the operation of animating statues, any deity of the Kemetic, Greek, and Roman pantheons is appropriate, and other pantheons may be explored after some research.

Assumption of God form places emphasis on the position of the deity. Study images of the deity. What is their characteristic pose? Seshat provides an excellent example, depicted holding a stylus in one hand and a long narrow tablet in the other. Osiris folds his hands on his chest. Artemis holds a spear and shield, Poseidon holds a trident, Fortuna cradles a cornucopia, Hermes holds a caduceus, Mercury carries a purse.

Synthema

Synthema can be used in invocation as well as evocation. We may create or consecrate a piece of jewelry that will hold the force of the deity. It is helpful to begin with a stone or metal already associated with the deity; for example, the Sumerian goddess Inanna loves lapis lazuli, while blood-red stones such as garnet are appropriate to Ares and Mars.

We may also create a robe dedicated to the deity, in a color appropriate to the deity, even embroidered with the deity's symbols. Just as we offer incense to living gods, essential oils carry the power of deity, and we may anoint your forehead and wrists with cedar for Inanna, rose for Venus, myrrh for Hathor. If using cinnamon oil for Mars or Ares, be careful—it burns!

Prepare Space

The primary ritualist may conduct the Ritual of the Theurgist. If an experienced group is working together, they may proceed with their own ritual space, such as the Witchcraft circle, the Lesser Banishing Ritual of the Pentagram, or any other ritual that is comfortable to the practitioners. The primary ritualist, who should be the caller, should include all participants in the purification and consecration.

Call Deity

The receiver takes the characteristic pose of the deity, imagining the force of the deity surrounding her. Again, women can assume male deity, men can assume female deity, people of all genders or physical attributes can assume any form of deity. The caller reads prayers and hymns to the deity, concluding by saying, "I call on you, (deity name), to enter your priest/ priestess/vessel!"

The caller should always assume that the invocation has succeeded and proceed as if this is so, addressing the receiver by the name of the deity and asking the questions or conducting the rite at hand. Your sense of confidence transmits directly to the receiver.

Just as the caller does, the receiver should always assume that the invocation has succeeded and proceed as if this is so. For the receiver the depth of the experience varies tremendously, from "Did that really happen?" to woozy entrancement. The receiver may feel a prickling at the back of the neck or a sensation of heaviness in the head.

As the caller asks questions, the receiver may hear the answers in their mind and verbalize them, or they may have the sensation that the deity is speaking directly through them.

Release Deity

When the working is concluded, the caller can say, "(Deity), we thank you for your presence and release you." Immediately the caller and receiver should both act as if the deity is no longer present, calling the receiver by their own name. If at any time either caller or receiver detect or suspect the entity responding is not the deity called, either or both should end the operation immediately.

Once the ritual is ended, but before leaving the space, the caller and receiver can compare notes. It may be helpful to record impressions immediately as these fade rapidly. This is the time to express the assessment either had about the depth of the engagement. Over time, particularly as two people work together, they will be able to quickly detect when a given deity is deeply present or is not clear.

Ground

Before engaging in invocation, as a caller, receiver, or both, prepare to ground the receiver and yourself. Once the operation is concluded, separate yourself from the energy. Touch the ground. Move out of the temple space, take off the jewelry, wash off the oil. Turn up the lights, turn on cheerful music, eat, and drink.

It is quite normal to feel somewhat disoriented and to need time to move back into the everyday world. The conscientious caller should pay close attention to the state of the receiver, who has moved into a vulnerable space and may need some support.

As always, give thanks and record the working.

Outline

1. Perform Ritual of the Theurgist to the Working section.

2. Add and activate synthema.

3. Call deity to object or person.

4. Perform working (ask questions, consecrate talisman, etc.).

5. Release deity.

6. Perform Conclusion from Ritual of the Theurgist.

RITUAL OF INVOKING DEITY INTO YOURSELF

This operation has all the same steps as the operation to invoke deity into someone else. The difference is that the operator is both caller and receiver.

First, purify and protect yourself. Put on a stone necklace or hold stones in hand. Bathe in herb water. Light incense. Put on a protective lamen. You may perform the "Ritual of Honoring the Ancestors" and ask specifically for protection against any forces that would seek to interrupt your journey.

You may use a recording device to capture your experience while it is happening. Once the ritual is complete, make your notes immediately. Shifting consciousness from seeing visions to directing the ritual takes time to master, and information can be lost when transitioning from trance to ritual action.

Once the operation is complete, it is very helpful to get out of the house: go out to eat, meet with a friend, or find another way to reconnect with the rest of the human world.

Outline

1. Perform Ritual of the Theurgist to the Working section.

2. Add and activate synthema.

3. Call deity to object or person.

4. Perform working (ask questions, consecrate talisman, etc.).

5. Release deity.

6. Perform Conclusion from Ritual of the Theurgist.s

RITUAL OF RISING THROUGH THE WORLDS

This is the culminating ritual of the theurgic system. The goal of the rite is to perform the Ritual of the Theurgist to the Working section.

Evoke the Teletarches

I call on the Teletarch Pistis.
Guardian of the Material and Sensible World,
Fill me with the power of theurgy, theourigikes dynameos.
I call on the Teletarch Aleitheia.
Guardian of the Intelligible World,
Fill me with the divine philosophy, theias philosophias.

I call on the Teletarch Eros.
Guardian of the Empyrean World,
Fill me with erotikes manias, the madness of love,
And let me rise!

Call Personal Daimon

Call your personal daimon using the rite you have constructed.

Ascend

Lie on the floor. Permit the soul to rise to the sun, guided by the personal daimon. If challenged for a password, use the password provided by your personal daimon.

Conclusion

At the conclusion of the vision, turn the mind toward earthly things. Perform the Conclusion from the Ritual of the Theurgist. Remove ritual jewelry. Record the working.

Outline

1. Conduct the Ritual of the Theurgist to the Working section.

2. Evoke the teletarches.

3. Invoke personal deity.

4. Invoke personal daimon.

5. Ascend.

6. Perform Conclusion from Ritual of the Theurgist.

EIGHTEEN

THE STORY YET TO BE WRITTEN

A woman sits on a bench in the cool of the temple and reads the account of Eunapius on the life of Sosipatra. She is black and considers herself a daughter of Neitokrity, who she learned about in school.

A white man enters the temple to make an offering, picking his way among the shrines of the loa, the place spirits, the many Celtic and Roman deities, until he comes to the Greek section, to the shrine of Athena. He lays a single flower at the feet of the statue and closes his eyes to pray.

The temple guardian, watching unobtrusively from a shaded balcony, looks at them both and smiles. This one considers themself gender fluid, male or female, neither or both as the occasion warrants. They carry DNA from Africa, Europe, and Asia, a true citizen of the world, fully welcomed and fully represented in the temple.

These three people will be taught as children that the gods have always walked among us. Some people have never forgotten this even though they were commanded to do so; they remained faithful until the gods and their people could meet openly again, in city and in country, in caves and on mountaintops, on house altars and in glorious newly built temples housing hundreds of shrines.

These three are our spiritual children, as yet unborn. They can pray out loud in public because of the work we do today. It is our responsibility to tell the stories of our teachers and pass them on. Then when they light the ancestor candle, we will be included in that act, and their gratitude will flow to us.

We call on those who are yet to come,
Descendants of our bodies and spirits.
You are the ones who will walk in the world,
The future to which we link.
Be strong, be peaceful, remember who you are.
Remember that gods are stars, and the stars are our true home.
We can return to that home at any time,
So soon as we remember the way.
Rise!

APPENDIX A
THEURGY FAQ, A DIALOGUE
BETWEEN TEACHER AND STUDENT

Imagine a sunny courtyard. The tile paving is cool, shaded by trees outside the wall. A woman sits in a simple chair working a drop-spindle. A man sits respectfully on the paving at her feet asking questions. The woman spins thread while she answers.

"What is theurgy?"

"The definition of the word *theurgy* is 'god-work.' Depending on how you look at it, this can mean the work the gods perform or the work we accomplish with the gods."

"Who practiced theurgy?"

"The first people who practiced theurgy were upper-class Pagan teachers at the dawn of the Christian era. As Christian emperors and bishops outlawed open Pagan practice, these teachers sought to preserve the knowledge of the gods, both their own philosophical rituals and the religious practices of the people."

"What kind of philosophy?"

"They studied the work of Plato. Today we call them 'Neo-Platonic' but they called themselves 'Platonist.'"

"Who was Plato?"

"He was a Greek aristocrat born in the late fifth century BCE. He was educated in Athens by the finest teachers of his time and in particular studied with the philosopher Socrates. After Socrates died, Plato left Athens and travelled to Egypt, called Kemet by its people, to study. Plato eventually returned to Athens to teach. He used what he learned in Kemet to reform the *paideia*, the Hellenic cultural and educational matrix that included knowledge of the gods. Plato thought deeply about the gods, the nature of the universe, human life and our place in the cosmos, and the soul and what happens after death. His numerous texts are still widely studied today."

"Who were the Neo-Platonists?"

"These were people responding to the urbanization of their world. About a thousand years after Plato, a city was founded in Egypt that drew students and teachers from the Mediterranean world. In Alexandria people from Egypt, Greece, Rome, Syria, and as far away as India rubbed shoulders and traded goods, stories, and philosophical discussions. In this environment Platonic philosophy took a particular turn, adapting to the flood of new ideas and the needs of the people studying it. The philosophers from the Alexandrian school are called Neo-Platonic to distinguish them from the other schools of philosophy of the time and to emphasize their connection to Plato."

"Were women also Neo-Platonists?"

"Women have been involved in writing and teaching Neo-Platonism from the earliest times to the present. Plato credited the priestess Diotima as being one of his most important teachers. Platonic and Neo-Platonic circles often included women."

"Were all the Neo-Platonists white and European?"

"Alexandrian Neo-Platonic philosophers inherited their knowledge from Africa, Europe, and Asia. In antiquity these philosophers were white, black, brown. Many of the most important ancient and modern thinkers went to Egypt to learn. One of the earliest Neo-Platonic philosophers in Alexandria, Plotinus, was probably Egyptian himself. Many Neo-Platonic philosophers came from Syria, a country with a mix of indigenous, Semitic, Arab, Greek, and Roman peoples."

"Is Neo-Platonism dead?"

"Neo-Platonism has been continuously developed to the present day. Parts of this philosophy were brought into the religions of Judaism, Christianity, and Islam, influencing the theological development of these religions. The emergence of this philosophy in medieval Europe helped to spark the Renaissance and found the scientific revolution."

"Is Neo-Platonism just a philosophy?"

"The study of Neo-Platonic philosophy has been linked to Pagan religion from its inception to the present day. Despite the widespread adoption of Neo-Platonic ideas among non-Pagans, the core of these ideas is fundamentally Pagan. Wherever Neo-Platonic works have emerged, Pagan religion revives. In our lifetime, the ancient rituals themselves have been relinked with the texts that explain them."

"Why does this matter?"

"Studying Neo-Platonism confronts us with the major questions of Neo-Paganism in our time. Why do we think the way we think? What are the predecessors of our culture? What are the origins of the way we look at the world? Who should we accept as our teachers? What texts can help us understand the people who came before us? How are we different from those people? How can we understand our religion as alive and evolving?"

"What does philosophy have to do with ritual practice?"

"Theurgy comes from the gods themselves. The rituals call the gods to speak to us and bring them into our spiritual sight. The ancients recorded what they saw and heard and how they brought themselves into a state to hear, see, and understand. The gods instruct us to harmonize our actions in the world with the life-giving patterns of the world. They beckon us to experience ourselves as participating in the divine."

"What does a theurgist do?"

"A theurgist lights incense at his altar to ask his gods for their aid and thank them for their gifts. A theurgist steps outside and turns to greet the sun, chanting vowels to bring the sun's energy into herself to start the day. A theurgist falls into trance while his partner quietly asks him questions about what he is seeing. A theurgist opens the door of the shrine and makes offerings to the living presence of her goddess."

"How do I practice theurgy now?"

"If you have an altar and make offerings to a god you have already started. Our practices are contiguous with the practices of the past. You can read the Neo-Platonic texts. You can also study the lives of the teachers—they show the way."

The student touches his forehead to his teacher's feet. She smiles and touches his head for a moment before resuming her spinning.

APPENDIX B
THEURGIC STUDY COURSE

We have seen that theurgy is a literate tradition; following are some of its most notable works. They include English translations of ancient texts and contemporary interpretations of the texts. Each student is free to chart a personal course through reading these works.

How to Read the Texts

The original texts are written in many languages, including hieroglyphic and demotic, Latin and Arabic. Where there is more than one translation, it can be illuminating to read different versions, as each translator draws on his or her own training and perspectives.

Many are written in Greek. Some translations take a different word in English than the Greek word; my favorite example is "magic," which can stand in for any of a number of different words, including "goes," meaning practical magic with a shading of disreputable, and "pharmakon," meaning an herb or object charged with healing or cursing properties. Taking the time to learn the Greek alphabet allows us to find the source word in the text and make our own decisions about what it might mean.

In addition to reading the texts on our own, we may be inspired to read the texts as part of a reading group with other people who are interested in the practice of theurgy. Every group is smarter than the smartest person in it; group study is a great way to leverage that power.

AFRICAN WISDOM TEXTS

Hieroglyphic inscriptions on stone and wood are primary sources for ancient Egyptian religious thought and practice.

THE PYRAMID TEXTS

The Pyramid Texts begin with the pyramid of Unas at Saqqara dated to about 2345 BCE. The texts assist the pyramid's inhabitants in their after-life journey to join the gods among the stars.

- Samuel Mercer, *The Pyramid Texts*, available online.
- R. O. Faulkner, *The Ancient Egyptian Pyramid Texts*, considered definitive by academic scholars.
- Miriam Lichtheim, *Ancient Egyptian Literature: Volume I: The Old and Middle Kingdoms*, includes selections from the Pyramid Texts.

COFFIN TEXTS

While the Pyramid Texts date to the Old Kingdom, the Coffin Texts were produced in the first Intermediate Period and the Middle Kingdom. They sometimes copy the Pyramid Texts, but there are new additions here as well. Like the Pyramid Texts, they assist the coffin's inhabitants in their post-life journeys.

- R. O. Faulkner, *The Ancient Egyptian Coffin Texts.*

BOOK OF GOING FORTH BY DAY

By the New Kingdom, the rituals guiding the deceased in their journeys had become widely available as funerary scrolls. The 1250 BCE Papyrus of Ani, titled the *Book of Going Forth By Day*, is the most complete of these texts.

- E. A. Wallis Budge, *The Egyptian Book of the Dead: The Papyrus of Ani in the British Museum*

- R. O. Faulkner, *The Ancient Egyptian Book of the Dead*
- Maulana Karenga, *Maat, The Moral Idea in Ancient Egypt*. Karenga extensively analyses the Papyrus of Ani and the coffin texts.
- Eva Von Dassow, editor, *The Egyptian Book of the Dead: The Book of Going Forth by Day*
- Wasserman, James, *The Egyptian Book of the Dead: The Book of Going Forth by Day*.

Kemetic Ritual Practice

Each morning the priestesses and priests in the temples would approach the statues that provided earthly bodies in which the deities could manifest. The temple walls and papyri are inscribed with instructions on how to perform these rites. The Opening of the Mouth ceremony could be performed on a statue of deity or on the mummy of a recently deceased royal or noble to enable that physical presence to receive offerings.

- E. A. Wallis Budge, *The Book of Opening the Mouth*.
- Richard Reidy, *Eternal Egypt, Ancient Rituals for the Modern World*. Reidy adapts rituals for bringing deity into statue and interacting with that statue daily.
- Robert Ritner, *The Mechanics of Ancient Egyptian Magical Practice*. Ritner discusses the work of temple priests and priestesses and the interaction of temple and home.
- Serge Sauneron, *The Priests of Ancient Egypt*. Sauneron describes the daily ritual practice in the temple.
- Mark Smith, *The Liturgy of Opening the Mouth for Breathing*.

The Works of Plato

Plato's works have survived in some number. They encapsulate the works of Pythagoras, Socrates, and Diotima. Scholars note that it is difficult to decide which of Plato's thoughts are attributable to him, but we can certainly consider the corpus of his work to include the thoughts of his predecessors, including his unnamed Kemetic teachers.

One approach to this learning would be to read the works in the order Iamblichus designated. Neo-Platonic philosophers held that reading the works in this order constitutes something of an initiation, with earlier texts providing the foundation for later thought. Here is the order:

- *Alcibiades I*
- *Gorgias*
- *Phaedo*
- *Cratylus*
- *Theaetetus*
- *Sophist*
- *Statesman*
- *Phaedrus*
- *Symposium*
- *Philebus*
- *Timaeus*
- *Parmenides*

These are available in many translations online and in print. Benjamin Jowett's readable translations from the early twentieth century are posted courtesy of MIT. If you can read only one of these works, read *Timaeus*.

- Mary Ellen Waithe, *A History of Women Philosophers*. Waithe specifically discusses the thought of Diotima and other women Platonic philosophers.

Platonic Philosophers

PLOTINUS

Plotinus's student Porphyry arranged and edited six of his lectures into the Enneads.

- Stephen MacKenna, *The Enneads*. This translation is available online through MIT. The work includes Porphyry's biography of Plotinus.

- Algis Uždavinys, Algis, editor. *The Heart of Plotinus: The Essential Enneads Including Porphyry's On the Cave.* Uždavinys provides a readable overview of Plotinus's work in his introduction to the book.

IAMBLICHUS

Some of Iamblichus's surviving works have a Pythagorean character, including his biography of Pythagoras. Most important for the theurgist is his book *Theurgia or the Mysteries of Egypt*, sometimes called *De Mysteriis*.

- Emma Clarke, John M. Dillon, and Jackson P. Hershbell, *Iamblichus On the Mysteries*, 2003. The excellent introduction to the translation provides a helpful analysis of the work.

- Thomas J Johnson. *Iamblichus, the Exhortation to Philosophy: Including the Letters of Iamblichus and Proclus' Commentary on the Chaldean Oracles.*

- Thomas Taylor. *Iamblichus' Life of Pythagoras.*

- Gregory Shaw, *Theurgy and the Soul: The Neo-Platonism of Iamblichus*. This analysis is enormously helpful to the practitioner seeking to understand the theory behind the practice of the rites.

HYPATIA

Claudius Ptolemais wrote the *Almagest* in 150. Hypatia's biographer Dzielska argues that Hypatia herself edited her father Theon's edition of Ptolemais's *Almagest* and largely wrote the commentary attributed to her father. The *Almagest* formed the foundational text for the practice of astronomy and astrology in medieval Europe. Reading the *Almagest*, which is not lengthy, reveals something of Hypatia's preoccupation with universal harmony. Bruce MacLennan brings Hypatia's thought back to life in *The Wisdom of Hypatia*; we owe him a tremendous debt for permitting us to sit at her feet again.

- David Blitz, *Ptolemy: Almagest, Book I.*
- Bruce MacLennan, *The Wisdom of Hypatia.*

PROKLOS

Proklos wrote prolifically; five of his commentaries on Platonic dialogues and six of his books survive. The work of Proklos certainly encompasses the thoughts of his teacher, Asklepigenia. In *A History of Women Philosophers*, Mary Ellen Waithe discusses Asklepigenia's thoughts on metaphysics and magic. Most notably, Asklepigenia taught that fate was not immutable, but could be altered by ritual action. Proklos also wrote many hymns; five that have survived were translated by Thomas Taylor.

- E. R. Dodds, *Proclus' Elements of Theology.*
- Kenneth Sylvan Guthrie, *Marinus' On Happiness, the Life of Proclus*, available online
- Thomas Taylor, *Proclus's Platonic Theology.*
- Thomas Taylor, *Proclus, Five Hymns.*

Ritual Texts

CHALDEAN ORACLES

We have previously discussed the oracles in their ancient context. While Plethon was the last Pagan to have access to the complete poem, numerous scholars have collected the existing fragments. Hans Lewy translated the available fragments in 1956. He separated fragments into "theurgical" and "magical." The most recent translator, Ruth Majercik, does not replicate this division.

- Sarah Iles Johnston, *Hekate Soteira*. Johnston's work makes a substantial contribution to our understanding of the oracles.

- Ruth Majercik, *Chaldean Oracles, Text, Translation and Commentary*. This version is the current and the definitive translation, treating nearly two hundred hexameter verses, reproducing the Greek texts with facing translations. She includes an exhaustive bibliography of primary and secondary sources, along with the best summation of classes of beings mentioned in the texts, the cosmology of the Oracles, and theurgic practice as found in the text.

- G. R. S. Mead, *Chaldean Oracles*. Mead's version deserves more attention than it gets. His volume gives an overview of texts where the fragments were found, the historical context, the cosmology of the oracles, and some idea of theurgic techniques.

- Thomas Taylor, *Collection of the Chaldean Oracles*. Taylor was the first to translate the fragments into English.

- William Wynn Westcott, *Chaldean Oracles*. The Golden Dawn founder relates the cosmology of the oracles to the Qabbalah.

KEMETIC AND GREEK RITUAL TEXTS

- Hans Dieter Betz, editor, *The Greek Magical Papyri in Translation: Including the Demotic Spells.* This is the current definitive collection.

- Eleni Pachoumi, *The Greek Magical Papyri: Diversity and Unity, A Thesis submitted for the Degree of Doctor of Philosophy.* Pachoumi links specific ritual techniques back to the philosophical doctrines that explain them.

- Stephen Skinner, *Techniques of Graeco-Egyptian Magic.* Skinner has analyzed the texts and provided a tabulated guide to the techniques.

Graeco-Egyptian Source Works
HERMETICA

The Corpus Hermeticum was assembled in Alexandria in the second century BCE from a much larger body of earlier texts. The Hermetica are presented in the form of a dialogue or teaching, most given by Hermes Trismegistus to various disciples, some of which contain ritual as well as theology and philosophy. They were known to Psellos and were redacted by Byzantine editors. The Hermetica were among the writings purged from the libraries of Western Europe and re-introduced to the West through Marsilio Ficino's translations in the time of the Florentine academy. Since Ficino's time, this collection has been enormously influential to esotericists and magicians.

Copenhaver notes that two earlier editors, Walter Scott and Andre-Jean Festugiere, divided the works into two categories, "philosophical" and "popular," with the "popular" works containing details of ritual practice. Fifteen "philosophical" texts form the currently translated canon. The "popular" or technical works were published by A. J. Festugiere volume I of *La Revelation d'Hermes Trismegiste*, copies of which can be located in a few university libraries, although I have not seen one.

- Brian Copenhaver. *Hermetica: The Greek Corpus Hermeticum*. This is the current definitive edition.
- Garth Fowden, *The Egyptian Hermes: A Historical Approach to the Late Pagan Mind*. This work remains the most useful and authoritative commentary on the context and content of the Hermetica, and forms an essential companion volume to Copenhaver's translations.
- G. R. S. Mead, *Thrice Greatest Hermes*.

APPENDIX C
GLOSSARY

Word	Pronunciation	Meaning
Aleitheia	ah-**lay**-thay-ah	Truth
Daimones	die-**moan**-ez	Spirits
Eros	**air**-os	Love
Iynges	**eeyoon**-ges	Wheels
Iynx	**eeyoon**-ks	Wheel, singular
Pistis	**pee**-stis	Trust
Symbola	**syoom**-bola	Physical objects that carry the power of the gods
Synoches	syoo-no-kez	Guardians
Synthema	syoon-**thay**-ma	Chants, songs, words that carry the power of the gods
Teletarches	tele-**tar**-khez	Pistis, Aleitheia, and Eros, the guardian spirits of theurgy

BIBLIOGRAPHY

Alic, Margaret. *Hypatia's Heritage: A History of Women in Science from Antiquity through the Nineteenth Century.* Boston: Beacon Press, 1986.

Allen, James P. *The Ancient Pyramid Texts.* Atlanta, GA: Society of Biblical Literature, 2005.

Asante, Molefi Kete. *The Egyptian Philosophers: Ancient African Voices from Imhotep to Akhenaten.* Chicago: African American Images, 2000.

Aslan, Reza. *Zealot: The Life and Times of Jesus of Nazareth.* New York: Random House, 2013.

Axon, William. *Thomas Taylor, the Platonist: A Biographical and Bibliographical Sketch* (1890). Available at: www.archive.org/stream /thomastaylorplat00axonrich/thomastaylorplat00axonrich_djvu.txt.

Ayad, Mariam F. *God's Wife, God's Servant: The God's Wife of Amun, ca. 740–525.* New York: Routledge, 2009.

Barrett, Helen M. *Boethius: Some Aspects of His Times and Work.* Cambridge, UK: Cambridge University Press, 1940.

Bell, Lanny. "The New Kingdom 'Divine' Temple—The Example of Luxor," in *Temples of Ancient Egypt,* edited by Byron E. Shafer. Ithaca, NY: Cornell University Press, 1997.

Betz, Hans Dieter, ed. *The Greek Magical Papyri in Translation: Including the Demotic Spells.* Chicago: University of Chicago Press, 1992.

Betz, Hans Dieter, ed. "The Delphic Maxim 'Know Yourself' in the Greek Magical Papyri," *History of Religions* volume 21, no. 2. Chicago: University of Chicago Press, 1981.

———. *The Mithras Liturgy.* Tübingen, Ger: Mohr Siebeck, 2003.

Blanton, Crystal, ed. with Taylor Ellwood and Brandy Williams. *Bringing Race to the Table.* London: Immanion Press, 2015.

Blanton, Crystal, ed. *Shades of Faith.* London: Immanion Press, 2011.

———. *Shades of Ritual: Minority Voices in Practice.* London: Immanion Press, 2014.

Blitz, David. *Ptolemy: Almagest, Book I.* bertie.ccsu.edu/naturesci /Cosmology/Ptolemy.html.

Blum, Paul Richard. *Philosophy of Religion in the Renaissance.* Burlington, VT: Ashgate Publishing Company, 2010.

Broadie, Sarah. *Nature and Divinity in Plato's Timaeus.* Cambridge, UK: Cambridge University Press, 2012.

Brown, Vincent. *Pyramid Texts Online.* www.pyramidtextsonline .com/.

Budge, E. A. Wallis. *The Book of Opening the Mouth: The Egyptian Texts with English Translations.* London: Kegan Paul, 1909.

———. *The Egyptian Book of the Dead: The Papyrus of Ani in the British Museum; the Egyptian Text with Interlinear Translation, a Running Translation, Introduction, etc.* New York: Cosimo Classics, 2010. First published 1895 by British Museum.

Burkert, Walter. *Greek Religion.* Cambridge, MA: Harvard University Press, 1985.

Burnett, John. "Parmenides On Nature," *in Early Greek Philosophy*. London: A & C Black, 1920.

Churton, Tobias. *Jerusalem!: The Real Life of William Blake*. London: Watkins Publishing, 2015.

Cicero, Chic, and Sandra Tabitha Cicero. *The Essential Golden Dawn: An Introduction to High Magick*. St. Paul: Llewellyn, 2004.

———. *Self-Initiation Into the Golden Dawn Tradition: A Complete Curriculum of Study for Both the Solitary Magician and the Working Magical Group*. St. Paul, MN: Llewellyn Publications, 2003.

Clarke, Emma, John M. Dillon, and Jackson P. Hershbell. *Iamblichus: On the Mysteries*. Atlanta, GA: Society of Biblical Literature, 2003.

Copenhaver, Brian. *Hermetica: The Greek Corpus Hermeticum and the Latin Asclepius in a New English Translation with Notes and Introduction*. Cambridge, UK: Cambridge University Press, 1992.

Crane, Eva. *The World History of Beekeeping and Honey Hunting*. New York: Routledge Taylor and Francis Group, 2013.

Crowley, Aleister, Mary Desti, Leila Waddell, and Hymenaeus Beta, eds. "ASTARTE vel Liber BERYLLI sub figura CLXXV" in *Magick: Liber Aba, Book Four, parts I–IV*. Boston: Weiser Books, 1994.

Crowley, Aleister. *Book Four*. York Beach, ME: Red Wheel/Weiser, 1980.

Crowley, Aleister. "Energized Enthusiasm, A Note on Theurgy", in *The Best of the Equinox, Sex Magic, Vol. III*. San Francisco: Weiser Books, 2013.

———. *Magick in Theory and Practice*. (1929).

———. "The Star Ruby," in *The Book of Lies*. York Beach, ME: Weiser Books, 1981.

Culling, Louis. *Complete Magick Curriculum of the Secret Order G.B.G.* Woodbury, MN: Llewellyn, 2010.

d'Aragona, Tullia. *Dialogue on the Infinity of Love.* Translated and edited by Rinaldina Russell and Bruce Merry. Chicago: University of Chicago Press, 1997.

Derksen, Louise D. "Anne Conway's Critique of Cartesian Dualism." www.bu.edu/wcp/Papers/Onto/OntoDerk.htm.

d'Este, Sorita, and David Rankine. *Hekate Liminal Rites.* London: Avalonia, 2009.

Diop, Cheikh Anta. *The African Origin of Civilization, Myth or Reality.* Translated by Mercer Cook. Chicago: Lawrence Hill, 1974.

Dodds, E. R., trans. *Greeks and the Irrational.* Berkeley, CA: University of California Press, 1951.

———. *Proclus' Elements of Theology.* Oxford, UK: Clarendon University Press 1992.

Dzielska, Maria. *Hypatia of Alexandria.* Translated by F. Lyra. Cambridge, MA: Harvard University Press, 1995.

Easlea, Brian. *Witch Hunting, Magic and the New Philosophy: An Introduction to Debates of the Scientific Revolution, 1450–1750.* Brighton, UK: Harvester Press 1980.

Farrar, Stewart, and Janet Farrar. *The Witches' Goddess: The Feminine Principle of Divinity.* Carlsbad, CA: Phoenix Publishing, 1987.

Faulkner, R. O. *The Ancient Egyptian Coffin Texts v. 1–3.* Oxford, UK: Aris and Phillips, 2004.

———. *The Ancient Egyptian Pyramid Texts.* Oxford, UK: Clarendon Press, 1910.

Faulkner, R. O. "The Bremner-Rhind Papyrus: IV." *The Journal of Egyptian Archaeology, volume 24* no. 1, Jun., pp. 41–53. Egypt Exploration Society, 1938.

Frew, Don. "Gardnerian Wica as Theurgic Ascent." theurgicon.com /gardnerian.pdf.

———. "Harran: Last Refuge of Classical Paganism," in *Pomegranate: The International Journal of Pagan Studies*, issue 9. August 1999.

Frankfurter, David. *Religion in Roman Egypt: Assimilation and Resistance.* Princeton: Princeton University Press, 1998.

Frischmann, Nina Ellis. *The Academy Under Proclus: Perfecting Women through Neoplatonic Education in Late Antiquity Athens.* Colorado Springs, CO: University of Colorado, 2013.

Gordon, Hayim, and Rivca Gordon. *Heidegger on Truth and Myth: A Rejection of Postmodernism.* New York: Peter Lang, 2007.

Grandin, Temple, and Catherine Johnson. *Animals in Translation: Using the Mysteries of Autism to Decode Animal Behavior.* Orlando, FL: Harcourt 2005.

Gregorios, Paulos Mar, ed. *Neoplatonism and Indian Philosophy.* New York: SUNY Press, 2001.

Gundert, Beata. "Soma and Psyche in Hippocratic Medicine," in John P. Wright and Paul Potter (eds.) *The Psyche and Soma, Physicians and Metaphysicians on the Mind-Body Problem from Antiquity to Enlightenment.* Oxford, UK: Oxford University Press, 2000.

Guthrie, Kenneth Sylvan, trans. *Fragments from Proclus's Commentary on the Chaldean Oracles.* Yonkers: The Platonist Press, 1925.

Guthrie, Kenneth Sylvan, trans.. *Marinus' On Happiness, the Life of Proclus*. www.platonic-philosophy.org/files/Marinus%20-%20On%20Happiness.pdf.

Hiebert, Paul G., and R. Daniel Shaw. *Understanding Folk Religion: A Christian Response to Popular Beliefs and Practices*. Grand Rapids, MI: Baker Books, 1999.

Huxley, Aldous. *The Perennial Philosophy*. New York: Harper Publishers, 1945.

Isaac, Benjamin. *The Invention of Racism in Classical Antiquity*. Princeton, NJ: Princeton University Press, 2004.

Jaffe, Irma B., and Gernando Colombardo. *Shining Eyes, Cruel Fortune: The Lives and Loves of Italian Renaissance Women Poets*. New York: Fordham University Press, 2002.

Jeanneret, Michel. *A Feast of Words: Banquets and Table Talk in the Renaissance*. Chicago: University of Chicago Press, 1991.

Johnson, Thomas J., trans. *Iamblichus, the Exhortation to Philosophy: Including the Letters of Iamblichus and Proclus' Commentary on the Chaldean Oracles*. Grand Rapids, MI: Phanes Press, 1988.

Johnston, Sarah Iles. "Animating Statues: A Case Study in Ritual." *Arethusa* 41 (2008): 445–477.

———. "Charming Children: The Use of the Child in Ancient Divination." *Arethusa* 34 (2001): 97–117.

———. *Hekate Soteira*. Oxford, UK: Oxford University Press, 1990.

———. "Rising to the Occasion, Theurgic Ascent in Its Cultural Milieu," in *Envisioning Magic*, edited by Peter Schafer and Hans. G. Kippenberg. Leiden, NL: Brill, 1997.

Jowett. Benjamin. *Ion*. classics.mit.edu/Plato/ion.html.

Jowett, Benajmin. *Meno.* classics.mit.edu/Plato/meno.html.

———. *Phaedo.* classics.mit.edu/Plato/phaedo.html.

———. *Phaedrus.* classics.mit.edu/Plato/phaedrus.html.

———. *The Republic and Other Works.* New York: Anchor Books, 1993.

———. *Timaeus.* ebooks.adelaide.edu.au/p/plato/p71ti/.

Kahane, Henry, Renee Kahane, and Angelenia Pietrangeli. "Hermeticism in the Alfonsine Tradition," in *Mélanges Offerts* à *Rita Lejeune,* volume 1. Gembloux, FR: Editions J. Duculot, 1969.

Karenga, Maulana. *Maat, The Moral Ideal in Ancient Egypt.* Los Angeles: University of Sankore Press, 2006.

Kazhdan, Aleksandr Petrovich, and Annabel Jane Wharton. *Change in Byzantine Culture in the Eleventh and Twelfth Centuries.* Berkeley: University of California Press, 1985.

Kingsley, Peter. *In the Dark Places of Wisdom.* Inverness, CA: Golden Sufi Center, 1999.

———. "The Paths of the Ancient Sages, A Sacred Tradition Between East and West," in *Crossing Religious Frontiers,* edited by Harry Oldmeadow. Bloomington, IN: World Wisdom, 2010.

Kraemer, Christine Hoff. *Seeking the Mystery, An Introduction to Pagan Theologies.* Englewood, CO: Patheos Press, 2012.

Küng, Hans. "A Global Ethic: The Declaration of the Parliament of the World's Religions." Presentation. parliamentofreligions .org/_includes/FCKcontent/File/TowardsAGlobalEthic.pdf via www.parliamentofreligions.org/content/toward-global-ethic -initial-declaration.

Kupperman, Jeffery. *Living Theurgy: A Course in Iamblichus' Philosophy, Theology and Theurgy.* Glastonbury, UK: Avalonia Press, 2014.

Lichtheim, Miriam. *Ancient Egyptian Literature: Volume I: The Old and Middle Kingdoms.* Berkeley, CA: University of California Press, 2006.

———. *Ancient Egyptian Literature: Volume II: The New Kingdom.* Berkeley, CA: University of California Press, 2006.

———. *Ancient Egyptian Literature: Volume III: The Late Period.* Berkeley, CA: University of California Press, 2006.

MacKenna, Stephen, trans., *The Enneads.* London: Penguin, 1991.

MacLennan, Bruce. *The Wisdom of Hypatia.* Woodbury, MN: Llewellyn: 2013.

Majercik, Ruth. *The Chaldean Oracles: Text, Translation and Commentary.* Leiden, NL: Brill, 1989.

Mathers, Samuel Liddell MacGregor. *The Sacred Magic of Abra-Melin the Mage* (Mineola: Dover, 1975).

Mead, G. R. S. *Chaldean Oracles.* Originally published 1908. gnosis.org/library/grs-mead/grsm_chaldean.htm.

———. *Thrice Greatest Hermes: Studies in Hellenistic Theosophy and Gnosis, volume 2.* London: Theosophical Publishing Society, 1906.

Mercer, Samuel A. B. *The Pyramid Texts.* Originally published 1952. www.sacred-texts.com/egy/pyt/index.htm.

Meyer, Marvin W. *The Mithras Liturgy.* Missoula, MT: Scholars Press, University of Montana, 1976.

Mierzwicki, Tony. *Graeco-Egyptian Magic, Everyday Empowerment.* Stafford, UK: Immanion Press, 2006.

Mikalson, Jon D. *Greek Popular Religion in Greek Philosophy.* Oxford, UK: Oxford University Press, 2010.

Mishev, Georgi. *Thracian Magic Past and Present*. London: Avalonia Press, 2012.

Momigliano, Arnaldo. "Cassiodorus and the Italian Culture of his Time" in *Proceedings of the British Academy 41*, 207–245. London: Oxford University Press, 1955.

Morkot, Robert G. *The Black Pharaohs, Egypt's Nubian Rulers*. London: The Rubicon Press, 2000.

Muller, Max. *The Upanishads Part 1, Sacred Books of the East, volume 1*. Originally published 1879. www.sacred-texts.com/hin /sbe01/index.htm.

———. *The Upanishads Part II, Sacred Books of the East, volume 15*. Originally published 1884. www.sacred-texts.com/hin /sbe15/index.htm.

Murray, Gilbert. "On the Gods and The World by Sallustius" in *Five Stages of Greek Religion, Studies Based on a Course of Lectures Delivered in April 1912 at Columbia University*. Oxford, UK: Clarendon Press, 1925.

Nasr, Seyyed Hossein. *An Introduction to Islamic Cosmological Doctrines*. Albany, NY: State University of New York Press, 1994.

Nieves, Yvonne E. "Paganism and the Path Back to Africa," in *Shades of Ritual, Minority Voices in Practice*. Edited by Crystal Blanton. London: Immanion Press, 2014.

Nock, Arthur. *Sallustius: Concerning the Gods and the Universe*. Cambridge, UK: Cambridge University Press, 1926.

Obrebski, Joseph. *Ritual and Structure in a Macedonian Village*. Amherst, MA: University of Massachusetts, 1977.

Pachoumi, Eleni. *The Greek Magical Papyri: Diversity and Unity.* Newcastle upon Tyne, UK: School of Historical Studies, Newcastle University, 2007.

Paper, Jordan. *The Deities Are Many: A Polytheistic Theology.* New York: SUNY Press, 2005.

Pennington, Bruce. "The Death of Pythagoras" in *Philosophy Now, A Magazine of Ideas*, September/October 2013.

Pessin, Sarah. "Solomon Ibn Gabirol [Avicebron]" in *The Stanford Encyclopedia of Philosophy*, spring 2013 Edition, edited by Edward N. Zalta. plato.stanford.edu/archives/spr2013/entries/ibn-gabirol.

Philips, William D. *Slavery from Roman Times to the Early Transatlantic Trade.* Manchester, UK: University of Minnesota Press, 1985.

Pomeroy, Sarah. *Pythagorean Women: Their History and Writings.* Baltimore, MD: Johns Hopkins University Press, 2013.

Porphyry. *Elements of Theology.* Translated by A. C. Ionides. Sequim, WA: Holmes Publishing Group, 2001.

———. "Letter to Anebo," translated by Thomas Taylor, 1821. www.tertullian.org/fathers/porphyry_anebo_02_text.htm.

———. "On Abstinence from Animal Food," translated by Thomas Taylor, 1823. www.tertullian.org/fathers/porphyry _abstinence_01_book1.htm.

Regardie, Israel. *Ceremonial Magic: A Guide to the Mechanisms of Ritual.* London: Aquarian Press, 1980.

———. *Foundations of Practical Magic: An Introduction to Qabalistic, Magical and Meditative Techniques.* London: Aeon Books, 2007.

———. *The Golden Dawn: A Complete Course in Practical Ceremonial Magic.* St. Paul, MN: Llewellyn, 1989.

Reidy, Richard. *Eternal Egypt: Ancient Rituals for the Modern World.* Bloomington, IN: iUniverse, 2010.

Remes, Paulina. *Neoplatonism.* Stocksfield, UK: Acumen Publishing, 2008.

Riad, Henri. "Egyptian Influence on Daily Life in Alexandria," in *Alexandria and Alexandrianism,* edited by John Walsh and Thomas F. Reese. Malibu, CA: J. Paul Getty Museum, 1993.

Ritner, Robert. *The Mechanics of Ancient Egyptian Magical Practice.* Chicago: Oriental Institute, 1997, 2008.

Roscoe, Henry Enfield, and Carl Schorlemmer. *A Treatise on Chemistry, Volume 2, the Metals.* London: MacMillan and Company, 1912.

Sauneron, Serge. *The Priests of Ancient Egypt.* Ithaca, NY: Cornell University, 1960.

Sewter, E. R. A. *Fourteen Byzantine Rulers: The Chronographia of Michael Psellus.* London: Penguin Books, 1966.

Shaw, Gregory. *Theurgy and the Soul: The Neo-Platonism of Iamblichus.* University Park, PA: Pennsylvania State University Press, 2010.

Siniossoglou, Niketas. *Radical Platonism in Byzantion: Illumination and Utopia in Gemistos Plethon.* Cambridge, UK: Cambridge University Press 2011.

Siorvanes, Lucas. *Proclus: Neo-Platonic Philosophy and Science.* Edinburgh, UK: Edinburgh University Press, 1996.

Skinner, Stephen, ed. *Michael Psellus Dialogue On the Operation of Daemons.* Singapore: Golden Hoard Press, 2010.

———. *Techniques of Graeco-Egyptian Magic.* Singapore: Golden Hoard Press, 2014.

Slavenburg, Jacob. *The Hermetic Link: From Secret Tradition to Modern Thought*. Lake Worth, FL: Ibis Press, 2013.

Smith, Mark. *The Liturgy of Opening the Mouth for Breathing*. Oxford, UK: Griffith Institute Publications, 1993.

Taylor, Thomas. trans. *Proclus's Platonic Theology*. archive.org/details /ProclusOnTheTheologyOfPlato-ElectronicEdition.

———. *Collection of the Chaldean Oracles*. www.masseiana.org /chaldean_oracles.htm.

———. *Iamblichus' Life of Pythagoras*. Rochester, VT: Inner Traditions, 1986.

———. *Proclus, Commentary on Timaeus*. archive.org/details /ProcluscommentaryOnTheTimaeusOfPlato.

———. *Proclus, Five Hymns*. www.tertullian.org/fathers /proclus_five_hymns_01_text.htm.

Teeter, Emily. "Celibacy and Adoption Among God's Wives of Amun and Singers in the Temple of Amun: A Re-Examination of the Evidence," in *Gold of Praise: Studies on Ancient Egypt in Honor of Edward F. Wente, Studies in Ancient Oriental Civilization No. 58*, Emily Teeter and John A. Larson, eds. Chicago: The Oriental Institute of the University of Chicago, 1999.

Trombley, Frank. *Hellenic Religion and Christianization*. Leiden, NL: Brill, 2001.

Troncarelli, Fabio. "Boethius from Late Antiquity to the Early Middle Ages," in *Boethius as a Paradigm of Late Ancient Thought*. Edited by Thomas Bohm, Thomas Jurgasch, and Andreas Kirschner. Berlin/ Boston: DeGruyter, 2014.

Uždavinys, Algis, ed. *The Heart of Plotinus: The Essential Enneads Including Porphyry's On the Cave.* Bloomington, IN: World Wisdom, 2009.

Von Dassow, Eva, ed. *The Egyptian Book of the Dead: The Book of Going Forth by Day—The Complete Papyrus of Ani Featuring Integrated Text and Full-Color Images.* San Francisco: Chronicle Books, 2008.

Waithe, Mary Ellen. *A History of Women Philosophers, vol. 1, 600 BC–500 AD.* Boston: Martinus Nijhof Publishers, 1987.

Wasserman, James. *The Egyptian Book of the Dead: The Book of Going Forth by* Day. San Francisco: Chronicle Books, 1994.

Welsh, James Jacob. "A Brief Note of Mr. Thomas Taylor, the Celebrated Platonist: With a Complete List of His Published Works." London: G. Balne, 1828.

Westcott, William Wynn. *Chaldean Oracles.* Originally published 1895. www.sacred-texts.com/eso/coz/index.htm.

Williams, Brandy. *Practical Magic for Beginners.* St. Paul, MN: Llewellyn, 2005.

———. *The Woman Magician.* Woodbury, MN: Llewellyn, 2011.

Wright, Wilmer Cave. *Philostratus and Eunapius: Lives of the Philosophers and Sophists.* London: William Heinemann, 1921.

Wroe, Ann. *Orpheus: The Song of Life.* New York: The Overlook Press, 2012.

Yates, Frances. *Giordano Bruno and the Hermetic Tradition.* Chicago: University of Chicago Press, 1964.

York, Michael. *Pagan Theology: Paganism as a World Religion*. New York: New York University Press, 2003.

Zimmern, Alice, and David R. Fideler. *Porphyry the Philosopher to His Wife, Marcella*. Grand Rapids, MI: Phanes Press, 1986.

INDEX

193, 206, 233–236, 245–248, 267, 310

Ficino, Marsilio, 171, 175, 179, 214, 283, 312

Florence, 167, 168, 172, 175, 177, 179, 181–184, 198, 283

Fons Vitae, 157

Frew, Don, 150, 200

G

Gardner, Gerald, 200, 283

Geb, 25

Gemina, 73, 74, 87, 184, 283

genius, 80, 81

Gennadios II, 173

goes, 65, 190, 215, 243, 305

Golden Dawn, 61, 197–199, 220, 259, 268, 269, 274, 292, 311

Greek Magical Papyri, see Papyri Graecae Magicae

Guerrino, 184

H

Hades, 57, 58, 141, 242, 244

Hadit, 199

Harran, 147, 148, 150–156, 161

Hatshepsut, 11, 73

Hegemon, 61

Hegias, 133, 134, 283

Heimarmene, 117

Hekate, 209, 229, 235, 236, 240, 242, 254, 262, 276, 284, 286, 311

Heliodorus, 129, 283

Helios, 104, 210, 240, 254, 276

Henad, 238, 239

Hephaestus, 58, 284, 286

Hera, 51, 58, 239, 284, 286

Hermes, 58, 77, 123, 149, 151, 154, 169, 171, 239, 240, 243, 261–263, 276, 284, 286, 292, 293, 312, 313

Hestia, 58, 66, 284, 286

Hierophant, 61

Hierus, 61

Hinduism, 19, 240

Hyparxis, 233, 235, 284

Hypatia, 18, 108–110, 112, 120–123, 127, 184, 200, 207, 245, 283, 310

I

Iamblichus, 26, 40, 51, 52, 67, 68, 99, 112–115, 123, 130, 155, 199, 201, 226, 229, 230, 232,

Syrianus, 112, 113, 119, 129, 132, 283

T

Taranis, 141

Tarot, 261

Tasso, Bernardo, 183

Tefnut, 25

Telesphoros, 115, 116

telestike, 253

Teletarch, 242, 243, 285, 296, 297

Thebes, 7, 10, 14, 53, 54, 212

Thelema, 199

Theon, 120, 283, 310

Theosophy, 196

Theurgicon, 200

Taylor, Thomas, 85, 114, 133, 187, 193, 283, 309–311

Thoth, 16, 77, 240

triumphalism, 125

truth, 69, 98, 181, 192, 195, 203, 204, 210, 214–216, 228, 236–239, 242, 243, 247, 285, 315

Tyche, 240, 272

Typhon, 240

U

Ulpian, 107, 108, 283

V

Valiente, Doreen, 200, 283

Varchi, Benedetto, 183

Venus, 77, 147, 254, 293

Vesta, 77, 78, 80, 141

Vulcan, 77, 141

W

Waset, 7, 8, 10, 11, 13–15, 29, 39–42, 53, 61, 209

Westcott, William, 283

Wica, 200

Wicca, 200

Witchcraft, 199, 200, 235, 251, 257, 266, 271, 293

World Soul, 64, 71, 232, 235, 236, 238, 244

Wretch, The, 184

Wunsch, Richard, 213, 220

Z

Zacharias of Gaza, 245

Zeus, 57, 58, 66, 124, 174, 175, 239, 284, 286